Occupying Habits

Occupying Habits

*Everyday Media as Warfare in
Israel-Palestine*

Daniel Mann

I.B. TAURIS
LONDON • NEW YORK • OXFORD • NEW DELHI • SYDNEY

I.B. TAURIS
Bloomsbury Publishing Plc
50 Bedford Square, London, WC1B 3DP, UK
1385 Broadway, New York, NY 10018, USA
29 Earlsfort Terrace, Dublin 2, Ireland

BLOOMSBURY, I.B. TAURIS and the I.B. Tauris logo are trademarks
of Bloomsbury Publishing Plc

First published in Great Britain 2022
This paperback edition published 2023

Cover image: Tel-Al-Hawa, Southern Gaza City, Kent Klich, 2009

ISBN: HB: 978-0-7556-3390-6
         PB: 978-0-7556-4689-0
         ePDF: 978-0-7556-3391-3
         ePUB: 978-0-7556-3392-0

Typeset by Integra Software Services Pvt. Ltd.

To find out more about our authors and books visit www.bloomsbury.com
and sign up for our newsletters.

For and with Ayala

Contents

Figures

Acknowledgements

The ideas collected in this book are in large part the outcome of invaluable conversations with friends and colleagues. Among them are Mirna Pedalo, Hannah Martin, Ifor Duncan, Sasha Litvintseva, Ariel Caine, Helene Kazan, Neda Genova, Stefanos Lividis, David Burns, Ruthie Ginsburg, Or Ben David and Ziv Berkovich with whom I shared earlier drafts, images, seminars, concerns, speculations, regrets and many cups of coffee. I am especially indebted to my friends Laliv Melamed and Eitan Efrat, whose insightful and nuanced readings and general vision helped me enlarge my understanding of this project.

I am fortunate to have been a member of the Centre for Research Architecture (CRA) at Goldsmiths. This truly unique forum gathers artists and researchers as one community around one famously round table. My PhD advisors at Goldsmiths, Susan Schuppli and Pasi Valiaho, provided formative advice at all stages of the research and writing; I want to express my appreciation for their encouragement and for sharing with me their thoughts and suggestions. I learned much from working as their research student. At the CRA, I also received guidance from Eyal Weizman, whose reflections on the politics of the audio-visual continue to be an inspiration. I thank Sean Cubitt, Zach Blas, Lorenzo Pazzani, Erika Balsom, Ayesha Hamid and Ryan Bishop for reading bits and pieces of the manuscript and contributing important suggestions for improvement. The research seminars at King's College and Cambridge University challenged and expanded the scope of this book. The generous support I continue to receive from the Leverhulme Trust and the Film Studies Department at King's College London enabled the completion of the project.

Discussing the material collectively with writers, activists and filmmakers from many backgrounds at numerous conferences and film festivals enabled me to sharpen the focus on the implicit meanings of audio-visual media. I thank Sophie Rudland and Yasmin Garcha, my editors at Bloomsbury. Their insights and editing recommendations were essential for making a book out of a manuscript. I also feel greatly indebted to the SOAS Palestine Studies series editors Dina Matar and Adam Hanieh for their trust in the project.

I am especially grateful to Ayala Panievsky, Itamar Mann, Eytan Mann and Gabriela and Kenneth Mann, who remain my closest confidants and most critical readers. In a book about homes and nations, all thoughts begin in the family and are inevitably devoted to unsettling its very foundation.

Introduction

Habits provide the ability to change one's tendencies, to reorient one's actions to address the new, and to be able to experience the unexpected. – Elizabeth Grosz[1]

'People don't go from the private into the public anymore because they can be better informed at home', wrote media theorist Vilém Flusser from his apartment in 1985, 'there is essentially no public space left to which to go'.[2] Media, as Flusser suggested, perhaps hyperbolically, will ultimately obliterate the public realm, driving us all into the enclosed spaces of the home, sending us into eternal quarantine. While others celebrated media and communication as the precondition for public space, Flusser foresaw the dwindling of shared life and the possibility that with the embedding of media into the everyday, individual users would gradually become separated, isolated and insular. Rather than connecting people, media could ultimately divide.

Flusser's premonition resonates through a new training facility recently built by the Israeli military (IDF). Revealed in 2020 on an Israeli security blog, the cutting-edge training simulator built for the IDF at the Tse'elim military base in the south of Israel imagines a war fought from the interiors of homes.[3] At first glance, the new facility appears to simulate an ordinary domestic interior: the living room is adorned with freshly picked roses, framed photographs are carefully positioned on the furniture, and in them contours of smiling faces (Figure 1). But a closer examination discloses an uncanny offset, as if life had been sucked out of the room, leaving behind hollowed-out cinematic props of what could have been a home. Initially, the window appears to overlook a strangely blue and two-dimensional urban landscape, but another glance reveals that this is an interactive screen. 'The structure of the apartment and the walls are real', explains an executive from the IDF's subcontractor, 'but the sights visible from the windows are virtual'.[4]

Figure 1 A snapshot of 'The Apartment', a simulation facility in the Tse'elim military base (Source: 'Israeli Defense Blog', 2020).

Soldiers and officers are invited to dwell in this 'home' and spend time observing the landscape through the fake window, analysing the pixelated world, learning the urban topography and carefully planning raids, arrests and assassinations in Palestinian cities. War is waged in the simulator from the interiors of an occupied homes, taken over for military purposes of reconnaissance and surveillance.

To conceal the violence that it regulates under a seemingly quotidian function, the IDF named this fake abode, 'The Apartment'. The interactive window-turned-screen allows IDF soldiers to freely switch 'locations' and reside in homes at various and interchangeable Palestinian villages and cities in the West Bank and the Gaza Strip, a kind of military Video On Demand. The window-turned-screen supports the illusion that change takes place outside while the interiors offer a comfortable, static and shielded cocoon. But this unique simulator simulates more than battle. 'The Apartment' simulates for the Israeli soldier the experience of being in a stranger's home; training in waiting, eating and sleeping in someone else's bed; surveying the topography through someone else's eye. Tactics of combat are absorbed into domestic habitus, to facilitate a practice of being at home that undoes the essence of 'homeliness', even negates it. Essentially, 'The Apartment' simulates a colonial fantasy of not only occupying the home, but also weaponizing it against the very dwellers that once inhabited it. It is a colonizers' 'dream house', at once a target and a weapon; a space where domestication and occupation strangely collapse into one space. 'Even before we step outside, we are engaged in battle', the architecture historian Beatriz Colomina once wrote, 'as we all know but rarely publicize, the house is a scene of conflict'.[5]

Resonating with Flusser's premonition, the home is the theatre of operations for Israel's security regime, imagined by the IDF as the ultimate shelter (if it is Jewish), or the source of the threat itself (if Palestinian). 'The Apartment' is the emblem of a militarized perception that conceives of a world wholly absorbed into the space of mediation, where domestic habitat is no longer shielded or exempted from the sacrifices of war. Further echoing Flusser's perception of media, it demonstrates that communication technologies can be weaponized through their capacity to eradicate public spheres, separating collectives into isolated individuals.[6] Communication, as the media historian John Durham Peters tells us, is not simply synonymous with 'connection', but can also mean division. The Latin *communicare*, which means sharing, is often invoked as the only origin of the meaning of the word communication, but the rarely cited but equally relevant is the Greek term *koinoō*.[7] Like *communicare*, it means to make common, communicate or share, but it also entails dividing, parcelling, separating or quarantining. This rarely considered etymology of the word 'communication' seems to undergird one of the main arguments of this book: media flexibly breaks down collective existence by expanding the private realm and separating individual users. This, I will show, makes it a powerful weapon for the Israeli state.

Drawing on extensive archival research as well as data produced and circulated by IDF soldiers during their routines of policing, raiding, guarding, patrolling, arresting and photographing in the West Bank, East Jerusalem and the Gaza Strip, this book builds on the assertion that media have gradually become an integral, if volatile, part of life in Israel-Palestine. The thoughts collected here stem from the assumption that media is deeply enmeshed into the very fabric of being and that the use of cameras, mobile phones and social media by IDF soldiers and Palestinian civilians cannot be easily couched on a competition over 'a narrative' covered by news, radio, cameras, and Facebook posts. Instead of reading photographs and videos that document Israel's abuses of power in Palestine, I will ask how media alter the very modus operandi of military power, and more specifically, how it is embedded within a routine of occupation in Palestine as an 'omnipresence'.

In the last three decades, constant and pervasive documentation using predominately handheld cameras by both Israeli soldiers and Palestinian activists has routinely exposed grave abuses of state power, such as illegal arrests or unlawful killings. The increasingly visible use of excessive military force by the IDF has posed a new problem for it and Israeli society at large: violent incidents have been photographed and filmed, providing representations of punishing acts performed by Israeli soldiers. Yet, three decades on, it seems as though the Israeli authorities have not only learned to cope with the deluge of images, but in fact re-appropriated the everyday habits of communication in flexible and at times even innovative ways.

With this in mind, this book explores the profound impact that habits of using cameras, mobile phones and social media have had on Israel's security regime. Inasmuch as media practices pose a threat to Israel's legitimacy in the West Bank and Gaza, today it is simultaneously paving the way for new modes of control that are becoming ever more ubiquitous. These modes are founded on the IDF's ability to delegate the responsibility of image production and distribution to soldiers and civilians, usurping their habits of snapping, tagging and sharing images for military ends. In doing so, Israel has expanded its capacity to shape the narrative of the military occupation of Palestine, while sometimes transferring the burden of political, legal and ethical liabilities to individuals as an immunitary measure against the hyper-visibility of its routine procedures of control and repression.

In using the term 'immunitary', I draw on the Italian philosopher Roberto Esposito, for whom communication and immunization are deeply enmeshed through the Latin *munus*, which means 'gift' or 'sacrifice'. Immunization, Esposito contends, is directly linked to the figure of the individual and the threat that the over proximity of community poses on clearly demarcated individuality. Against this threat of undifferentiated community, Esposito tells us, an immunitary apparatus is urgently needed. Immunity, he argues, is what saves the communal space by setting up new protective borders against what is outside the group as well as among its very own members. 'In a world in which individuals who are naturally at risk confront one another in competition whose stakes are power and prestige', writes Esposito, 'the only way to avoid a catastrophic outcome is to institute among them sufficient distance so as to immunise each from everyone else'.[8] This immunitary figure of the individual, as I will illustrate below, emerges as an imperative protective shield used and abused by the state against ethical and legal responsibility.

Much of the material I present here is based on the declassified documents found in the IDF military archives in Israel, where I flipped through the often excruciatingly dreary military protocols that register the IDF's approach to media coverage, and more specifically, to the integration of visual media into their strategies of public relations and propaganda. Curiously, the more media technologies were incorporated into the very fabric of the occupation, the less evidence I could find of its application by the IDF. The gradual disappearance of any direct mentioning of distinct media such as film, photography, television or radio gestured to the ebbing of media into the very infrastructure of security and indeed into the lives of both civilians and soldiers in Israel-Palestine. References to the use of cameras vanish from the military archives as cameras become absorbed into the background of a premediated military occupation. As I will argue throughout this book, in reaction to the excess of information flows and round-the-clock usage of cameras, mobile phones and social media, the IDF has been slowly adapting to an environment that is always already documented in some way or form. The absorption of media into life intensifies the securitization in the West Bank, East Jerusalem, and the Gaza Strip and allows military power to change over time and according to need. Rather than relating or attending to a close reading of representations such as photographs, videos and oral testimonies, I am concerned with the ways in which *mediation* alters the very condition of life in and under military occupation.

In using the term *mediation*, I draw on writers, practitioners and activists for whom the term means something more than the circulation of photographs and videos that are deemed 'newsworthy' occurrences, and extends to the potentiality to generate unprecedented connections and unexpected events. 'Mediation', write media scholars Joanna Zylinska and Sarah Kember, is 'a key trope for understanding and articulating our being in, and becoming with, the technological world, our emergence and ways of interacting with it, as well as the acts and processes of temporarily stabilising the world into media, agents, relations, and networks'.[9] Through the notion of *mediation*, I attempt to move beyond questions that pertain to what is told or untold, seen or unseen, shared or unshared, to the ways in which the military presence in the West Bank, East Jerusalem and Gaza is shaped by constant interaction with technology as part and parcel of life itself. I therefore seek to broaden the definition of media and its entanglement with security in Israel-Palestine by considering media to be the infrastructures of being, the habitats and materials through which civilians and soldiers act.[10] Drawing on the writings of John Durham Peters, Helga Tawil-Souri, Rebecca Stein, Benjamin Bratton and others, I argue that communication itself should be seen not only as messages, but also as conditions for existence that organize forms of life.[11] I ask whether the absorption of media into life abates state power, or instead, facilitates its re-emergence in other formations, and if so, what do such new formations of power entail?

Today, all IDF soldiers *mediate*. Engaging with their own smartphones and social media profiles, the wide angles of remote surveillance cameras are split into numerous close-ups recorded with personally held cameras. The centralized vantage point of authority is thus multiplied and dissected into a variety of perspectives that do not always congeal to a singular, coherent image. Top-down logics of military technologies of surveillance and control are turned upside down, resulting in a more diffused form of 'soft power', as Brian Massumi suggests, when the civil is no longer clearly distinguished from the military, nor offense from defence, to the point where it becomes impossible to say where the exercise of state power begins and ends. Or in Massumi's more poignant phrasing: 'military affairs bleed across the spectrum'.[12] The use of media technologies by the IDF, which has traditionally been delegated to specific units, such as the spokeperson's office or the IDF's intelligence unit, is now in the hands of individual users of media, dissected by algorithms. A key argument in this book, therefore, addresses the extension of state power through the everyday habits of mediation exercised by individual users, both civilians and soldiers. Examining media practices means looking at the historical contexts and political climates that facilitate the gradual absorption of media practices into a routine of policing. Yet, habits do not simply appear in photographs and videos. Evading representation, habits are not easily recorded by the visible traces of military rule of Palestine. Rather, habits are made perceptible through the juxtaposition of various images, bodies and spaces with information flows and algorithms that together form assemblages of media infrastructures and data.

Habitual media

Drawing on media theorist Wendy Hui Kyong Chun, what I call 'habitual media' pertains to practices that are today increasingly re-appropriated by state actors who aim to undermine and obstruct the counter-visualities of resistance. In her seminal book, *Update to Remain the Same: Habitual New Media*, Chun defines 'habitual media' as ubiquitous technologies that dictate a routine of perpetual crisis. Habitual media are sustained by the constant and repetitive engagement of users, on the one hand, and a permanent need to update and recalibrate practices of media, on the other. Chun conceptualizes habit through the seemingly paradoxical duality of repetition and change, whereby the very dynamic of change is incorporated into the everyday and embodied by users. Habitual media, for Chun, are inseparable from the perpetual crisis of economic instability and risk, which requires alertness and flexibility as a means of coping with contingency.[13] 'Through the analytic of habits', writes Chun, 'individual actions coalesce bodies into a monstrously connected chimera'.[14] Crucially, drawing on Chun, I argue that media generates imagined networks that in turn, generate *individuals* rather than *collectives*. These individuals, shaped through the act of sharing data, are defined by their personal, asynchronous habits, rather than by mass ceremonies and events.

In Israel-Palestine, this 'connected chimera' has, in turn, become an instrument of military power, reliant on the countless minute gestures of individual soldiers and civilians. The permanent crisis of instability is replaced with a permanent emergency. Accordingly, in the context of the Israeli occupation, war is no longer a one-off occurrence, waged by a nation state; rather, it is increasingly replaced by an enduring condition, which can no longer be captured by a singular media event. Effectively, perpetual emergency feeds and sustains habits, which in turn changes the nature of an authority determined by how numerous interconnected individuals record, upload, share and tag images.

Due to the rapid increase in the production and circulation of images, and the use of cameras and mobile phones by civilians, it is crucial to examine how sovereignty makes use of habitual media practices, updating its tactics in reaction to the shifting media ecology. State power has not been left unabated by the incorporation of habitual media into its everyday practices; rather, as Benjamin Bratton has argued, today sovereignty is made out of a patchwork, weaved together from institutions, private companies, and most significantly, technology itself, which dictates certain behaviours and habits.[15] I therefore attempt to shed light on the imperceptible force of habit that accompanies and underpins state authority. Habit, in this context, operates as a cumulative force that works its way up, from the body of the individual, to the level of the institution and the state apparatus.

The notion of habit might be intuitively understood as stasis, normalization and equilibrium. But as I will argue here, it can also suggest dynamics, change and transformability. On the one hand, the notion of habit relates to the force of repetitive performance and training for combat. This aspect of habit concerns training schemes that every soldier goes through. On the other hand, habit also allows a subtle transformation to take place. This second aspect of habit emerges from the sudden interruption of the first and produces a creative force. These two notions of habit – the first pertaining to repetition and stasis and the second to a potential transformation – recall two historical strands of thought through which to approach a definition of habit. In the first, habit is understood as a mere bodily reflex, threatening to undermine the rational autonomous subject: 'Pure mechanism, routine process, devitalisation of sense, habit is the disease of repetition that threatens freshness of thought and stifles the voice, repeatable but never stale, of the categorical imperative.'[16] But the second historical strand of habit, developed by Felix Ravaisson, John Dewey, Elizabeth Grosz and others, contends that habit is not only acquired, but is contracted by transformation, with respect to the very change that gave birth to it. As Ravaisson puts it, '[h]abit is the remains of repetition, not the repetition itself'.[17] Rather than being simply the force of past experience dictating the present action, the residual being of habit opens up new possibilities. Like Ravaisson, Grosz distinguishes habit from the reflexive, internalized actions ingrained into the body. For Grosz, habit points to a new kind of relation between life and its surrounding support systems. Grosz defines habits as inherently modifying, creating new, and changing the disposition to action: a new virtuality, a new tendency to act and a new potentiality. Habits:

> [b]ring about a new ability, the capacity to persist, thrive, change and grow in the face of a world that is itself subject to endless and often random change. Habits provide the ability to change one's tendencies, to reorient one's actions to address the new, and to be able to experience the unexpected.[18]

Through habit, the role of media technologies in war and as warfare also changes. While media technologies can contract habits that sustain the patterns of activities of soldiers in routine operations, they also constantly demand updates. 'Habituation dulls us to the new', writes Chun, while at the same time, introducing a change that requires recalibration and re-habituation.[19] This duality, underlining Chun's exploration of the intersection of media and habit, permeates routines of policing and securitizing. Effectively this means that the IDF utilizes media as part of its mode of functioning, while at the same time facing the need to remain updated. For instance, while the IDF might attempt to prevent soldiers from uploading pictures from their deployment in Gaza, Facebook actively encourages them to share and circulate their images. After dozens of such photographs make their way into social media, the IDF is forced to not only accept that these are now inevitable outcomes of habitual media practices, but also, and more crucially, reconsider how such habits can be co-opted into security. To maintain its mode of operation, the IDF paradoxically needs to constantly modify its use of media in accordance with the habits of individual soldiers. How habits of mediation are co-opted into the security regime in Israel-Palestine is the core inquiry of this book.

A focus on *habitual media* can expand the prevailing analysis of representations of violence that have come to dominate the critical literature addressing the Israeli occupation. In their important book, *Digital Militarism: Israel's Occupation in the Social Media Age*, Rebecca Stein and Adi Kuntsman argue that the use of mobile phones and social media by IDF soldiers is another facet of an entrenched militarism and its normalization.[20] The surge of images is thus considered as a symptom of an already established civil-military complex that is deeply connected to the Israeli state. Kuntsman and Stein, however, do not consider the use of new technologies by soldiers during their everyday military procedures as an active force that deeply alters the very operation of state power. Habitual media, I will argue, are not simply another tool in the arsenal of a normalizing military occupation; they also enable the military to flexibly change and recalibrate how media is used. How habits dictate the integration of media into the armed conflict in Israel-Palestine, and the implication of habitual media on military power have not yet been adequately examined.

Habitual use of media has become inseparable from the security regime in Israel-Palestine. The notion of security, as it is often defined, refers to a condition in which the state of exception has become the rule.[21] In the West Bank and East Jerusalem, this so-called exception lies at the core of the legality of the military rule. Various procedures exercised in the West Bank are legitimized under the authority of extraordinary legislation enacted by the British Mandate over Palestine. Although the British Mandate was terminated in 1948, Israel decided to adopt the declared state of exception from 1967, shortly after taking control of the West Bank.[22] The Israeli military authorities began using the British Defence Regulations against the population in Occupied Palestine and have resorted to them to justify various actions such as arrests, detentions, house demolitions and spontaneous curfews. This legal infrastructure allows Israel to use and abuse security for different and flexible needs and interests. The shift towards a paradigm of security means that war becomes an interminable condition, without any clearly defined frontlines, and the traditional distinction between war and everyday life becomes increasingly muddled. 'War', write Michael Hardt and Antonio Negri, 'is becoming the primary organising principle of society, and politics merely one of its means or guises'.[23] Under these circumstances war is aimed not only at controlling the population but also at producing and reproducing all aspects of social life. It operates not only through violence but also by permeating everyday life with regular routines. 'Security is a form of biopower', Hardt and Negri argue, 'in the sense that it is charged with the task of producing and transforming social life at its most general level'.[24] Due to its permeation into all aspects of life, security dissolves fixed distinctions between the military and civil spheres, conflict zones and private homes, inside and outside. It consists of everyday routines and unconscious actions, cumulatively perpetuating national ideologies of defence.

Where war is gradually replaced by security routines indistinguishable from the patterns of everyday life, the role of habit is amplified.

This notion of security is nowhere more pronounced than in Israel-Palestine. Established in 1967, the military rule was set as a temporary solution, according to the restrictions prescribed by the Hague Convention of 1907. Several decades on, this 'temporary' state of affairs has become a permanent condition, in direct violation of international humanitarian law.[25] While the military rule of the West Bank and East Jerusalem is predicated, under Israeli law, on Emergency Regulations initially put in place by the British Mandate in 1945, the Israeli parliament (Knesset) has authorized the renewal of these emergency regulations every year since the state was established in 1948. In practice this means that Israel upholds a permanent legal condition of emergency, which allows its government and military to use a variety of procedures, such as trying prisoners in military courts, house demolitions and unlimited detention of non-Israeli Palestinians, as well as continuing its heavy military presence in civil centres. The substitution of the spatial and temporal categories of war with the indefinite temporalities of a permanent emergency blurs the distinction between the everyday and wartime.

Personalizing occupation

Due to this enduring legal perception of a 'permanent emergency', the use of media technologies by individual users rapidly increases. With the use of social media such as Facebook, YouTube and TikTok, traditional forms of power have been giving way to what the media theorist Geert Lovink calls 'personalization'. Personalization allows companies and governments to target individual users, while encouraging them to interact with online platforms.[26] For Lovink, the conceptual leap that is most relevant to grasp is the move from collectives, groups, forums and communities to the empowerment of loosely connected individuals in networks. This shift, writes Lovink, 'had already begun in the neoliberal 1990s, facilitated by growing computing power, storage capacity and internet bandwidth, alongside simplifying interfaces on smaller and smaller devices'.[27] This transformation has been slowly redefining the meaning and role of media by linking together visual outputs with the users that produce and circulate them. These adaptations in the lives of civilians and soldiers in Israel-Palestine introduce a kind of 'personalized occupation', whereby everyday media practices, together with the infrastructure that isolate and separate users, facilitate new modes of governmentality.

Throughout the chapters of this book, I argue that the ubiquitous use of cameras and social media has been gradually sharpening the resolution of state security, allowing it to hone in on the individual user as a key political figure within the Israeli security regime. The availability of personal camcorders has allowed Israel to make use of the amateur practices of filmmaking to tackle security. Indeed, from the early 1990s, the ubiquity of personal cameras facilitated the integration of individualized viewpoints that witness and record war and armed conflict. In this model, civilians and soldiers are not only nodes within a faceless system but in fact coerced agents of state power. I thus consider the personal engagement of individual users with media technologies and the capacity of media to isolate users as a core function in contemporary warfare. The use of media by soldiers does not only yield representations, i.e. snapshots and videos, through which particular acts and events are made visible and tangible, but also and more substantially enable Israel to shed responsibility by isolating individual soldiers who are deemed 'bad apples' in an otherwise allegedly benevolent occupation. This process of shedding responsibility works in the favour of the IDF when soldiers are encouraged to mediate routine procedures of policing, raiding and arresting. The habitual use of personally held mobile phones and social media profiles set these borders via algorithms that dissect the uniformity of military actors, while the contemporary media ecology produces a new field of operation in which IDF soldiers can no longer hide under the cloak of a faceless authority and collective action.

The habitual use of media expedites a process that the legal scholar Gabriella Blum has called 'the individualization of war'. The process of individualization addresses the noticeable change in the nature of the military threats faced by states and growing intervention of private companies in providing state security. 'States no longer enjoy a monopoly over the use of significant military power', writes Blum; instead, 'individuals and groups of individuals are nowadays capable of dealing physical blows on a magnitude previously reserved for regular armies'.[28] For Blum, technological innovation allows for more precise identification and targeting of distinct individuals and objects, and more significantly, a shift of legal accountability to the individual. The IDF has recognized this shift as an advantage that allows it to pin down individuals when it fits its incentives and goals. This procedure of individuation – in which soldiers act for and in themselves – could seemingly safeguard modes of legal accountability and even limit abuse of force; indeed, at times, it does. Yet, the intensifying military presence in East Jerusalem, the West Bank and the Gaza Strip has shown that this process of individuation works to the advantage of Israel by allowing authority to become modular, fragmented and flexible, and to outsource the task of documentation to dispersed users who intimately engage with producing information.

A key concept weaved throughout this book is what I call the 'individuation of media', according to which individual users become extremely valuable for the Israeli state and the military. Where others emphasize the interdependency of individuals in their coming together in the political realm, I wish to underline the division and isolation dictated by the usage of media technologies and its operation in conjunction with a defensive perception of home and household. I draw here on the compelling work of political philosopher Hagar Kotef, which sensibly defines the individual – which she calls the 'colonising self' – as inherently tethered to the notion of state and home.[29]

In my attempt to explicate the way in which individuated practices of media become both risky and beneficial for the IDF, I am also attentive to attempts made by the IDF in the late 1990s and early 2000s to resist it through the advent of digital technologies, and the promise of anonymity, opacity and flexibility couched in network theories. As I will claim in Chapter 2, the techno-militarized vision of the smoothly operating soldier, fashioned around the euphemistic notion of 'Netwar', envisioned as a faceless swarm of combatants that moves fluidly within the refugee camps, has since been proven to be a militaristic pipe dream. Indeed, on the cusp of the twenty-first century, digital images and the rise of network formations mesmerized IDF officers who were versed in continental philosophy and saw themselves as tech savvy, resulting in a flurry of new military tactics informed by lofty ideas predicated on speed and flexibility and inspired by cyberculture. Some of those dreams came true when the military began contracting Israeli high-tech companies to design new weapons. 'The state', suggested Achille Mbembe 20 years ago, 'may transform itself into a war machine [...] by borrowing from regular armies while incorporating new elements well adapted to the principle of segmentation and deterritorialization'.

Twenty-five years later, things look quite different. If IDF think tanks desired to conceive of soldiers as metamorphing units that perform manoeuvres within dense cities, under the contemporary mediascape soldiers are pinned back to concrete identities. The shapeshifting military squads of the late twentieth century have been replaced with atomized users who cannot escape their tailor-made algorithms. If, as Chun has argued, mobile phones and social media are tools that latch onto the habits of documenting, storing and distributing images and videos, today media is coerced into military power as a 'personalizing' force, allowing the IDF to choose whether to hide or expose its actors. In Chapter 5, I will argue that by allowing civilians and soldiers to exercise their habits of snapping photographs and circulating data, the IDF absorbs a dosage of what could harm it.

This personalizing force is the state's response to the use of media technologies by Palestinians and activists that gather to resist military power. The promise embedded in media can potentially resuscitate a collective voice that has been denied from Palestinians. Through video advocacy, so the argument goes, a common and collective demand can be articulated, one that resists the personal voice to achieve anonymity, opacity, impersonality and plurality. In his book, *The People Are Not an Image: Vernacular Video after the Arab Revolutions*, filmmaker and writer Peter Snowdon suggests that the stream of videos of the popular revolution in Syria amounted to demands made by a faceless collective, wherein individuality is replaced with a revolutionary 'we'.[30] Snowdon argues that the plural, anonymous, impersonal dynamics that traverses the videos streamed during the Syrian uprising already 'transcend the perspective of the empirical individual who made them *at the moment when they were uploaded to the internet*' (italics in original). According to Snowdon, those videos are unchained from individuality to migrate virally online.

If Snowdon looks at the aesthetics of the plural within videos, the Israeli media theorist Ruthie Ginsburg appeals to the collaborative production of videos and pays close attention to the practice of filmmaking. Ginsburg contends that the emancipating potential of audio-visual media is pronounced through the concerted and collective action that media practices inscribe. She makes the crucial move from what the image shows to the ways in which images are made. Looking at particularly violent events that took place in Palestine and were caught in the lenses of civilians and activists, Ginsburg's prism focuses on the collective and impersonal modes of image production. Such analyses continue to be imperative for the task of imagining a common ground, despite and against the immense efforts made by police, military and private companies to pin down, parcel and separate.

This book attempts to openly converse and exchange with the work mentioned above under the assumption that to fully understand how to resist the state, it is today urgent to trace the ways in which Israel and the IDF cultivated the *individual* – both figuratively and as user – as a core agent of state power. Hopefully, the ideas collected here will cast new light on the vital work that had already been done to investigate the role of everyday media in Israel-Palestine and to make legal, political, ethical and social claims with audio-visual media.

From representation to circulation

To see the military occupation in Palestine, a different aesthesis strategy must be considered. In her book, *Visual Occupations: Violence and Visibility in a Conflict Zone*, Gil Hochberg asks how certain constellations of images come to function as 'representations' of a complex and ongoing conflict.[31] 'Looking at the vast majority of images that make up the international media spectacle of the Israeli-Palestinian conflict', she observes, 'one cannot fail to notice how severely limiting these images are and how violently they restrict our ability to read them'.[32] The images she has in mind include the all-too-familiar photographs of Palestinian masses crowded at checkpoints, ruins of demolished houses, armed Palestinian militants, the damage left by Hamas rockets and, of course, Israeli soldiers. 'The repetitive dissemination of these images', Hochberg argues, 'constructs a highly restrictive visual framework. Palestinians and Israelis appear in this predetermined visual field, time and time again, as familiar objects with pre-assigned roles'. Indeed, within the confines of this familiar visual frame, the occupation begins to seem almost banal, while Palestinians are seen through a fetishized lens of destruction, violence and loss, deprived from political agency. Instead of looking at images published by official media outlets, Hochberg turns her attention to artworks by both Palestinians and Israelis that have the potential to redistribute and undermine established frames of reference. At stake in this move towards visual art are both the reaffirmation of representation as the dominant force within visual culture, repudiation of new modes of image production and circulation that transform the role and meaning of images. Hochberg's thorough analysis risks reinforcing the dichotomy between what is seen and unseen, and as such undermining the vast range of images and data that do not make it into newspapers, press releases and galleries.

It seems that the aesthetic lure manufactured by war and surveillance technologies has eclipsed the mundane use of media and their rapid habituation into the daily itineraries of policing to be exuberantly adopted by the 'boots on the ground' that uphold and enforce the Israeli occupation day-in, day-out. The media practices adopted by soldiers are today not only changing how we sense and make sense of the military presence in Israel-Palestine but also reshaping the routine conduct of the IDF. Looking at the role of media in a routine of policing, today we should reconsider whether the focus on photographs and videos, and their close optical examination and analysis, paradoxically eclipses the violence. The affective capacity of representations is curtailed by other functions of media in warfare that remain outside of the frame. Instead of homing in on representations, perhaps we should zoom out to bear witness to the patchwork of images, infrastructures and users that together make up a space of mediation, where civilians and soldiers become agents that serve the state. With mediation, the state does not simply decline, but rather, as Benjamin Bratton has already noted, the contemporary condition is qualified both by a 'debordering perforation and liquefaction of the system's ability to maintain a monopoly on political geography', and by a fragmentation, manifest through the pinpointing of individual users.[33]

To adequately define the use of media in war, there is a growing need to recognize that wartime is no longer distinguished from the temporalities of the everyday. Both soldiers and civilians at home determine which photographs circulate by interacting with online platforms such as Facebook, YouTube and TikTok, as a way of taking part in an essentially invisible economy of information spread patterns that are determined by algorithmic operations. Encouraged by companies such as Facebook and YouTube to 'like' and 'share' photographs and videos, users push certain images to the fore, while undercutting the capacity of others to be seen. By thinking of images as data we move beyond the legacy of mobilizing action, on the one hand, and compassion fatigue, on the other, and towards the realm of functions and operations. Once we do so, other problems ensue. For instance, how can we think with and against visual cultures – which elevates human vision – in times when the role of images is no longer determined solely by the visible? Why must we reconsider how war and security operate in light of the rise of information flows?

While scholars of visual culture recognize how both photographic images and everyday media can articulate a collective claim against centralized state power, it is rarely considered how such modes of engagement can be incorporated into the state apparatus itself and re-appropriated by military authorities as a strategy to expand their control over a rapidly changing media sphere. In fact, the very dichotomy between everyday media and state media often serves to maintain the traditional divide between top-down mechanisms of image projection and bottom-up vernacular media practices, where the former is attached to state sovereignty and the latter to political dissent and civic emancipation. This dichotomy, however, risks concealing how the state, together with private companies, adopts and appropriates media practices as part of its unofficial media strategy.

As we are confronted with the demise of representational modes of bearing witness to Israel's occupation of Palestine, we must further problematize the promise couched in photographic images as bearers of justice. The capacity of images to mobilize dissent or shame is severely weakened by the multiplication of sources and flood of information that fills up our screens. Emancipatory media has come to an abrupt end and in its place emerged a more diffused and ever-present realm of mediation that, while making abuses of power spectacularly visible, unpredictably hampers the legibility of photographic and audio-visual material. For instance, the IDF has initiated contacts with private telecommunication companies to program search engines that probe into private messages between users of social media. In 2018, a leaked document mentions the need to pre-empt the actions of what the IDF has called 'lone terrorists'. The IDF responded to the leak by claiming that what they had done had become standard practice in the corporate world. Why, they asked, should they be condemned for something that was so widespread?

Indeed, top-down surveillance is made partially superfluous by the participation of soldiers and civilians who willingly share information. These prevailing forms of surveillance are predicated on the everyday use of media and wilful dissemination of information. Claire Birchall named this condition, whereby governments and private companies harvest information directly from the individual users who willingly share their private information, 'shareveillance'.[34] Considering the enhanced transparency of personal data, Birchall seeks out opportunities to salvage the concept of 'sharing' to imagine a collective subjectivity that could emerge from within this sociotechnical moment.[35] The use of the term 'share' refers to a range of platforms and applications that facilitate the harnessing of surplus time, skills, goods, and capacities is only the latest incarnation of sharing's articulation within the digital context. Birchall notes that human and non-human actors are involved in the dissemination of data, documents, photos, feelings, opinions and news across space and time.[36] Rather than thinking about sharing primarily as something that soldiers and civilians *do* on the internet, it is today necessary to focus on the idea that sharing is integral to omnipresence mediasphere that has engrossed concrete space.

Alexander Galloway calls this mediasphere the *protocological* level, meaning, standards that 'govern how specific technologies are agreed to, adopted, implemented, and ultimately used by people around the world'.[37] The idea of sharing as protocological is posited here to emphasize the fact that specific modes of sharing are determined by ideologically charged dispositions. As Galloway puts it, 'protocol is how technological control exists after decentralisation'.[38] Crucially, the conditions of sharing today inflect a subjectivity that makes a particular call on, and imposes a limitation to, the agential capacities of citizens.

Galloway insists that we think about images as mere interfaces of much deeper operations. 'Algorithmic interfaces', he writes, 'even as they flaunt their own highly precise, virtuosic levels of detail – prove that something is happening behind and beyond the visible'.[39] While images and videos that document Israel's military presence in Palestine appear on our screens, they expose only the edges of much larger constellations linking media infrastructure, media habits and algorithmic calculations that remain, at least for the most part, invisible. The question of how images of abuses of power affect us is revived through new modes of sharing and circulation. But is the violence representable, or does it remain, to a large extent, outside of the image?

Galloway deviates from the established discourse around photographs and their ethical force. He invokes Jacques Ranciere's essay, titled 'The Future of the Image', in which the power of the image is put to the test. In this essay, Ranciere asks what happens when graphic images of state-sponsored torture circulate within the mass media? What do pictures want? Galloway's main difficulty with Ranciere's position, and those sympathetic to him, is that the question is in fact never exclusively one of representability, but more around the capacity of images to implore a reaction. The question is one of affective response:

> Occasionally (Ranciere) plays the part of the nervous liberal, worried whether certain images will escape into the wild, and if they do whether or not the spectators witnessing them will exhibit the proper emotional responses. His position is therefore at root allied with the creation and maintenance of proper subject positions. His is a discourse of visual culture that is quite familiar: the power of an image relies exclusively on its circulation as hidden or visible; images exist either as triggers for emotional responses within populations, or as cynical evidence of that same population's numbness to them. Either seen or unseen, either affecting or impotent – such is the trap of representation today.[40]

Galloway sees the trap of representation in its link to the dichotomy of visibility and invisibility, and the weighing of the image as a photograph, with the affective response that it generates. He turns to Gilles Deleuze and his society of control to pave a new way towards another kind of violence that does not crop up as a spectacular image, but is no less insidious and pervasive in its particular deployment. By doing so, he asks us to reflect on the violence embedded into the ubiquity of a society of control.

In his essay 'Data Visualization and Documentary's (In)visible Frontiers', Kris Fallon builds on Galloway to argue that power does not reside in the image, but in networks, computers, algorithms, information and data.[41] But Fallon also points to Galloway's injunction to 'cast away' considerations of image spectacle and the risk of missing the extent to which one regime – the regime of information – is entangled in the regime of representations. One is inseparable from the other. Fallon's critique of the over-determinations of protological operations is essential in understanding the tension between the spectacular aspect of the images and how, underneath the level of representations, certain links and operations are unleashed. Images merge the level of representation – with its capacity to mobilize and shape emotions – with the protological level that lies beneath the visible interface. Representations are thus not the central object of my analysis, but the entry point to habits and automated activities that lie beneath. Although my examination will focus on representations, it is the habitual production and circulation of information that I seek to better define. Yet, if attention should move away from the one-dimensional gaze at images that beckon us to look closer, where we do find ourselves investing our critical efforts in exposing the role of everyday media in Israel-Palestine?

Chapter breakdown

Each of the six chapters of this book addresses the influence of habitual media practices on security and warfare from a different angle. The case studies that structure each chapter delineate the gradual embedding of individuated media into the state's mechanisms of vision. Following a chronological sequence of events, the structure of the book aims to trace how, from 1991 to the present day, the Israeli state and the IDF have gradually incorporated habitual media into their arsenal of weapons, and how the spontaneous media practices of individual civilians and soldiers have been appropriated to cater to security interests.

The first chapter focuses on the First Gulf War (1991) to trace the demise of mass communication technologies as unidirectional top-down channels of communication between the state and the citizen. In January of 1991, Iraq launched missiles at cities in Israel, unleashing panic amongst civilians. In its effort to protect the public against the threat of missiles, the Israeli state and the military distributed uncertainty, instability and fear. Israeli officials prepared civilians for a threat it asserted loomed over their private homes. Government and military officials repeatedly emphasized that citizens should remain at home whenever possible. The private household became the recommended form of shelter against the obscure threats posed by Saddam Hussein in his attempt to deter the US expulsion of Iraq from Kuwait. While pretending to contain the panic that the missiles unleashed, IDF officials were implicitly inflaming the fear of a potential chemical missile strike, urging individuals to prepare themselves for the worst and to hermetically seal their homes against nerve gas. Consequently, as this chapter shows, fear rapidly penetrated the everyday and reshaped the ways in which Israeli civilians extend the nation's security apparatus. Where the official state communication channels failed to record and contain the unfolding crisis, amateur filmmakers filled in the gaps. For the first time, predominantly homemade images framed war. This marked a shift towards personal use of media that would give rise, over the next two decades, to an apparatus of visualization, whereby habitual modes of image production and circulation redefine the visuality of Israel's security regime.

The second chapter begins with the eruption of the al-Aqsa Intifada (2000) and the military operation that followed (2002). It explores the role of the IDF's Military Film Units, particularly those under the IDF spokesperson's office, which were assigned to record photographs and video footage of military operations deep within Palestinian towns and refugee camps in Jenin, Nablus, Ramallah and the Gaza Strip. The chapter focuses on the IDF's attempt to orchestrate the upsurge of images produced by numerous 'user-soldiers' in the course of their daily lives. Beginning with the al-Aqsa Intifada, the Israeli soldier was no longer a mere cog in the war machine; he or she was also an independent producer and consumer of media. As I demonstrate in this chapter, the fragmentation introduced by media technologies has presented both a threat and a new opportunity for the Israeli army. Incorporated into the routines of the military occupation, media technologies rendered visible what until recently remained hidden or obscured, such as grave abuses of power by soldiers and systemic violations of human rights. While this new visibility exposed unlawful activities, it would later serve to further obfuscate the military occupation and expand the capacity of surveillance technologies to trace and monitor ruled populations.

The third chapter returns to the notion of the home and the domestic interior to look at the binary opposition between two perceptions of privacy at the core of a colonial imagination. It attempts to define an imagination that elevates one home as a sanctuary that shelters life while vilifying the other, perceiving it as the core of the menacing secret. I claim that this biopolitical opposition is driven by the fallacy that Jewish and Palestinian homes hide under their roofs opposite relations to life. The soldiers' habit of filmmaking mediates this foundational split at the heart of the Israeli perception of security. This chapter questions how, through personal habits of filmmaking, the space of the home is either reaffirmed or stripped of its very essence. The comparison reveals that media habits are at once integral to *inhabiting* and *occupying*; they emerge as the Janus face of Israel's perception of security. But to address this question it is first important to contextualize the use of mobile phone cameras and applications such as Facebook as the prime communication channel through which soldiers become double agents: both individual users and representatives of state power.

The fourth chapter returns to the figure of the individual to argue that the soldier's face has emerged as a new site of politics, driven by the use of everyday media in warfare. The image of the soldier's face, I suggest, has become the Achilles' heel of a military apparatus struggling to maintain its centralized power. Once captured on camera, the image of a soldier's face can potentially weaken a centralized military apparatus that depends on presenting its soldiers as generic representatives. In this way, the face fragments the body politic and its idealized unity. Looking at such images of faces that have been circulated on social media, this chapter asks what the hidden face has to hide, and why its uncovering poses a new threat to military authority. I go on to argue that individuated media technologies have begun to shift the focus of warfare onto the individual. While soldiers' everyday media practices are fragmenting the IDF's official media outlets, warfare is gradually changing its resolution, increasingly focusing on individual suspects and alleged terrorists.[42]

In the fifth chapter I turn to those who are most affected by the co-option of media technologies into warfare. I examine the use of cameras and mobile phones by Palestinian civilians and activists who document their encounters with Israeli soldiers in the West Bank and East Jerusalem. Habitual media practices, in this context, become acts of resistance and self-defence against a visuality that renders them invisible. Activists' capacity to collect and share visual evidence has been drastically improved by widespread access to image production (mobile phones) and channels of circulation (social media). Visual documentation has been further encouraged by the Israeli NGO B'Tselem, which initiated a project in 2007 called 'Shooting Back', intended to distribute small cameras to civilians living in the hearts of cities and villages in the West Bank, where friction between Israeli soldiers and Palestinians is worst.[43] B'Tselem has assisted Palestinians in recording confrontations with either IDF soldiers or Jewish settlers, both to document the normalized violation of human rights and to deter excessive use of force. The technological superiority of the Israeli military and its advanced weaponry thus met an unlikely challenge from dedicated individuals with handheld cameras, carrying out a daily routine of recording and sharing images.

But against the emancipating potential of such practices, I suggest that by 2015 the IDF had developed new techniques to disarm civic media.

In this chapter, I also argue that, confronted with the efficacy of such images, the IDF has had to incorporate and internalize media practices in order to obfuscate its actions. What I will refer to as 'visual obfuscation' aims to increase the flow of data even further and to bring it to the point of excess, to a point where attention is thwarted from a particular photograph or video. Here my analysis draws on Helen Nissenbaum, who theorizes obfuscation as the deliberate addition of ambiguous information in order to interfere with data collection.[44] At its most abstract, Nissenbaum argues, obfuscation is the production of noise to make data more unintelligible, and therefore less valuable.[45] Similarly, in the context of the Israeli occupation, visual obfuscation responds to the inevitable visibility of spaces and bodies by adding additional, competing images. No longer monitored solely by the state, spaces and bodies are always already caught in the net of cameras carried by individual civilians and combatants. Visual obfuscation thus aims at discrediting one image by posing numerous others. It defies the evidentiary mode of representation through conjuring multiple additional images that complicate, obscure and cloud a given document. I will argue that due to the omnipresence of media and its integration into life, representation is replaced by circulation.

The sixth and last chapter focuses on the tension between the individual and the community to rethink how liberal individuality comes to permit and organize the violence against the Palestinian population. Focusing on two videos produced in 2018 and 2021, this last chapter explores the politics of transparency and opacity through the figure of the single sniper and the angry masses. Here I return to the core idea of the book: the figure of the liberal individual as the source of state violence.

Domestic inspectors: The First Gulf War and the militarization of the home

We are, we seem to be, on the edge of war. At the threshold. A line has been drawn. Literally, a deadline. In crossing that line, we go to war. We go outside. We leave the homeland and do battle on the outside. But there are always lines in the interior, within the apparently safe confines of the house. Even before we step outside, we are engaged in battle. As we all know but rarely publicize, the house is a scene of conflict. The domestic has always been at war.[1]

Following several weeks of uncertainty and a few hours after the US air force commenced an intensive airstrike on Bagdad, in 17 January 1991, the Iraqi military fired an Al Hussein scud missile in Israel's direction. Scrambling to report on the long-dreaded attack, the live public television broadcast aired one slide with the word *alert* flickering in six languages to signal to civilians that the time has come to take cover (Figure 2). But despite the alarming sound of sirens, one anonymous civilian intuitively grabbed his personal camera and directed it to the dark skies above. The grainy footage recorded that night depicts a small flare crossing a dark screen, until hitting the ground with a white flash.

I found this video buried deep in the IDF archives, between dozens of trivial papers from the early 1990s that document exchanges between military officers. According to the archive's search history, I was the first to view the tape since it was filed in the archive, almost three decades ago. Watching the tape for the first time on the monitor in the archive, it seemed odd that this video would be of any significance to the IDF. Nevertheless, the 30-second clip captured what state-run television failed to record: the first missile fired in Israel's direction by the Iraqi army during the 1991 Gulf War. The video was later obtained by the military spokesperson and broadcast on television for all to see.

The details in the frame are barely legible; instead, the singular perspective of the amateur filmmaker is the communicated massage. The audio-visual

Figure 2 A frame from the live television broadcast during the bombardment, 1991
(Source: https://www.youtube.com/watch?v=PVFV6RTvP28s).

document registers something that does not appear in the frame. That is, it
documents practices of domestic filmmaking re-appropriated for the first time,
to document a national emergency. The sharp movements of the camera and
the agitated zoom-in on the incoming missile are the seismograph registering
the rapid activation of the individual user of media as part of the Israeli security
apparatus.

Indeed, more than mere unintelligible noise, the homemade video marks the
intersection of two distinct transformations that took shape in the early 1990s.
On the one hand, the availability of personal cameras and the rapidly growing
market of camcorders for domestic use. Analog video format for camcorders
was introduced by Sony in 1989 and found eager consumers. On the other
hand, the escalating sense of uncertainty that permeated homes in Israel due to
threats made by Iraq. Together, the two opened a window of opportunity for the
Israeli state to incorporate new sources of visual media into their public relations
apparatus that absorbed the private use of domestic cameras.

Looking at the circumstances that led to the filming of this homemade
video and others like it, in this chapter I suggest that the fusion of available

technologies and collective national paranoia enabled the rapid militarization of the everyday, and the enlisting of civilians as amateur filmmakers that do not merely film their own routines but supplement the state's vision. This chimera that merges available technologies and collective paranoia surfaced in the First Gulf War and paved the way for the state to co-opt the personal use of media.

Only some months before the amateur video was filmed, the Israeli government had declared a state of emergency. Saddam Hussein, in an attempt to deter the United States from mobilizing a military intervention into Baghdad, threatened to target Israeli cities with missiles that potentially carry nuclear, chemical and biological warheads. Arming Iraqi soldiers to engage in war, Hussein had warned in December of 1990 that if the Iraqi people 'must suffer the first blow, whether at the front or here in Baghdad, and whether or not Israel participates directly in the aggression, they will suffer the second blow in Tel Aviv'.[2] The United States perceived Iraq's invasion of Kuwait as an attempt to challenge the regional order and to assert hegemony over the Middle East. Of course, there was also the incentive to protect their financial interests by intervening in the local geopolitics and standing with Saudi Arabia to secure access to oil. Considering its longstanding alliance with the United States and its long-standing occupation of Palestine territories, Israel became a target by proxy.

Jewish-Israeli citizens in Israel, usually well-shielded from the violent clashes in Gaza and the West Bank, were now, if only momentarily, exposed to direct missile strikes and to the invisible threat of nerve gas. Catching Israel at the height of a bloody intifada in the West Bank and the Gaza Strip, the missile attack was not only a threat to Israel's otherwise well-protected civil sphere ('Homefront'), but was also perceived as a public relations opportunity that, if presented correctly, could potentially resuscitate the public image of Israel as a small state under the looming threat of annihilation. This was a contrived fantasy designed by Israel from its inception to justify the occupation of Palestinian territories. By winning over the urge to retaliate, the Israeli Prime Minister Itzhak Shamir believed that the crisis might well be a chance to restore Israel's status as victim, for the world to see.

With no distinct military frontline, the crisis was handled by the Military's Technological and Logistics Directorate (TLD), an administrative agency that would later turn into the 'Homefront Command'. The TLD ordered every family and private household in Israel to convert one room into a shelter by taping up all windows and doors against the potential use of nerve gas by the Iraqi military.[3] Meanwhile, Israeli media proclaimed the demise of the public shelter, which until the winter of 1990 continued to be a symbol of Israeli resilience.

'The public shelter is no longer a shared space', concluded one headline, 'it is now the private home that will save you'.[4] Tasks that in the past belonged to state institutions were gradually transferred to civilians. 'Private homes would be the first destination of chemical warheads', announced another headline in one of Israel's major newspapers.[5] The home, no longer imagined as a refuge from the public realm, was now the centre of concerns over security and defence.

To deal with the probability of an Iraqi attack, Israel triggered Civil Defence Regulations that were drafted with the establishment of the Israeli state in 1948 and adopted as a basic law in 1951. These regulations lay down the scheme of communication between the government and the civil population during times of emergency. The crisis resuscitated the need for civil defence and for a strategy that would allow the IDF to efficiently distribute information to each and every citizen, individually. With the looming threat of an attack that would hit private homes, buildings and infrastructure within city centres, Israel delivered a message that communicated a simple principle: *protect yourself*. This refined resolution of defence singled out the individual as the core unit of national security. By delimiting the home as the target of war, the government was able to delegate responsibilities that are usually handled by the IDF to individual civilians. Simultaneously, the borders of the state, usually marked by fences, barrier and walls, were suddenly shrunk to the scale of private homes. This, as I will show in this chapter, blurred the private and national conceptions of security and helped to reroute domestic media practices to national interests. Civil Defense Regulations, I argue in this chapter, are the unexamined history of what would later shape the appropriation and weaponization of habits.

Civil defence

Although the trail of paper traces the Civil Defense Regulations back to the very foundations of the Israeli state, they were not fully implemented until the beginning of the 1990s. 'Until 1991 the home front in Israel was fairly protected from terror', stated Aharon Farkash, the former chief of military intelligence, 'but with missiles launched from Iraq life has changed: the notion that "my home is my fortress" has crumbled'.[6] The inability to preempt what will be the consequences in case Iraq targets private households in Israel quickly replace procedures of self-defence.

Civil defence is more than anything a long list of regulations and protocols that instruct citizens on what to do in case their lives are directly threatened.

A closer look reveals the role of these regulations in formulating a channel of communication between the state and the individual. By training, regulating and guiding the civilian to a set of practices, the state can reach directly into the privacy of his or her home and the individual body that inhabits it. More than reproducing the inert subject of disciplinary power through demands and orders, the individual shaped by civil defence becomes actively and intimately engaged in matters concerning security. This activating force, what Michel Foucault would call 'pastoral power', is incremental to the personal use of media technologies and their integration into the core of emergency routines.[7]

The first legal stature of civil defence was formulated in the aftermath of the 1948 war. Its aim was to introduce communication channels between the Israeli state and civilians at home. As early as 1951, these communication channels were institutionalized through the Civil Defence Law that specified the growing need to implement schemes to prepare civilians to manage direct security treats to their private households.[8] The new law grounded the necessity to take all measures required to protect the civilian population against attacks by hostile forces, or to limit the adverse results of such an attack, emphasizing the need to save lives. The law further stated that under the unpredictable condition of imminent threat, military procedures should be consigned to the civilians themselves: 'individuals should take fate into their own hands'.[9]

The 1951 document titled *Civil Defence Regulations* opens with the main goals behind civil defence and the defining procedures aimed at mobilizing civilians during times of continued national emergency. The opening words of the chapter allude to the individuating element of the entire scheme, articulating a conception of security that revolves around the single individual:

> The defensive layer whereby the individual harnesses any available means to minimise threat through the use of technologies, individual defense kits and the preparedness of the private household for crisis [...] the responsibility of one's safety is in the hands of the individual himself.[10]

The 1951 Civil Defence Law reflects strong ties between the military and civil sectors of Israeli society. One of the most important factors enabling the strengthening of these ties was the nourishing of the idea of a ubiquitous threat to the survival of the Israeli state. 'Israel's national security policy', writes Anver Yaniv, 'begins from the assumption that the Arab-Israeli conflict is inherently and unalterably asymmetrical and that the Jews are and will always remain the weaker party'.[11] The new civil defence regulations were shaped according to this fallacious notion and by existential fears embedded within the Israeli social fabric.

Such fears were expressed in 1951 by Israel's first prime minister David Ben-Gurion who declared that:

> A small Island surrounded by a great Arab ocean extending over two continents
> [...] this ocean is spread over a contiguous area of four million miles, an area
> larger than that of the United States in which 70 million people, most of which
> are Arab speaking Muslims, live.[12]

The Civil Defence Law was backed by Ben Gurion's assumption that 'Israel must eliminate the common but pernicious misconception that the army alone can guarantee state security'.[13] Security, consequently, must be habituated and personalized. The notion of self-defence poignantly captures this personalizing necessity.

The gist of 'self-defence' regulations and the programme for imbedding them into the everyday were largely inspired by experiments and procedures within the United States. In the early to mid-1950s, the US government invested substantial scientific and economic resources into re-imagining the private sphere as the ultimate defence against nuclear warheads.[14] Israel's civil preparation for wartime followed US President Truman's lead. At the time the Israeli Civil Defence Law was passed, Truman had just inaugurated the new Federal Civil Defence Administration (FCDA). This government office was charged with integrating science, technology and entrepreneurship to develop plans for making people and property safe from attack.[15] The FCDA invested all of its resources to find a curative for the nation's nuclear blues, calling 'all statesmen and citizens alike to prepare for a new kind of war that would show no mercy for home front civilians'.[16] In the 1950s, civil defence was devised as 'a security program that domesticated war and made military preparedness into a family affair'.[17]

Anthropologist Joseph Masco argues that the American civil defence project of the early 1950s was not predicated primarily on protection and security of the home, but rather on a national contemplation of ruin.[18] In other words, imagining the dismal consequences of a nuclear bomb became the means of perpetuating emergency regulations. By the mid-1950s, it was no longer a perverse exercise to imagine one's home ruined and devastated. Imagining one's home up in flames was 'a formidable public ritual – a core act of governance, technoscientific practice and democratic participation [... Thus,] it become a civil obligation to collectively imagine the physical destruction of the nation-state'.[19] Focusing on the private home and its maintenance, the state in the early 1950s sought to 'emotionally manage' citizens through fear. By militarizing everyday life, civil defence authorities attempted to both normalize a catastrophic future and politically deploy an image of it. Both US and Israeli civil defence officials argued that citizens should be prepared every second of the day to deal with a potential aerial attack. 'It was up to the citizens to take responsibility for their own survival'.[20] In 1953, Val Peterson, the director of the newly founded The Federal Civil Defence Administration declared, 'if there's an ultimate weapon it may well be mass panic – not the A-bomb [… ;] war is no longer confined to the battlefield. Every city is a potential battleground, every citizen, a target'.[21] Peterson's tone and the official message of the civil defence officials was that citizens should act as 'soldiers' at home. Jackie Orr has powerfully shown that by unleashing panic, 'the national security state remade the individual as a permanently militarised node in the larger system'.[22]

The state's central strategy, both in Israel and the United States, was to empower the individual to take control over his household. The strategy was predicated on the capacity to contain panic while at the same time instilling fear. Fear, it was imagined, was a sort of immunization against contingency. The distribution of images that depict annihilation were thus crucial for the task of mobilizing the citizen.

In 1952, David Ben-Gurion sought inspiration from President Truman, carefully learning how to communicate with citizens and to mobilize fear as part of the war efforts. Beginning in 1945 and based on the support the newly appointed US president provided to the Zionist aspiration of national determination, Truman and Ben-Gurion founded a keen friendship. Truman was lionized by supporters of Israel as the person who made the birth of Israel possible. His interest in establishing an intimate relationship with the Israeli state was driven by a combination of Zionist emotions and Cold War strategies. Israel was perceived to be an ally in the Middle East, close enough to become a strategic asset. Ben-Gurion found security in his ally and was directly inspired by how that ally, the United States, perceived foreign and domestic politics.[23]

Curiosity kills

Inspired by the Second World War military policies in the United States and the UK, the newly organized Israeli Defence Forces identified the need to communicate directly with the civil sector. A direct communication line between the military and civil sphere was advanced by a Jewish lawyer in 1944. Lieutenant Mordechai Nimsabisky approached the British Mandate officials in Palestine to acquire special permission to arm civilians against the 'Arabs in the region'.[24] Under his advice, the 'Civil Section' of the pre-state defence organizations recruited new immigrants who arrived from Germany as Zionists to form a paramilitary civilian task force.[25] Taking his prime example from the British 'Home Guard', the zealous lieutenant Nimsabisky opened the Civil Guard office to advise the Jewish Agency in matters pertaining to the mobilization of civilians.

With extensive experience in print advertising and propaganda, Nimsabisky foresaw the engagement of non-military actors with national security as a communication project bridging the state and civil society. His office published an instructional booklet titled *Your Home as a Shelter During Aerial Bombardment*.[26] This booklet, together with approximately 50 other such publications, provided sketches instructing civilians in how to fortify their homes and prepare their families for a potential attack. Sealing one's home and remaining safely within the interiors of the house were repeatedly emphasized as the core of defence.

Civil preparedness was tested in April 1948 when war was imminent and air raids seemed likely. The assumption was that once the British Mandate in Palestine ended and the British officers had departed, air attacks could be expected from the air forces of Egypt, Iraq and Syria against the main Jewish population centres. The Head of the Military Staff urged that immediate action be taken to improve the readiness of the city by establishing a local civil defence system to address the threat from the skies.[27] On 6 May 1948, the Civil Guard prepared residents' homes for the possibility of air raids. Israeli civilians were ordered to tape over windows to prevent them from breaking, to install bomb shelters and prepare for air raid sirens. These preparations were accompanied by an informational campaign to instruct civilians on how to behave in emergency situations. During the fighting in May 1948 and before the first lull in June, a total of 146 high explosive bombs and 32 incendiary bombs fell on Tel Aviv.[28]

To prevent mass panic, Nimzabisky requested that the use of heavy-weight bombs not be disclosed to civilians. The informational campaign distributed by Israel's civil defence office singled out the private domain of the household as the best available shelter against aerial bombing. Leaflets were distributed throughout the Jewish settlements. One such leaflet distributed by the Civil Guard campaign shows a man standing in his pyjamas on the balcony of his home looking outside to witness the spectacle of bombs coming from above. Behind him, his family sneak a peek with dread while a cartoonish bomb makes land near their house (Figure 3). A large caption in Hebrew reads: 'curiosity endangers life'.[29]

Figure 3 'Curiosity Endangers Life', poster by Civil Guard (Source: IDF Archives).

The slogan 'curiosity endangers life' marks the clear boundary between the private and public spheres, evoking the traditional political model of the liberal subject, and redraws the contours of the individual as both the target of state power and its most valuable agent. The centrality of the individual in the discussions of security at times of emergency draws the outline of a liberal individuality fundamentally predicated on access to the home. The man on his porch operates according to a governing rationality that grants a degree of freedom to individuals. The figure of the man on the edge of his porch illustrates the close relation between the home and the shelter, a more so, between individuality and property. How does an illustration of a man standing on the edge of his domestic porch symbolize the fuzzy line between everyday life and wartime, self-defence and military deployment, home and state?

Oikonomia

Diagrams drawn elegantly and included within the civil defence protocols illustrate the levels of risk that might disrupt everyday life. Onion layers of 'protective shields' begin with the outermost shell and continue inwards to the centre and core of 'security' (Figure 4). At the heart of the diagram, the individual

Figure 4 Layers of defence, from the individual at the centre, through the family, community and the government at the edges. 'The Fundamentals of Home Front Command', 2009 (Source: IDF Archives).

appears isolated from the world, enveloped by a family, a community and national borders that circle the inner spheres.[30] The centrality of the individual in the model draws the outline of a liberal individuality that is fundamentally predicated on access to the home. 'Having a property in one's own person is the ultimate point where propriety meets property', writes Etienne Balibar, such that 'where "to be" rejoins "to have"'.[31] The home, according to this basic idea, is not only a place of residence but also the precondition for any public politics to arise, with the divide between *oikos* and *polis* at its core. In conveying the relation between the domestic and political spheres, Balibar claims that external frontiers of the state have to be imagined constantly as a projection and protection of an internal personality, which each individual carries within herself and that enables her to inhabit the space of the state.

The man on the edge of his balcony captures the erosion of the Aristotelean divide that separates the private from the public spheres. Drawing on this Aristotelean divide, 'life' (*zoe*) at home takes on a unique significance, when explored by a historical trajectory that maps out precisely what is regarded as 'outside' of politics (*bios*). As has often been noted, Aristotle began his discussion on politics by distinguishing the qualifications required for the management of the household from that of the state. Further distinguished as an element within the household, the 'family' in Greek antiquity was *genea*, which connoted not only the lineage, but also temporal sense of generation. The maintenance of the household as opposed to the political engagement in the polis originates from Aristotle's *Politics*. Economy, or *oikonomia* – derived from the word *oikos* (household) – was for Aristotle the practice of maintaining and taking care of the private realm, including not only the family, but also the servants and slaves of the household. Underneath the definition of the home, the notion of *oikonomia* is grounded in the habits, chores and activities of life at home. Those, at least in the traditional modality, were not political.

No doubt this divide between the political and the domestic has been challenged, scrutinized and repositioned in various constellations.[32] Chief among the critics of this foundational divide was Michel Foucault, for whom the living body, and the biological life of the domestic sphere (*zoe*), is the central object of all politics. Indeed, there are no politics that are not body politics, according to Foucault. But for him, the body is not first a given biological organism on which power then acts. Rather, the very task of political action is to fabricate this body, to put it to work, to define its modes of production and reproduction, to foreshadow the modes of discourse by which that body is fictionalized to itself until it is able to say 'I'. Foucault's entire oeuvre can be understood as a historical analysis of different techniques by which power manages the life and death of bodies and populations. For Foucault, the techniques of biopolitical government spread as a network of power that goes beyond the juridical spheres to become a horizontal, tentacular force, traversing the entire territory of lived experience and penetrating each individual body.

Foucault tells us that 'life' at home takes on a unique significance when investigated through a historical trajectory that maps out precisely what is regarded as 'outside' of politics – most notably through Foucault's notion of *biopolitics*, "which he describes" as an explicit rupture in the attempt to trace political processes. He analyses the historical process through which 'life' emerges as the central political strategy, as biopolitics stands for a fundamental transformation in the order of politics. 'For millennia', Foucault famously writes, 'man remained what he has was for Aristotle: a living animal with the additional capacity for a political existence; modern man is an animal whose politics place his existence as a living being in question'.[33]

Foucault distinguishes 'two basic forms' of the power over life. On the one hand, it comes to discipline the individual human body and on the other, it is the regulatory governing power of populations. By 'population' Foucault does not imagine a legal or political entity but an independent biological corpus, a 'social body' that is characterized by its own processes and phenomena, such as birth and death rates, health status, life span and the production of wealth. The totality of the concrete process of life in a population is the target of a technology of security.[34] Thus, the domestic sphere, or the realm of the 'household' as Foucault terms it, is where biopolitical technologies are adopted as a form of *government*. Foucault gives a very broad meaning to the term 'government' to show that up until the eighteenth century the problem of government was placed in a more general context. Thus, government was a term discussed not only in political tracts but also in philosophical, religious, medical and pedagogic texts. 'In addition to the management of the state or administration, government also address problems of self-control, guidance for the family and for children, management of the household, directing the soul and other questions', writes Foucault.

Yet, there is a third modality of governance that appeared in Foucault's later writing that becomes productive in understanding the relation between institutional power and the domestic sphere in which freedom of action, and not docility, is a tool for governance. This more allusive form of governance has been termed *techniques of the self* to address the instigation of the individual, its springing into action. Differing from the institutional power inferred by the hospital, the school or the prison with which Foucault identifies disciplinary power, the home is the domain of self-control. To understand how crisis activates the usage of media, this latter formation should be better defined.

In *Undoing the Demos*, Wendy Brown examines the transference of responsibilities from the state to individuals who seek self-control and self-interest.[35] Brown emphasizes the increasing erosion of participation in political life and communal existence. In describing this, Brown substituted the dichotomy of private and public with a model proposed by Foucault in his Collège de France lectures.[36] In his 1979 lectures, published as *The Birth of Biopolitics*, Foucault defined the neo-liberal figure of rationality par excellence: 'The surface of contact between the individual and the power exercised on him, and so the principle of the regulation of power over the individual, will be only this kind of grid of *homo oeconomicus*. *Homo oeconomicus* is the interface of government and the individual'.[37] The rise of *homo oeconomicus* is predicated on entrepreneurship, while the function of state power equally mutates, adopting a new governing rationality. This governing rationality is no longer one of strict regulation and disciplinary power; rather, it grants a degree of freedom to individuals. With that transformation, which Foucault calls 'governmentality', the liberal polarity of subjectivity and power ceases to be plausible. From the perspective of governmentality, government is a continuum, which extends from political government right through to forms of self-regulation, namely 'technologies of the self', as Foucault calls them.[38] But governmentality reveals that the neo-liberal forms of government do not simply lead to a reduction in state or its limitation to some basic functions.[39] On the contrary, the state in the neo-liberal model not only keeps its traditional roles, but also takes on new tasks and functions.

Domestic inspectors

Perhaps the notion of *Homo oeconomicus* is most clearly pronounced in yet another clause of the civil defence regulation titled 'House Guard' or 'Domestic Inspector' (*Pa'kach Beiti*). In a folder extracted from the IDF archives, dated May 1953, a full section is devoted to 'self-defence techniques'.[40] Three main clauses underline the procedure of preparation towards self-defence:

> (1) Every individual must learn about the dangers that the enemy poses and about the civil defence regulations to take any measure to protect himself, his family and his home.

(2) Experience has shown that the more the individual, his family and the household make efforts to follow civil defence regulations, the more misconduct and panic are prevented.

(3) civil defence is more efficient when members of the household help each other.

In the 1950s, these defence guidelines were supposed to be implemented by appointing a member in the family that would act as a 'domestic inspector'. The 'domestic inspector', civil defence protocols emphasize, would be a competent individual within a given family that could take the responsibility of policing the household.[41] In the words of the IDF: 'The home is the basic idea behind civil defence. An efficient organization of self-defence within the home may prevent misery and save human lives. The "Domestic Inspector" is responsible for installing the defense mechanism in the home; a connecting link between the residents of the household and the army'. Other descriptions require all residents to accept the domestic inspector as an 'instructor, a teacher and a friend'; therefore, his personality and behaviour must fit the task.[42]

The appointed domestic inspector was meant to wear a tag on his shoulder bearing the symbol of a wide-open eye (Figure 5). This eye would supplement the state's monitoring technologies that could, under certain conditions of difficult visibility, be shortsighted. Most significantly, the domestic inspector was in charge of communication, in the event that state technologies failed to inform civilians at home about the unfolding events outside. The domestic inspector's round-the-clock presence in the home was seen as crucial in conducting the tasks of maintaining order within the household. Thus, the guidelines for civil defence relied upon recruiting a family member to take on a new role. The domestic inspector was put in charge of replacing faulty equipment only to become a messenger in his own right.

While the alert system was defined by the 1953 Civil Defence as 'messages from the state that are communicated in every means possible', it would be inherently flawed and therefore likely to break in cases of immediate danger. The task of the domestic inspector was to supplement the state's alert systems. According to the self-defence regulations, the domestic inspector should be ready to assume control of public messaging', taking over from mass media in ensuring the connection between the state and the household. 'A crucial precondition for securing the efficiency of monitoring is communication', the protocol continues: 'personal communication is the extension of the alert'.[43] Here, it seems the inspector was expected to be ready to embody media itself.

Figure 5 Domestic inspector shoulder badge (Source: IDF Archives).

The illustration of the open eye expresses a new form of interdependency that cannot be adequately addressed by the military or the nation-state. Risk, as the German sociologist Ulrich Beck defined it, is integral to the process of activating individuals. The more risk is embedded into the everyday, notes Beck, the less control institutionalized power has over its containment. This is the key for the individuation of security itself. 'The individual', Beck continues, 'is forced to mistrust the promises of rationality of key institutions' and 'as a consequence people are thrown back onto themselves, they are alienated from expert systems but have nothing in place thereof'.[44]

The distribution of uncertainty and risk during the First Gulf War exposed a component within Israel's perception of security that usually remains hidden.

This component is not about exercising top-down governance that subjects civilians to military power, but rather a kind of freedom, or independency given to civilians to act on their own accord. Yet, as I will show in the next chapter, this so-called freedom does not mean that the state weakens, but instead, that it can delegate responsibilities to individuals only to deepen its grip on the narrative. By demarcating the home as the precondition for security, the Civil Defence Regulations establish a link between property and security.

Although the domestic inspector is an archaic role invented to cope with a potential communication breakdown in wartime, its essence continues to fuel the media strategies shaped by the IDF. The domestic inspector lingers as an allegorical figure that stands in for the increasingly blurred boundaries between civil and military realms, where a civilian instantly takes on tasks that are otherwise exercised by a state agent (police or military). Furthermore, in this allegory, home and nation are barely distinguishable, collapsing into each other. Through the model shaped by the Civil Defence Regulations, a much vaster disposition is revealed, in which perceptions of security are drawn and shaped by the movement from the public to the private realms, or from the plurality of the social sphere to the single and defensive individual.

The inspector, reincarnated

In the winter of 1990, the domestic inspector was summoned back from the archives. At the same time, the refined scale of security equally intensified the personal use of media technologies. 'Taking fate into one's hands' often meant interlacing everyday habits with emergency routines. Habits of filmmaking within the private homes of families were redirected to capture the events outside. Key to this process of re-appropriation was the distribution of fear and its infiltration into the home, or as one headline poignantly stated: 'we are all eyes protecting the same body'.[45]

The aesthetics of domestically produced videos, such as the video this chapter starts with, clashed with the audio-visual documentation of heavy bombs destroying dots on maps of Baghdad. In parallel to the videos captured by domestic cameras in Israel, a surge of images capturing the machinic points of view of advanced missiles hitting targets in Iraq flooded television screens around the world. 'Operation Desert Storm', as it was coined by the coalition forces on the eve of the massive aerial attack against Iraq, became synonymous with the emergence of a seamless and disembodied vision of war machines. The images of abstracted targets unleashed throughout the 1990s, prompted critical writing that addressed the aesthetics of a detached and remoted theatre of operations, taking place on the TV screen more than in any real place. With machines producing the images, the role of human agents in documenting war changed dramatically. The arrival of the coalition forces to Baghdad was timed perfectly to coincide prime time television in the United States. Bombers from England, Spain, Saudi Arabia and the remote island of Diego Garcia dropped their payloads. Stealth airplanes entered Iraqi airspace and fired smart bombs. Ten minutes into the attack much of Iraq's infrastructural network, including the Baghdad power grid, had been disabled. The CNN broadcast of the destructive assault in the desert quickly sparked a critical debate around the modes of spectatorship that remote wars generate. The infrared images of abstracted targets hit by smart missiles nourished a fetishistic celebration of advanced warfare, while also desensitizing viewers, who sat at home in front of television sets.

Jean Baudrillard's controversial essay on the topic suggested that the war took place on screens rather than in real cities, destroying real infrastructure and killing civilians. Baudrillard's critique addressed the retreating sense of the 'real'. 'It is strange to see this disaffection, this profound indifference to one another, played out at the very heart of violence and war', wrote Baudrillard in his essay 'The Gulf War Did Not Take Place'.[46] Echoing Baudrillard's critique, Paul Virilio stressed the transformative role of information technologies in an era of 'desert wars', shaped by a vision of conflict that maintains total control over public reception through televisual informatics. In *Desert Screen: War at the Speed of Light*, Virilio argues that televisual data has transformed the political landscape.[47] According to Virilio, what made the First Gulf War distinct is how it cropped up, at great speed, from the battlefield to the screen. War at a distance meant both military ammunitions blasted from high up in the air to wreak havoc, and a military campaign documented and transmitted 'live' via television to enclosed and private spaces. The inauguration of 'electro-optic perception', to use Virilio's term, alongside the deployment of smart bombs, GPS technologies and cameras attached to warheads, ushered a virtuality that totally masked the gruesome consequences of armed conflict. The erasure of targets on military monitors was broadcast repeatedly on television, feeding the perception of war as a rolling stream of 'shock and awe', an unstoppable catastrophe.

But parallel to the detached voyeur, defined by the consummation of images on television, emerged a more active participant, implicitly invited to produce audio-visual footage. Indeed, the grainy videos caught by Israeli civilians from their homes bore a profoundly different meaning, altering the relation between visual media and the spectacle of war. The uncertainty unleashed by the Iraqi missiles in 1990 replaced the passive viewer, sitting at home and consuming the spectacle of bombs destroying targets in a far-flung battle, with the highly engaged user. This transition from passivity to activity was born out of the direct threat to the home and the profound sense of *crisis* leaking into the interiors. The importance of the otherwise insignificant barrage of home movies produced during the First Gulf War lies in the way it reshaped habits, intuitions and practices of engagement with communication technologies. The direct threat to the private realm replaced the experience of witnessing a catastrophe with reacting to a crisis, and the difference lies in the tension between the two.

Film scholar Mary Ann Doane suggests that if the distant and uncontrolled progression of an event is akin to a *catastrophe*, a *crisis* requires intervention. The remote military assault that takes place far away can appear 'live' on a television screen, but without the viewers' capacity to do something about it. For Doane, the real-time televisual broadcast of an unfolding catastrophe, such as the 1991 bombardment of Iraq, is inextricably linked to a fascination with annihilation and death, and hence to the irreversibility of time.[48] Doane argues that television privileges catastrophe because catastrophe 'corroborates television's access to the momentary, the discontinuous, the real'.[49] Catastrophe underscores television's greatest technological power: its ability to be there 'both on the scene and in your living room'.[50] The catastrophe, inextricably linked to mass media, is unstoppable, and as such, produces a docile subjectivity. It unfolds in front of our eyes, uncontrolled, irreversible and fatalistic.

In contrast to the catastrophic event that unfolds on the screen without the human capacity to intervene, crises prompt an active choice and action.[51] 'Crisis', writes Wendy Chun, 'cuts through the constant stream of information, differentiating the temporally and temporarily valuable from the mundane, offering its users a taste of real-time responsibility and empowerment'.[52] Chun suggests that crisis is tamed by rehearsing routines repeatedly, strengthening the sense of individual security in confronting the unpredictability of a 'risky' future. The escalating sense of risk and riskiness stimulates, galvanizes and motivates a reaction. Crisis is embedded into the momentary failure of state-run television to broadcast a live transmission of the incoming missile. Indeed, this failure ushers the transition from a potential catastrophic event, manifested by passive viewers at home, to a crisis that implicitly encourages the involvement of onlookers in the potentially hazardous missile strike.

If the US military ushered an aesthetic of fetishized military force that communicated total control, in Israel-Palestine the media projected chaos and confusion, injecting fear directly into domestic life in a part of Israel that usually remains protected from the threats of war. In Israel-Palestine, the anticipation and dread around the incoming missiles turned out to be more significant than the event itself, steering a perpetual crisis, rapidly co-opting everyday practices into defensive strategies. With the 1991 crisis, the deeply entrenched idea of self-defence was suddenly aligned with the rapid diffusion of media technologies into the lives and homes of disparate individuals. Advanced media technologies were becoming more enmeshed with mundane life at home.

For instance, 'Bezek', the largest telecommunication company in Israel, began promoting its BITNET, an early version of networked communication

Figure 6 Advertisement, 1990: 'Intelligence through an individual computer' (Source: News Archive Tel Aviv).

(Figure 6). Rather than waiting for information to be transmitted through official media outlets, BITNET users were stimulated to 'remain always updated' and informed about a potential attack from the air. One civilian even went so far as to write his own reports of the war on BITNET[53] while sitting in his domestic shelter. Robert Werman wrote: 'I began recording the events and my perceptions and posting those reports on the BITNET computer network. Other network users read my reports and immediately began posting as well'.[54] The online diary fittingly titled 'Notes from a Sealed Room' was thus one of the first blogs to emerge in Israel.

Meanwhile, a local magazine told the story of Berl Schur, an engineer by training, who installed telephone and television connections within his domestic shelter to enable continuous communication (Figure 7). In case of a communication failure or a blackout, the Schur family was prepared to produce

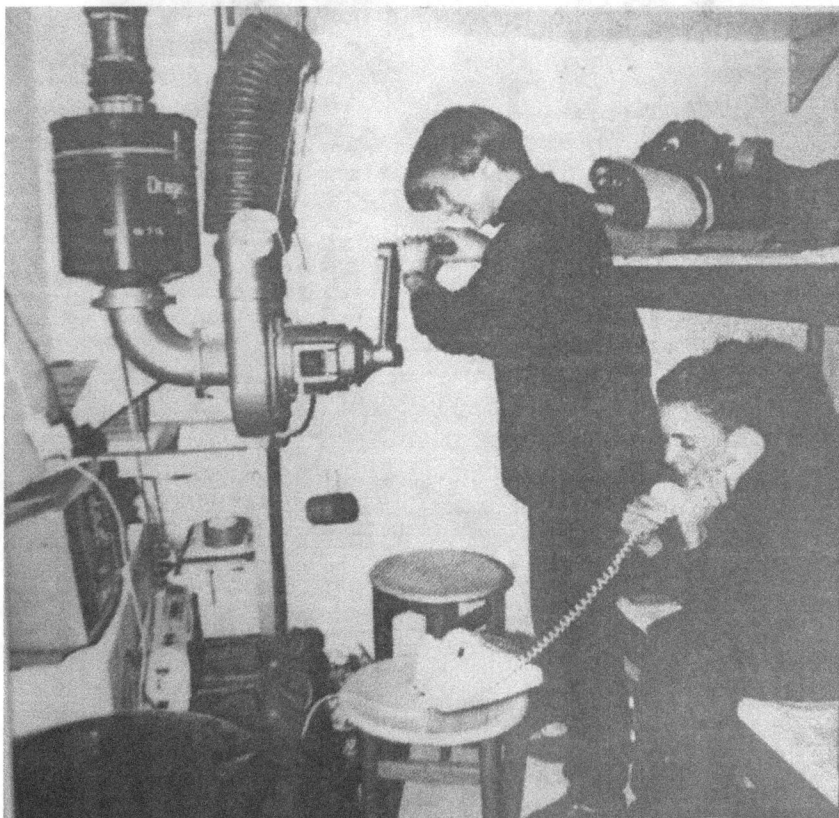

Figure 7 The Schur family, producing energy at home to enable self-sufficiency, 1990 (Source: News Archive Tel Aviv).

energy by manually spinning a turbine.[55] Another report tells of a resident from a small town elsewhere in Israel that took upon himself the responsibility to solve a pressing problem: civilians around the neighbourhoods could not hear the civil defence alarm systems. Yaacov Vismonsky then recorded the oscillating sounds of the alarm on VHS tapes, positioned his stereo speakers outside of his living room and played the alarm directly from his videocassette recorder at times of emergency.

Such instances demonstrate the ways in which the crisis transformed and mutated everyday habits of mediation and engagements with technologies. Mediation emerges as part of a defensive strategy, rapidly individuating security. The intersection of available technologies and the abstract threat outside complicate the dichotomy between a consumer and maker of media. But in activating media users in such a way, the state was drawing on an expanded notion of freedom to act, one that comports with liberal core in the Israeli social fabric, which can be militarized when needed. Crisis and security threats emerge as the raison d'etre of the personal use of media. In a society that bases itself on the omnipresence of a security threat, each crisis is the motor and the goal itself. Through this logic, a state of emergency mobilizes individual users of media, who in turn extend the vision and visuality of the state. As I will show in the next chapter, this movement towards the individual user is not only designed by the state and military, but also serves to deepen their grip on society.

The death of a cameraman: The al-Aqsa Intifada and the demise of the military film units

I am the camera's eye. I am the machine which shows you the world as I alone see it. Starting from today, I am forever free of human mobility. I am in perpetual movement. I approach and draw away from things – I am on the head of a galloping horse – I burst in full speed into a crowd – I run before running soldiers – I rise up with airplanes – I fall and fly at one with the bodies falling or raising through the air.[1]

One evening, in April 2003, a crew of military-trained cameramen accompanied a squad of IDF combatants to a raid deep in the residential areas of Rafah, in the Gaza Strip. The task of the cameramen was nothing out of the ordinary: cover the military operation, document the soldiers' manoeuvres in a flattering light and collect visual evidence of ammunition stashed in civilians' homes. But somewhere in the midst of this routine operation, gun shots were fired at the soldiers from one of the neighbouring houses. One of the IDF cameramen was directly hit. After he fell to the ground, his camera continued to record the unfolding event and to capture the seconds after the bullet hit him (Figure 8)[2]. Left behind on the ground, the camera continued to gaze eerily a darkened and grainy window. The sudden drop, and the stillness that followed, clearly designated the location where the soldier's body had been removed. A faint hint of a darkened interior thus came to demarcate the threshold between the home and the world. In this way, the window pane is framed through a mechanized eye displacing the inhabitants' gaze, the same inhabitants that fled that home with the ensuing gunfire.

Weeks later, soldiers testified that the cameraman had insisted on keeping his eye on viewfinder and to compose aesthetically pleasing shots of the soldiers running through Rafah. His fervour to get the best angle did not make him impervious to gunfire.

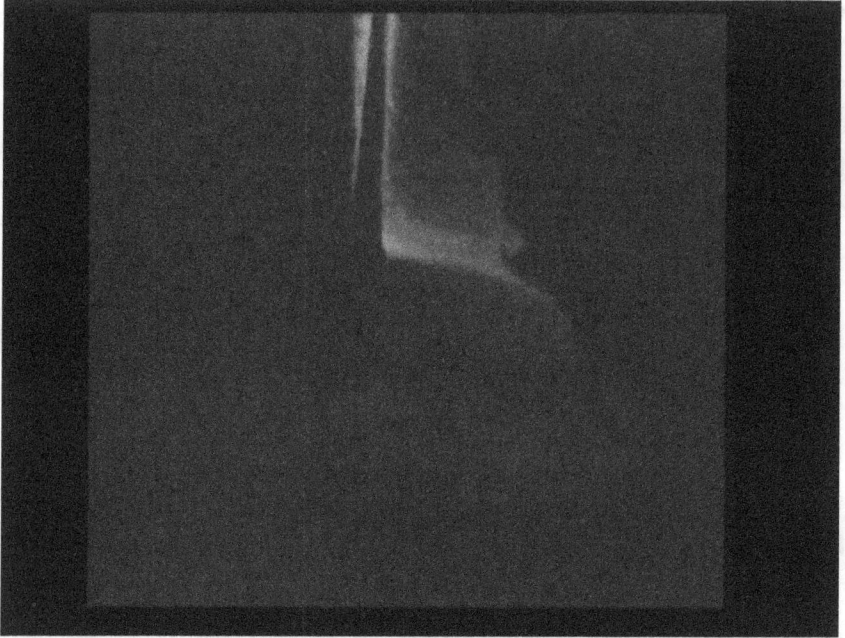

Figure 8 A frame from the video recorded by Lior Ziv after his camera dropped to the ground (Source: Dorel Gillerman, former IDF film unit soldier).

The falling cameraman, as I address it in this chapter, anticipates the demise of the IDF military filming unit. Recorded as mere seconds of video, the event consolidates what would unfold in the next decade: the multiplication of cameras, fragmentation of sources and activation of users that together denoted the rapidly shifting media ecology of the early 2000s. After the event, the IDF gradually abandoned the traditional and professional tasks of the film unit to adapt to a more visible environment and adopt the media habits of soldiers. Importing media habits into military routines meant collecting overwhelming amounts of information on both Palestinian civilians and the soldiers themselves. It also invited the excessive production of snapshots and videos of military procedures that Israel wished to hide for decades. Indeed, if in the early 2000s the individual soldier and his everyday use of media technologies threatened Israel's capacity to control the visibility of the occupation, by the end of the first decade of the twenty-first century, Israel had accepted that the scale of the singular user could be advantageous, in various and contradictory ways. How and why this happened is the main focus of this chapter.

The IDF film unit

A year before the incident in Rafah, Israel initiated a military operation in the West Bank and the Gaza Strip. With the stated intention of catching Palestinian militants, confiscating their weapons, and destroying weapon facilities, the operation (codenamed 'Defensive Shield') effectively targeted Palestinian Authority installations, carried out assassinations of political and religious leaders and imposed a series of collective punishments.[3] The operation entailed the deployment of several thousand armed IDF soldiers, tanks and bulldozers that roared through the cities and narrow streets, reaching into the civilian fabric of the West Bank. Entering into heavily populated refugee camps, the IDF often failed to distinguish between armed resistance and civilians. Ariel Sharon, the newly elected prime minister, declared that the purpose of the operation was to 'catch and arrest terrorists and, primarily, their dispatchers, to confiscate weapons intended to be used against Israeli citizens, to expose and destroy facilities and explosives, laboratories, weapons production factories and secret installations'.[4] To grasp the scale of it, during the al-Aqsa Intifada and the military operation that followed (2000–05), 3,135 civilians were killed by security forces in the West Bank and Gaza including 627 aged under 18.[5]

From the start of the operation, the IDF film unit was assigned to accompany combatants to the West Bank and the Gaza Strip. The professionally trained cameramen embodied the IDF's institutionalized point of view, which in the early 2000s aimed to provide well-composed, glorifying images that would enable Israel to control the mediascape. Established in 1948 as the military film branch, the film unit had been involved mostly in the production of scripted, produced and edited propaganda or instructional films for the purpose of training soldiers. Providing assistance to the local cinema industry or producing feature length films, the IDF spokesperson's office aspired to operate like a private production office. Until the 1980s, the unit dealt mostly with the representation of the IDF in local and international cinema, carefully curating the image of the military presence in Israel, as well as in Palestine and Lebanon. With the availability of handheld cameras and the increasing ability of Palestinians to document life under Israeli military occupation, the IDF's traditional assembly line of scripted and directed films was rendered mostly irrelevant. Scrambling to update its tactics, in 2000, the film unit ceased producing film and began sending crews with combatants, effectively mimicking the role of journalists. The IDF film unit, regularly involved in more traditional modes of filmmaking for propaganda purposes, confronted the need for continuous documentation of daily clashes between Israeli soldiers and Palestinian civilians within dense urban spaces. Consequently, highly trained cameramen were assigned to participate in raids into homes, run with a heavy analogue beta-cam on their shoulders and grab whatever they could.

The incident in Rafah, it seems, precipitated the demise of the traditional media coverage. It stirred within the IDF offices the need to reassess how visual media was used, particularly within a routine of policing. 'Following the event in which a cameraman had died, we were urged to rethink the embedding of soldiers from the unit into combat', wrote a former IDF commander in an article for a military journal in 2003: 'imagine 500 combatants, each holding a camera and recording everything!'[6] The incident laid bare the need not only to recalibrate the use of cameras by soldiers, but also, and more significantly, to face the shift from a visuality predicated on a highly controlled image production that takes on an fixed gaze, to a more flexible mode of documentation and circulation of images that considers both operational needs and the advent of habitual media. It became vital to re-evaluate the agency of the individual soldier, not merely as part of an organization aspiring to homogeneity, but as an active and deeply involved participant.

The al-Aqsa Intifada

During the 1990s the IDF was losing its mythical status as the backbone of Israeli society. The IDF's failures during the First Lebanon War in 1982 and the moves towards a negotiated peace with the PLO in the early 1990s, eroded the military's role in shaping all aspects of Israeli society.[7] At the core of this transformation stood the weakening of Israel as 'a nation-in-arms' and attrition of the hegemonic defence ethos as well as security threat perceptions.[8] Furthermore, during the 1990s, the public gradually elevated the pursuit of personal aspirations and achievements on both the personal and collective levels.[9] The liberalization of Israeli society saw it embrace individualism and self-interest, underlining personal prosperity as a staple value.[10] Alongside this renewed prosperity, the Israeli occupation of the West Bank and the Gaza Strip was no longer easily packaged as a temporary installation. The failure of the Camp David peace negotiations between PLO Chairman Yasser Arafat and Israeli prime minister Ehud Barak closed the window on what could have been an end to 30 years of occupation.[11] With Ehud Barak's refusal to accept East

Jerusalem as a Palestinian capital and to comply with Palestinian demands, the military was already preparing for what has been perceived by the IDF as the inevitable outbreak of another Palestinian popular uprising.[12] Israel's military grip tightened with renewed strength and ferocity.

Meanwhile, in an attempt to assert Israeli dominion over Jerusalem's Al-Aqsa (Temple Mount), Ariel Sharon – the leader of the hawkish right-wing party at the time – paraded into the Al-Aqsa compound, guarded by an armed entourage. Right after the provocative visit, Palestinian demonstrators threw stones at Israeli police, who responded with tear gas and rubber-coated metal bullets. The next day, demonstrations erupted at Al-Aqsa following the Friday prayers before rapidly spreading into the West Bank and Gaza Strip. By the end of this week, several Palestinians had been killed. Sharon's visit to the Al-Aqsa compound had sparked the outbreak of the second, much more violent, intifada.[13]

After attempts to reach an agreement with the Palestinian authority (PA) failed, there was a massive civil uprising in the West Bank, East Jerusalem, and the Gaza Strip. The definition of war, fought between nation-states, had been replaced with what the military echelon called 'asymmetrical warfare', which effectively meant armed soldiers cracking down on civilians. Israel's vast conventional superiority to the PA's security apparatus meant total freedom of action in the air and the ability to send ground forces into areas in the Gaza Strip and the West Bank.[14] With the spread of violent clashes throughout Israel-Palestine, the official IDF spokesperson's office focused on the attempt to control the surge of videos and photographs produced by Palestinian civilians and journalists.

In September of 2000, a global controversy erupted around a video clip that captured Muhammad al-Durrah, a 12-year-old Palestinian boy, being gunned-down by Israeli troops at the Nezarim Junction in Gaza. The footage of the young boy and his father desperately signalling for help seconds before being shot was caught by Abu-Rama, a freelance Palestinian reporter and broadcast worldwide through a French news agency (Figure 9). Israeli authorities concluded that Abu-Rama's footage could not prove that Israeli fire killed the child, and that the footage could have been staged.[15] The video exposed not merely the death of a young boy, but the 'Open Fire Regulations' in the West Bank. Following the diplomatic disaster that the footage of the killing generated, the IDF spokesperson's office was convinced that image-bans and restrictions on journalists entering parts of Gaza and the West Bank should be reintroduced. The IDF quickly re-established a policy that effectively impeded journalists from producing images. These censorship regulations expressed a desperate and futile attempt to resort to media blackouts and refuse to accept the expanding

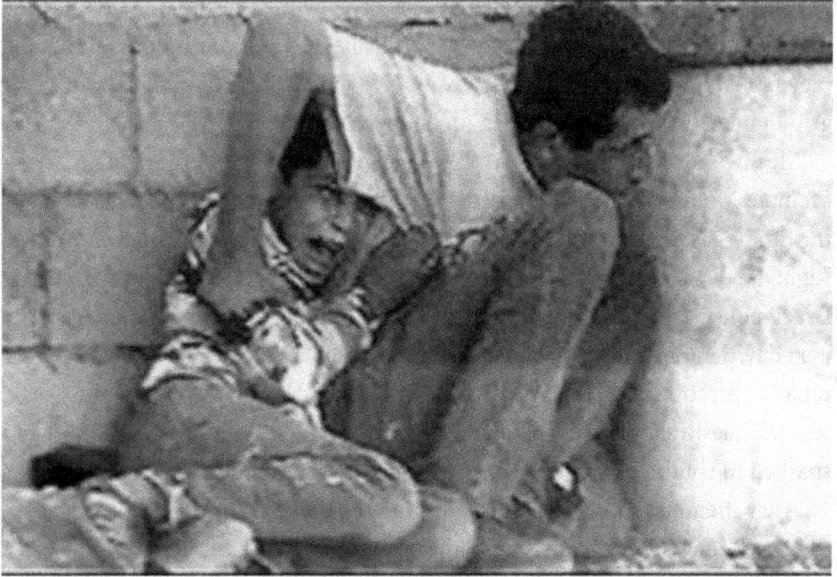

Figure 9 The killing of 12-year-old Mohammed al-Durrah in Gaza (Source: Talal Abu Rahma, FRANCE 2 agency, 2000).

role and agency of images. But direct accounts of the violence in the West Bank only aggravated the situation. Testimonies of grave violations of human rights and brutal acts perpetrated by Israeli soldiers in the refugee camps were quickly spreading, further inciting Palestinian rage.[16] To confront the increasing visibility of military activity, the IDF spokesperson relayed on its film unit to produce pictures and video clips that would look particularly favourable for Israel. The perception was that of two competing narratives: one Jewish-Israeli, and the other, Palestinian.

During the first months of the Intifada thousands of Palestinians were demonstrating in the West Bank and the Gaza Strip. Israel's response was quick and harsh: live bullets were fired at demonstrators, aggravating the collective rage. This was a further indication that Israel was steadily abandoning forms of control used to manage the lives of the Palestinian inhabitants residing in the West Bank and Gaza Strip.[17] 'The firing of a million bullets during the second uprising's first month', writes Neve Gordon, 'signified a change in the primary principle informing Israel's occupation, that is, a shift from the principle of colonisation to the principle of separation.'[18] The paradigmatic sentence best describing this principle is 'we are here, they are there'. The 'we' refers to Israelis, and the 'they' to Palestinians. But what does separation mean in this context?

The emblematic figure of this separation principle was a wall. 'The wall', writes Eyal Weizman, 'has become a discontinuous and fragmented self-enclosed barrier that can be better understood as a prevalent condition of segregation and a shifting frontier rather than one continuous line cutting the territory in two'.[19] The wall, Weizman argued, is not a fine line dividing two populations, but rather a jagged track dissecting and fragmenting space. The checkpoints and walls erected across and the Occupied Palestinian Territories were part of a development generally characterized as a shift from colonization and administrative control to what Wendy Brown has defined as 'domination achieved through the separation and deprivation of the Palestinian population'.[20] Walls and barriers, maintains Brown, were not simply a symptom of an intensifying state control over disputed territory, but an indicator of profound changes in how power operates and what it means. The separation principle, as it took shape in the early 2000s, designated a new conception of security that shrunk the powers of the state. This gave way to the rise of other modes of authority, which consolidated supranational, private and entrepreneurial agencies.[21]

But some of these new constellations were not all that visible. From the 2000s onwards, the rapid integration of technology into security occurred in parallel with the fragmentation of both spaces and political collectives. This, among other things, includes the ubiquitous use of personal cameras and mobile phones by soldiers who are otherwise part of a uniform military power. Integrated into a routine of policing and used individually by soldiers, media technologies fragment collectives into defensive 'users', breaking groups into singularities. Extending the 'us' and 'them' of two separated populations, another layer of fragmentation congealed on top of the already sliced geography. In this layer, 'us' and 'them' become 'Self' and 'Other'.

Advanced technology loomed over the West Bank and the Gaza Strip as a new weapon. Private companies established collaborative channels to connect soldiers together through communication technologies. This new layer that hovers over the territory, as Benjamin Bratton notes, is endemic of a state authority that continues by extending up and down into the new scales offered by multiple interdependent layers. Making communication technologies part and parcel of the IDF arsenal has gradually given rise to the notion of the 'user' as a singular node in a much wider abstract network. This so-called 'user', growing out of the fabrication of the atomized human individual, re-emerged and came to reorganize armed conflict in the early 2000s. While the separation principle was made tangible and very much concrete through walls and fences and guns, the looming presence of technologies gradually refined the scale of separation, honing in on singular bodies. The use of technologies by both soldiers and activists exposed faces of both occupied and occupier, further sharpening the resolution of warfare.[1]

Private telecommunication companies such as Motorola, for instance, provided the Israeli military with technological infrastructure for purposes of security and surveillance. In 2000, Motorola won a $100 million contract to provide the IDF with a specially designed cellular communications system.[22] The system allowed direct communication between commanders and soldiers, pre-empting the extensive use of mobile technologies as operational devices in warfare (Figure 10). The telecommunication technology was installed in a wide range of armoured vehicles and integrated with communications systems throughout the West Bank. The contract between Motorola and the IDF opened the door for rapid integration of mobile technologies into the routine of policing in the West Bank. In July 2000, Motorola sold to the IDF a sophisticated military encrypted voice and data communications system (GSM-900 military cellular network) code-named 'Mountain Rose'. The system went operational in 2004. This was a key component in helping Israeli forces control and subdue the Palestinian population and carry out its military operations in Palestinian territories. In

Figure 10 Soldiers communicating with the Motorola device, 2000 (Source: News Paper Archives, Tel Aviv).

return Motorola profited handsomely from selling the products developed for suppressing the Palestinians to a worldwide market – under the guise of the 'war on terror'. Forced to accept the inescapable presence of cameras, state authority had to gradually incorporate the very substance that threatened its operation for years: the integration of ubiquitous technologies into armed conflict.

In her important work on media infrastructure in Palestine, Helga Tawil-Souri argues that telecommunication companies in Israel further entrench the territorial slicing within the West Bank, dividing land according to infrastructure and connectivity, and thus perpetuating the separation principle that manifests itself through infrastructure.[23] 'While there exists a matrix that has seeped into Palestinian territory', Tawil-Souri suggests, 'the presence of Israeli cellular infrastructure, flows and signals demonstrates the extent to which the boundaries of the Israeli regime are much more fuzzy, wide-reaching, and dynamic that traditionally understood territorial presence'.[24] Tawil-Souri notes that while the infrastructure of telecommunication might be less visible than concrete walls and barriers, they are no less real and significant. The fragmentation of borders, which lies in the realm of the technical order, is shaped and maintained by the rapid integration of communication devices into everyday policing. This notion of fragmentation, which operates on the less tangible level of communication infrastructure, is not merely flipping the prevailing perception that communication can overcome material borders by connecting places and people, but suggests that the border itself is manifested in the realm of media infrastructure.[25] Where Tawil-Souri underlines material infrastructure as unevenly distributed to deepen Israeli control, my interest lies with the myriad of ways in which media infrastructure inscribes habits that in turn divide and atomize the military uniformity into individual soldiers and users. This refined division introduces new threats and opportunities for Israeli security.

While media infrastructure supplements borders and barriers, the imagination produced by mobile phone companies repeatedly evoked the home – one of the central figurations of this book. In 2002, Celcom, one of the largest telecommunication companies in Israel, attempted to take over the emerging 'boutique niche market' of soldiers wishing to communicate with their family members back home. The company's head of marketing stated: 'our goal is to be recognised with Israel's most precious asset, the soldiers themselves'.[26] Celcom offered gifts to IDF soldiers, together with other perks such as free donuts and juice. Special Celcom four-wheel vehicles cruised throughout the West Bank to offer soldiers 120 minutes of free cellular conversations with their families.[27] These third-party companies further lubricated the rapid dissemination of mobile phones into military theatres. The central role of cellular companies strengthened the knot between private communication companies and security. How to integrate the 'user' into a military machine oriented towards unity and homogeneity as its ideal was a question the IDF dealt with in a confused manner.

The integration of mobile technologies into military itineraries and the collaborations between the private sector and the IDF premiered as a televised advertisement video produced by Celcom.[28] The commercial presents a platoon of young soldiers in their basic training, on their way to becoming fully trained combatants in the IDF (Figure 11). Preparing themselves for their final initiation, dusty and exhausted after long days of basic military training, the soldiers begin the last stage of their journey into combat. But the final initiation takes an unexpected turn when the soldiers appear in the residential district of an Israeli city. After climbing up a staircase in a typical middle-class apartment building, they stall in front of a door and gently knock on it. The door opens and the soldiers 'raid' the interiors of the Israeli home, where one of the soldiers has been waiting for his friends, in his pyjamas. The men embrace their fellow soldier and celebrate the reunion. It is then that a title appears: 'With you – also at home'. Uncannily, the advertisement conflates the intimacy of domestic affection with the offensive manoeuvres of an operation. On one level, the video insinuates, the mobile phone permits uninterrupted communication between the battlefield and the home. But on a deeper level, the device latches onto the individual soldier, isolating him from the military unit. The staged scenario

Figure 11 Frame from the Celcom commercial, 'With you also at home' (Source: https://mizbala.com/offline/television/77855).

reflects the role of the soldier, not merely as a cog in a war machine, but as a mediator, a member of an expanded family.

The advert intimates that technologies move from their militarized application to the domestic realm. This one-directional modification has often been understood to reflect the deeply symbiotic relation between media and warfare, and moreover, that the integration of technologies into the civic life occurs only after their military application is exhausted. Friedrich Kittler went so far as to suggest that 'the unwritten history of technical norms is a history of war'.[29] The move of media technologies from the military to the home is for technological determinists a 'natural evolvement', a fait accompli of weapons that moves into civil life. According to this logic, military technologies such as Motorola's are bound to relive in civil life. Complicating this one directional move from war to home is the move from the everyday into military theatres, and the ways in which soldiers brings their habits into routines of policing in Palestine. The more singular soldiers engage with this new technology, the more the abstracted notion of military operations disintegrates.

New media, old problem

In the 1990s, the rapid spread of cyberculture penetrated into IDF think tanks, inspiring new ideas that were borrowed from continental philosophers and misappropriated by IDF generals. The role of the singular soldier emerged at the centre of such innovative concepts of warfare shaped by newly established collaboration between the IDF and Israeli researchers that advocated the incorporation of theoretical literature into warfare. The techno-enthusiasts saw the individual soldiers integrating into a vast war machine that would move and operate with no distinct epicentre. Such ideas were drafted in air-conditioned rooms and later tested in the cities and homes of Palestinian civilians. Within them, the soldier-user was reconceived as a futuristic combatant. What exactly this meant in terms of operational strategies was open for speculation. In attempts made by the IDF to refashion the conception of military power, the tension between uniformity, with a clearly defined leadership, and the role of the singular soldier in combat becomes an unlikely theoretical discussion.

The introduction of new media technologies in a routine of policing opened the gates for new ideas to enhance and improve the control over the Palestinian population. Scholars of international relations and IDF commanders became infatuated with the notion of 'low-intensity conflict', a catch-all phrase for Israel's use of intelligence information to carry out assassinations while obscuring the deadly nature of the military's official tactics and procedures. The popularity of the buzzword in Israeli military discourse and the desire of the Israeli political leadership to depict the conflict as 'low-intensity' are endemic of the state's particular efforts in this period to veil and blur the violence unleashed by military force. At its core was a perception that the enemy should be targeted individually through precise and surgical military operations. In reality, low-intensity conflict served to obscure the clear divide between civilians and armed combatants and engaging in face-to-face conflict with the local population.

The origins of the term 'low-intensity conflict' reflects the rhetoric adopted by IDF generals in the late 1990s. At the time, the IDF conceptualized low-intensity conflict as a new organizational structure influenced and informed by a 'systemic thinking approach', a military theory developed by the IDF's Operational Theory Research Institute (OTRI). Bringing together several retired IDF generals and scholars of security studies, OTRI was established to fill in knowledge gaps that kept the IDF from employing technology as its main strategy of warfare. The theoretical treatise titled *Low-Intensity Conflict* was published by the think tank in 2001 to present insights gathered about the nature of warfare.[30] Inspired by French phenomenology, the report argued that winning the war on perception meant, above all, reconsidering the various ways in which military operations are documented by cameras held by both soldiers and civilians.[31] Replacing the traditional frontline, the think tank envisioned combatants that operate as an interconnected network. The IDF became obsessed with an idea of military power that no longer adheres to the hierarchical structure of the nation-state.

OTRI combined military tactics with neo-liberal ideas of the market. It saw itself as a consultancy for the development of an 'experimental lab' that tests weapons and as an 'educational order' that would enlighten the IDF commanders to think critically and systematically about military affairs.[32] The guiding principles of OTRI were 'openness' and 'jointness', posing an alternative to the linear chain of command. 'Ideally', claims the Israeli national security expert Dima Adamsky, 'jointness blurred borders between services, left classical linear combat behind, and opted for simultaneous multidirectional warfare'.[33] Essentially, the members of OTRI sought to mirror their perceived enemy as a way to neutralize it, a technique they called 'netwar'. The notion of netwar idealizes guerrilla warfare that breaks down the uniformity of the military unit and separates it into 'nodes', or in other words, individual users. Like 'low intensity warfare', netwar was a euphemistic term for a military force that operates like a militia – organized yet flexible. It elevated the role of the singular soldier above the military unit.

Inspired by the American War on Terror and the 2003 invasion of Iraq, which coincided with the preparation for operation 'Defensive Shield', OTRI sought to implement the concepts associated with netwar.[34] Netwar, as its two most prominent advocates John Arquilla and David Ronfeldt called it, was aimed at developing military strategies and potentialities of information networks upon conflicts.[35] In *Networks and Netwars: The Future of Terror*, the two RAND analysts explain how 'through netwar, numerous dispersed small groups using the latest communications technologies could act conjointly across great distances'.[36] The ideal network, Arquilla and Ronfeldt write, is the all-channel network, in which communications are sporadic, by-passing the hierarchy, without having to pass through a centralized position: 'Ideally, there is no single, central leadership, command, or headquarters – no precise heart or head that can be targeted'.[37] By adopting this language, the military was attempting to salvage the perception that the military unit operates as one modular machine. It is built out of singular soldiers but moves and acts as a faceless entity—flexible, fast and deadly.

Samuel Weber notes that the 'netwar' is predicated on mimicking the dissent of civil uprising.[38] Combating a civil population that operates in a dispersed formation, notes Weber, requires mimicking the 'headless enemy'—a leadership without a distinct centre. Like Arquilla and Ronfeldt, Weber chooses to stress the importance of technology in shaping what he calls 'a horizontal function of power', not only by supplying new weapons, but also in outlining a new perception of the role of the singular soldier in the unit. Weber addresses two modes of mimicry that come to define how netwar operates. The first, which he calls *swarming*, aims to 'be able to coalesce rapidly and stealthily on a target, then dissever and re-disperse, immediately ready to recombine for a new pulse'.[39] The second, *blurring*, aims to blur the distinction between offense and defence, but also between civilians and combatants and times of wars against times of peace. Together, swarming and blurring act as idealized modes of operation that take their main cue from the ways in which the enemy moves (or at least how it is perceived by the state). In both 'techniques' the individual soldier is enmeshed into a wider war machine. Both modes of mimicry are based on rendering the singularity of the solider indistinguishable, unseen and generic. The ideas promoted by OTRI were flawed mostly because they further abstracted a concrete, physical and violent armed conflict. Moreover, whereas 'netwar' proposed a smooth and flexible war machine, technology hinted to the other way: it separated the military 'unit' into individuated users, each left to her own devices.

These half-baked ideas reflected the notion that the personalized use of technologies by soldiers should be repressed to maintain a faceless and flexible operational force. For decades, the suppression of the singular point of view had been underlined as a threat to the state's visuality.[40] Indeed, soldiers were using personal cameras to document war from the early days of photography and often against the will of the state. Personalized cameras, for instance, not much bigger than a mobile phone, were carried by individual soldiers as early as the beginning of the twentieth century and were co-opted into military theatres beginning with the First World War. Already in 1888 George Eastman's portable Kodak cameras reduced both the practical and financial barriers that had previously stood before would-be amateur photographers, making photography accessible to the hobbyists. By 1912, the company was marketing a 'soldier's Kodak'. Jon Cooksey shows how, by advertising the new camera, Kodak directly targeted solitary British soldiers who were preparing for war. The ad carried the slogan: 'There is a great deal of Europe and very little to a pocket camera, but with that marvel of portability, the Vest Pocket Kodak solves the problem'.[41] While militaries have been experimenting with new ways to integrate photography for reconnaissance for decades, they have not always welcomed the unwarranted use of individually held cameras that meddle with the military approach to representing war.

Although the accounts of the implementation of photography and film by soldiers far exceed the scope of this chapter, as a whole they testify to the difficultly of incorporating the singular soldier, with his or her personal use of visual media, into the established visuality of state authority. Bottom-up practices of photography were often a threat to how the state desired to see and to be seen. Uncontrollable, the everyday use of cameras by soldiers could potentially impede the abstracted and omnipresent power to visualize.

This principle of authority, argues Nicholas Mirzoeff, has always embodied in, and manifested as, the figure of the leader. 'The mystical and unclassifiable hero was nonetheless separated from all others by his ability to visualise history as it happened, thereby gaining an authority that was aesthetic', writes Mirzoeff. Mirzoeff refers to Karl Von Clausewitz's theory of war in which the battle is a complex event that does not resolve itself in a single moment or incident. War requires grasping topography '[…] imprinted like a picture, like a map', and is understood as the capacity to take decisions by deploying 'a power of judgment raised to a marvellous pitch of vision, which easily grasps and dismisses a thousand remote possibilities'.[1] Clausewitz called this capacity the 'sovereign eye of genius', bringing together the ability to imagine with the absolute authority of sovereignty. The singular soldier is therefore a potential threat to the visuality of authority. The singular soldier has always been an interruption to the uniformity of the militarized unit and thus a liability. This was often proven true during the great wars. But when war is replaced with a routine of policing, which is much more endemic to a colonial regime, and certain technologies such as the mobile phone become integrated into that routine, the place and role of this singular point of view within the visuality of the state change.

Mobile images

By 2006 the mobile phone coverage in Israel was immense. Nearly every soldier had a phone and nearly everywhere those phones had good reception. But more than that, nearly every phone also came equipped with a camera. For soldiers, being at war often meant producing numerous images. So it does not come as a surprise that hundreds of images were indeed taken during the Israel-Lebanon war by professional soldiers, conscripts and reservists, and less so by public affairs officers whose professional mission it is to bring back images of operations, such as combat camera units. Instead ordinary soldiers often brought digital cameras or camera-equipped mobile phones, even some 3G mobile phones with video capability, sometimes violating the restrictions banning the use of such gadgetry.

In 2008, 20,000 soldiers returned to the neighbourhoods of besieged Gaza as part of a ground operation aimed at dismantling Hamas and the Izz ad-Din al-Qassam Brigades.[42] To prevent soldiers from producing images that might expose the extent of the destruction in Gaza, the IDF attempted to restrict the use of private cameras and smartphones. Soldiers were not permitted to take their private mobile phones with them. A news item from 2008, titled 'Mobile phones with cameras? Not in our military bases', reported on the attempts made by the IDF to restrict the use of mobile phones on military bases.[43] 'Soldiers bring their smartphones into military bases, but are not aware of the danger that it poses', says a military commander, 'one thinks he is snapping a selfie, but he is actually exposing a military facility'.[44] Recognizing that the institution could no longer separate soldiers from their mobile phones altogether, only the use of the camera was banned. Curbing habits of snapping images and uploading online was the last futile attempt to limit the force of habituated media.

An instructional video produced by the IDF intelligence in 2008 shows a hand holding a smartphone camera directed at another soldier who sits in her office smiling as her picture is being taken. But behind the smiling soldier there

המצלמה שלך יכולה
להיות נשק
אל תכוון אותה נגדנו

Figure 12 'Your Camera could be a weapon, don't aim it towards us'. IDF
instructional video for internal circulation, 2008.

is also a map sketching out a military operation. The video then freezes and a
statement appears: 'your smartphone could be a weapon, don't point it at us
(Figure 12)'. Explicitly comparing the face and the map, the video signals a shift
in perception within the military, acknowledging that images do much more
than represent. Images uploaded into Facebook can provide further information
added to snapshots such as locations and timestamps.

In 2008, the IDF opened a filming course to ordinary combatants participating
in operations in the West Bank and the Gaza Strip. The statement issued by the
military announced that the new military filmmakers are first of all combatants
and then media users. This is how one of the commanders in the course describes
the purpose of the training:

> Infantry and paratroopers should hold their cameras just like they are holding
> their rifles. They often have no prior experience in photography apart from using
> their smartphone, but end up with a love for the practice of filmmaking. The
> media soldiers are trained by shooting 'selfies' and aiming the camera at each
> other – before going into a more intensive training scheme. They will eventually
> have to decide themselves what to document, therefore it is important to instruct
> them well.[45]

Once soldiers reach the final stage of their training, they are kitted out with
a helmet with a GoPro camera attached and a small hand-held video camera.
According to a combat media officer, '[T]he individual soldier is already
acquainted with cameras, after all today everyone does it back home. It's only
a matter of reusing these skills for operational needs'.[46] Similarly, internal

documents in the army suggest that the use of cameras is not only necessary for the sake of public relations, but also 'for collecting visible evidence of weapons and explosives hidden within private homes'.[47]

The peak of the training course takes place at a specified military facility built to be captured by images. Boaz Malkieli, the deputy commander of the spokesperson office in 2008 describes how: 'In between hills and olive trees, fake low houses typical of an Arab village were built especially to challenge photographers'.[48] A military instructor in the course notes that 'while officers prepare the solider for a final drill with a camera in hand, theatrical scenarios such as a woman giving birth, a family with a sick boy and ammunition stashed inside a private home' are put in place as part of the scene. 'Our objective is to train soldiers to capture every possible problematic event', he concluded.[49] The soldier, well trained to use weapons, was now also a filmmaker. Whereas the official military filmmaker is trained in the craft of formal filmmaking that includes shot coverage, focus and camera movement to bring in materials for a skilled editor, the new *combatant-turned-filmmaker* is able to grab images spontaneously, capturing not only 'war zones' but also mundane and quotidian military procedures.

The personal use of media technologies by soldiers has been recognized by the IDF as a threat and a potential breach of confidentiality. But, when the use of phones and cameras by soldiers was no longer external to military activity but integral to it, it became clear that the army could turn the tables on this problem. In other words, the army could now use this to fragment and dissect the military unit to unleash the tide of information and flood our screens. If at the beginning of the 2000s the military still maintained the top-down visuality of state authority by employing well-trained soldiers from the film unit, 15 years later the efforts made towards controlling the distribution of media gave way to habits dictated by technologies demanding round-the-clock updates. This process would only intensify towards the end of the first decade of the twenty-first century. With the gradual acceptance that the use of habitual media was inevitable, the centralized strategies of media, endemic to a state-run operation of an on-going military occupation of the Palestinian territories, was slowly replaced with an alternative configuration of power, which delegated more responsibility and freedom to individual users. As a result, the unity of the military establishment, and the figure of the collective body, was fractured and sliced into multiple bodies and selves. The spatial separations that were installed throughout the West Bank are today multiplied exponentially.

Throughout the first five years of the twenty-first century, the gradually intensifying scale of violence in the Occupied Palestinian Territories intersected with the equally increasing use of media technologies by IDF soldiers. If, at the beginning of this period, the IDF believed that advanced technology, tele-presence and network power would win the war over perceptions, by 2008 and with the military assault on Gaza, the engagement of soldiers and civilians with media technologies had laid the ground for a new media strategy. Indeed, while authority was often manifested through advanced technologies producing images from positions of power and superiority, from the 2000s the entanglement of individuals and media technologies has transformed not only how the military occupation is visualized, but also, and more significantly, how it operates.

In the next chapter, I will suggest that while habits imported from everyday life were perceived as a dangerous exposure of military tactics, they were effectively appropriated as a weapon in Gaza. Digital devices, once incorporated into everyday routines, have become entangled with the soldier's sense of self, "his or her" experience of embodiment, acquisition of knowledge and meaning making and the broader social relations. The sheer mobility and pervasiveness of contemporary digital devices and the fact that soldiers connect to the internet and thus to their online social networks from almost anywhere and at any time have had a major effect on the conduct of occupation.[50]

In the fourth chapter, I will take another step to show how the growing reliance of the military establishment on external companies, such as Motorola, Celcom, Facebook and Google, has been crucial in this reformulation, turning sovereignty into a patchwork of multiple agencies. Emerging from this fog of habituated war is the singular soldier who tirelessly documents her own life, conflating emergency with everyday life. Rather than exposing another aspect of an increasingly militarized society, based upon solidarity and unity, this newly born soldier-user is a by-product of a sovereignty increasingly dictated by habitual media.

The split wall: Homes to return to and homes to destroy

There are actually two walls: the external wall is turned towards dangerous aliens and potential immigrants; the internal wall is turned towards the dwellers of the house to guarantee their safety. The external wall is political and the internal wall, secret; and the function of the wall as a whole is to protect the secret from the sinister and the uncanny.[1]

On 8 July 2014, thousands of IDF soldiers were loading their gear and cleaning their rifles in preparation to enter the Gaza Strip. Pamphlets rained down on the Palestinian civilians across Gaza forewarning about the incoming aerial assaults, while armed platoons drove their way into residential areas, carrying orders to treat every man they encountered as a potentially hostile combatant.[2] Buildings were flattened with tank shells and D9 bulldozers.

According to data gathered by the UN, at least 2,133 Palestinians were killed during Israel's 2014 military campaign 'Protective Ledge' in Gaza. Of the initially verified cases, 1,489 were believed to be civilians, including 500 children. Many fatalities involved multiple family members, with at least 142 Palestinian families having three or more relatives killed in the same incident, for a total of 739 deaths. In addition, approximately 18,000 housing units were either destroyed or severely damaged, leaving approximately 108,000 people homeless. On the Israeli side, 72 people were killed during the war, 67 IDF soldiers and five civilians. These figures already point to a clear discrepancy with respect to the number and proportion of civilian deaths: 70 per cent of all those killed by Israel were civilians compared to the 7.5 per cent of deaths at Palestinian hands being civilian.[3]

In the lead up to Operation 'Protective Ledge', rockets were sporadically launched from Gaza towards city centres in Israel. Air-raid alarms sounded daily, sending Israeli civilians to immediate cover in their own homes. Although most rockets were intercepted in mid-air by Israeli anti-missile technologies, the immediate threat introduced a risk that penetrated deeply into everyday routines. Private homes and civil infrastructure in Tel Aviv – usually unscathed in contrast to the sheer destruction in Gaza – were exposed to long-range rockets.

By the end of August of 2014, the IDF pulled most of its ground forces out from the Gaza Strip to bring the military incursion to a temporary conclusion. Leaving behind utter destruction, the soldiers documented the anticipated return home with their mobile phones. What quickly became a viral 'genre' consisted of IDF soldiers switching their mobile phone cameras on, before entering their house to surprise their families. In most of those short videos, soldiers, still in uniform, show up at their parents' home unannounced, triggering an overwhelmingly emotional response from family members. The more exhilarated the response, the faster the video circulated on social media. In one such video, a soldier quietly sneaks into his own home. The continuous shot moves from the exteriors of the house, through the main entrance, and all the way into the bedroom, where the soldier finds his parents bewildered by his sudden intrusion. The long continuous shot that moves from the front door and inwards into the darkened spaces of the house resembles a raid. In another video, the soldier reunites with his pet dog, which frantically sniffs the military uniform in suspicion, like Argos nosing around the returning Ulysses in his disguise. Yet, another follows a soldier into a wedding celebration, where he instantly draws the attention of the guests. The bride approaches the soldier and bursts into tears of joy and relief to see her younger brother there, in uniform and fully armed. Significantly, all of the videos were uploaded by the soldiers themselves and reshared on the IDF Facebook page or Instagram account under the hashtag *#homecoming*.

While the *#homecoming* hashtag went viral in the summer of 2014, videos from the ground invasion into the Gaza Strip sprouted up all over Facebook like mushrooms after the rain. The regular use of mobile phones by soldiers deployed in the ground invasion bore a direct impact on the visibility of the immense destruction of civil infrastructure in the neighbourhoods and refugee camps in Jabaliya, Rafah and Gaza City. By August 2014, Facebook had become the main outlet for audio-visual footage that captured the forceful takeover of private homes, sometimes with the children and the elderly still sheltering inside. As a response to the devastation depicted in the rapidly mounting visual evidence of grave violations of international law, IDF soldiers began uploading videos of their own personal experience of entering the building and houses in the Gaza Strip. Recorded with GoPro cameras or smartphones, the videos featured soldiers brazenly performing raids on evacuated Palestinian homes, where ammunition was allegedly hidden in dark corners of bedrooms, or in tunnels dug underground. The procedure of raiding a home, 'cleaning', securing and sometimes erecting a temporary military post in it, was filmed by IDF soldiers who spontaneously picked up their mobile phone cameras to record and share videos. Although partially destroyed by the mortars and artillery, the interiors raided by soldiers were not completely stripped of the domestic qualities that tied them to the families that once inhabited them. The furniture, beds, books, domestic utilities and even framed family photographs appear as objects bound up with the absent inhabitants of the home, such that one can no longer separate the dispossession of the one from the destruction of the other. Bringing the camera into the home meant occupying the position that the camera would take if it were documenting the life of the family that lived there — the same family that had now been dispossessed of their home.

Focusing on the surge of videos that cropped up on social media and documented the soldiers' homecoming or raiding means asking what might bind or separate two homes, one Jewish and the other Palestinian. While the home movie celebrates familial life and builds the perception of home, is there a home movie that undoes the home? What kind of 'home movie' can be oriented to destroying it? Can the viral 'genres' undergird two parts of the same militarized imagination of *home*? How might the personal use of cameras by soldiers uncover a necropolitical logic that dictates whose lives are protected, and whose killed with impunity? Side by side, the audio-visual compilations that capture the entrance into the home raise vital questions about the role of media practices for the IDF. Recording the two homes with their personal mobile phone cameras, soldiers take part in the production of the spaces they frame and record. Their movement from the exterior of buildings inwards through the door, or the window, is often recorded in a single travelling shot that designates the concrete architecture, the narrow passages, the swerving and turning in the stairways, the treading through corridors and finally, the destination in the smaller rooms of homes, empty or inhabited.

The production of the two spaces through the lenses of personal mobile phone cameras could be understood as a procedure of 'homing' and 'unhoming'. 'Homing', on the one hand, means recording a space to reaffirm its uniqueness and intimacy as a home. Perhaps most clearly manifested through the home movie, the use of personal cameras is not merely documenting a pregiven space, but rather integral to the making the space itself. According to Patricia Zimmerman and Karen L. Ishizuka, the home video 'is a subset of the amateur film movement located within the individual and familial practices of visual recording of intimate events and rituals and intended for private usage and exhibition'.[4] The home movie takes part in the conversion of a space into a home through the construction of boundaries and shared experience. Rather than simply documenting the domestic realm and the lives that it hosts, the home movie is actively turning interior spaces into homes. Indeed, space, as Michel de Certeau famously claimed, is not preconceived but made by the practices that it hosts. Space, he writes, 'is actuated by the ensemble of movements deployed within it.'[5]

If *homing* relates to the production of familial intimacy and privacy, *unhoming* is the process of undoing that privacy, a practice of filming tailored to stripping out the domestic quality of the home and converting it into a dangerous place. Negating the home is equally negating the access to privacy and human dignity, enshrined in international human rights law.[6] By recording the interiors of homes as war zones, IDF soldiers take part in the violation of those spaces as homes. The privacy inherent to the home movie is inverted to become a kind of anti-home movie.

Together, the viral online videos are the output of practices that bear political and affective registers that never operate solely at the level of representation – the content displayed in an image or a sound file – but also as a practice, enacted at the structural level of how privacy and domesticity are conceived through a militarized imagination.

In the procedure of *homing* and *unhoming*, military practices become domesticated inasmuch as domestic habits become militarized. The habits that Israeli soldiers take with them into their routine deployments are spontaneously turned into a performance aimed at documenting military manoeuvres, a gesture that converts the privacy of homes into secrecy. I will address the transition from privacy to secrecy at the end of this chapter.

Connections between 'home videos' and military documentation emerge as two modes of filming that can produce either intimacy or enmity. The comparison between the videos reveals the binary opposition between two perceptions of privacy at the core of a *militarized imagination*, one that elevates one home as a sanctuary that shelters life while vilifying the other, perceiving it as the core of the menacing secret, an imaginary determined by the fallacious binary wherein Jewish and Palestinian homes hide under their roofs opposite relations to life.

Furthermore, the juxtaposition of the two ideals of homes suggests that media habits are at once integral to *inhabiting* and *occupying* while both emerge as the Janus-face of Israel's perception of security. Inhabiting and occupying are terms intermeshed with overlapping meanings. 'Inhabiting' is defined by the Oxford dictionary as 'occupying a space of living or dwelling'. Inhabiting is informed by *habi-* which comes from *habere*, meaning to have or to hold. 'Habitus is improvisatory, operating through human practice rather than through prior conscious thought', writes architecture historian Georges Teyssot.[7] Both the acts of inhabiting and occupying the home are defined through specific bodily practices that often overlap and appear indistinguishable, blurring the borders between the two. The photographs and videos recorded during military raids communicate the indecisive proximity between inhabiting and occupying and remind us of the power of images to take charge over life as a direct object. Inhabitation, notes Teyssot, 'consists in grasping routines that help to organize life, and in rethinking and transposing customary modes of action in response to the need to adapt to unfamiliar circumstances.' No doubt, inhabiting space is partially what makes it into a home.[8] Juxtaposing the two viral modes, occupation and inhabitation emerge as two sides of the same coin, intimately linked through the soldier's daily engagement with cameras and social media. The two viral videos attest to the practice of filming as a process of rendering interiors into defined spaces, where proximity and alienation are gauged through a personal point of view.

Drawing on philosopher Hagar Kotef, the home, in both its metaphoric and material senses, is not a domain outside of politics, but in fact comes to define it. The home and the domestic realm, Kotef contends, are weaponized to dictate a particular defensive, territorial and destructive individuality, which she calls the 'colonising self'. The home, as Kotef defines it, is a geography and an apparatus that orients colonial expansion, in which the construction of a home often means the destruction of the another. The 'colonising self', based on Locke's formulation of the individual, makes the home an extension of the body, and the state the extension of the home. The property-making unit must expand from body to household. Expansion further becomes essential to the household as a property unit and, with it, global expropriation and dispossession. The Lockean 'individual' is therefore linked to the household. Kotef's definition of home is particularly productive because it enables the combination of two elements, or components, that seem at first to be contradictory. On the one hand the home is a place of familial love and belonging, but on the other – in its colonial guise – it must include the dispossession of the other. In her words: 'The fantasy (or concept) it captures is a certain fantasy of home, as a sheltering, stable and peaceful space. The reality is that of violence – the violence of forced mobility, demolition, and dispossession.'[9] (8–9)

Recording Gaza

The 2014 war was not the first time IDF soldiers invaded the isolated Gaza Strip. Only three years after Israel disengaged from the Gaza Strip and ostensibly handed control to the Palestinians, in the winter of 2008–9, IDF fighter jets assaulted with full force. The aerial operation very quickly escalated into a full-scale war. On the eve of 3 January 2009, 20,000 soldiers made their way into the neighbourhoods of sieged Gaza as part of a ground operation aimed at dismantling Hamas and the Izz ad-Din al-Qassam Brigades.[10] Learning the lesson from the al-Aqsa Intifada and the 2006 Lebanon War, the IDF was well aware of the need to control the photographs and videos that expose the sheer destruction in the Gaza.

To prevent soldiers from recording videos, the IDF attempted to restrict the use of cameras and smartphones, while also acknowledging the growing popularity of Facebook, a new application that appealed to the teenage Israeli soldiers. An Israeli news item from 2008, titled 'Mobile phones with cameras? Not on our military bases', reports on the attempts made by the IDF to restrict the use of mobile phones in any military base.[11] 'Soldiers bring their smartphones into military bases, but are not aware of the danger posed', says a military commander, 'one thinks he is snapping a selfie, but he is actually exposing a military facility.'[12] Everyday practices of snapping images and recording videos held out the promise of creating potential links between a picture and a personal profile. Uploaded by individual users on Facebook, every image is a node within a constellation of images that creates movements and connections, linking the soldier's everyday life at his home with his activity as a soldier. Perfectly aligned with the rapidly escalating popularity of Facebook among teenage conscripts, the massive operation in Gaza was an unstoppable media disaster for the IDF spokeperson's office.

Acknowledging the challenge of limiting the soldier's habits of image production and circulation, the army decided to install what it called 'selfie machines' to allow soldiers to snap and send images to families back home.[13] Photo-booths were placed on military bases, and soldiers were invited to enter and grab a selfie. Sending a selfie to your parents has been officially encouraged as part of the initiation into soldierhood. Against the assembly line that turns individuals to soldiers, the IDF selfie machine appears to be anticipating that habitual practices of mediation are now bound to be integral to a military occupation. But as I mentioned in the last chapter, most often such clumsy attempts to tame habits proved redundant. With the technology receding to the background and becoming ubiquitous, the singular user slowly moves to the foreground.

But with the ground operation in Gaza and the availability of smartphones and new applications such as Facebook, the data genie was out of the bottle. According to Adi Kuntsman and Rebecca Stein, 'Israeli online communities first became militarised on a massive scale during the 2008–2009 military incursion in the Gaza Strip'.[14] While the IDF still implemented a ban on images and denied access to the international press, it launched a YouTube channel; the first social media platform with which the military would experiment. Given an enforced media blackout by Israel, this channel became the main source of information. While the army gradually embraced social media as a channel of distribution, it reaffirmed the top-down vertical line of vision to flaunt its use of advanced technologies. Kuntsman and Stein also note that it was not until 2012, with yet another military incursion into the Gaza Strip (codenamed 'Pillar of Defense'), that the IDF started publishing audio-visual material collected and disseminated by individual soldiers.[15] No longer organized solely by the state, soldiers were participating in the battle of information. During the course of the incursion, platforms such as Facebook and Twitter became wartime tools in their own right, transformed into so-called 'technologies of warning'. The military has struggled to keep pace with these practices, perpetually recalibrating its internal social media policy to match new media trends among this population of 'digital natives'. Kuntsman and Stein also recognize that the rise of a personalized idiom was at the core of these recent developments and a signature of what they call 'digital militarization'. 'The state and its violence were reduced to the individual', they write, 'even as military operations were represented as personal projects via family pictures, handwritten placards, and private moments of civilian life under fire'.[16] Personalization masked state violence through the patina of the private, functioning to disguise the brutality of the Israeli war machine.

This procedure of masking the sheer violence of the war in Gaza is nowhere more pronounced than in the snapshots of IDF soldiers sitting in abandoned Palestinian homes, sometimes resting, eating or drinking coffee. Often such photographs were taken in the moment of hiatus, where a soldier smiles pleasantly to the camera. One such snapshot depicts a soldier caught in the act of spraying the slogan 'we will return' on the interior walls of a home in Gaza (Figure 13). The promise to return uncannily evokes the soldier's return to his own home. Echoing the rhetoric of exilic romanticism, this vandalizing sentence recaptures the underlying ethos of Zionism, tying together the 'myth of return from exile' with military action. According to the metadata, the snapshot was taken in 2008 by an anonymous soldier, but then reposted numerous times in 2011 and 2014 with the IDF's return to Gaza and to the violence unleashed within. The promise of return thus captures the speech act of an Israeli soldier inasmuch as it reflects

Figure 13 The slogan 'we will return' being sprayed onto the interior walls of a Palestinian home in the Gaza Strip (Source: Facebook).

the circulation paths of information, appearing and disappearing repetitively on our screens, fulfilling the promise of return. The habits that produced this image and others alike are the result of the dissemination and appropriation of everyday practices to military ends. If the home is the ground zero of such habits, armed conflict is where they yield representations. The domestic use of cameras is turned inside out to abolish domesticity. The domicile, if indeed it is the breeding ground of habits, is uncannily also the target of those habits, closing full circle within the soldier's own home.[17] Spraying graffiti inside the home inverts it, turning the interior into an exterior. This snapshot perhaps captures the most direct expression of *unhoming*.

Converting homes into war zones

The intensity of the 2014 operation in Gaza was a reminder that the homes of Palestinian civilians are at the frontline of the fire. The IDF, it seems, transforms the very essence of home and its privacy as a way of justifying its illegal activities. By perceiving homes as the harbinger of dark secrets, the IDF is able to isolate them as targets, and most of the time, in violation of international law.[18] By August 2014, the United Nations Office for the Coordination of Humanitarian Affairs stated that 520,000 Palestinians in the Gaza Strip (approximately 30 per cent of its population) might have been displaced from their homes. The UN calculated that more than 7,000 homes of 10,000 families were razed, together with an additional 89,000 homes damaged, of which roughly 10,000 were severely affected. In Israel during the same timeframe of the operation, an estimated 5,000 to 8,000 citizens temporarily fled their homes due to the threat of rocket attacks from Gaza.[19]

At the end of the hostilities Amnesty International issued an urgent call to prompt an investigation by the International Criminal Court into the conduct of both the IDF and Hamas for targeting civilian areas.[20] In a document circulated at the end of the 2014 war, Amnesty International urged the acknowledgement of the unprecedented assault on Gaza and the dire consequences of the continuing military blockade on the Gaza Strip that began in 2007, as well as the continuing threat of Hamas rocket attacks on civilian areas in Israel. Amnesty emphasized that international law sets out standards of humane conduct and limits the means and methods of conducting military operations. A fundamental rule of international humanitarian law is that parties to any conflict must at all times distinguish between civilians and combatants, especially in that attacks may only be directed against combatants and must not be directed against civilians. Warring parties have obligations to take precautions to protect civilians and 'civilian objects' under their control from the effects of attacks by the adversary. As with precautions in attack, these rules are particularly important when fighting is taking place in residential areas with large numbers of civilians.

To fend off the mounting international criticism, the IDF turned to media representations. Using the steady stream of photographs and videos produced by IDF soldiers, the IDF spokesperson's office attempted to reaffirm an imagination that conceives of the most intimate place as unruly. Grainy, barely legible, videos of ammunition and hidden tunnels within domestic interiors were used to instil ambiguity, uncertainty and fear that there is something in these invisible spaces justifying the intrusion of the armed forces. As an invisible space, the 'home' was defined through a scrutinizing fiction that turns the interiors of living spaces into dark and threatening lacunae. The military agencies that mapped terrorist activity in the interiors of domestic spaces projected the home as the quintessence of secrecy, a perception well rooted in the modern history of domesticity. 'Domestic space is assumed to hide, in its darkest recesses and forgotten margins, all the objects of fear and phobia that have returned with such insistency to haunt the imaginations of those who have tried to stake out spaces to protect their health and happiness,' noted Anthony Vidler.[21] As the domain of the unseen, the home serves as a medical metaphor for both bodily and social well-being.

Two types of homes emerged from the flood of images during the 2014 war. The first framed the Jewish home as a shelter, and the second, homes in Gaza as battlefields. This profound fallacy is not simply propaganda. Rather, the mix between the two images exposed a meta division that until then remained intact. Maintaining this divide allows the IDF to take control of the visual field and police it efficiently. The term 'police,' Jacques Rancière tells us, stands for a partition of the sensible that is characterized by the absence of void and of supplement: society here is made of groups tied to specific modes of doing, to places in which these occupations are exercised and to modes of being corresponding to these occupations and these places. 'Police', taken in the Rancièrian sense, refers to dominant modes of sensing and thinking of what a home is, and in the process rules out other, potentially contesting modes, and thus establishes consensus and hegemony across culture, politics and the economy. In Rancière's idiom, the notion of 'police' obviously designates much of what 'politics' is ordinarily taken to mean, especially when it comes to the theory of power and governmentality as the establishment of an order of bodies that 'defines the allocation of ways of doing, ways of being, and ways of seeing, and sees that those bodies are assigned by name to a particular place and task'.[22] Encouraging soldiers to produce images both during their activity in Gaza and upon their return home is a strategy to maintain this policing divide. In other words, the individuation of media assists with maintaining a racist divide. Yet, it is crucial to shine a light on the conceit of this manufactured divide to reveal the true commonality of the two homes, and in so doing expose the uneven access to livelihood on the two sides of the buffer that separates Gaza from Israel.[23]

The difference between the two homes is essential because it encapsulates a division that Israel utilizes to maintain its perception of security. Echoing Rancière, Helga Tawil-Souri has argued that representations feed into much wider imaginations of a 'larger than life shadow'. Transformed into a narrow strip of land by Israel, fortified behind fences, weapons, walls, thick bureaucratic regulations, drones, and automatic guns, Gaza – for Israel – is an asset that generates fears, justifications and ideologies:

> Gaza helps Israel generate and actively produce political-economic values to remain 'at war' with Gaza; it rationalises larger 'defence' expenditures and new military technologies, generating even more forms of income, even as it also requires and produces more fear, more protection, more barriers, more

techniques and technologies rendering Gaza small. Gaza becomes a military test site, a marketing bonanza for Israeli surveillance and 'security' companies, an experimental case for drone warfare for others to emulate.[24]

The two images of home are the most pronounced cast of this 'larger than life shadow'. Habits of mediation exercised by soldiers in Gaza and Tel Aviv generate a symmetry that folds perfectly into two opposites.

The tenacious fissure that separates 'types' of homes was evident in various images of illustrated dichotomies circulated by the IDF during the 2014 military operation in the Gaza Strip. The illustration appeared on the IDF Instagram page during the 2014 war, seeking to communicate for Israeli and international followers what the IDF saw as the essence of the conflict between Israel and Hamas. One after the other, the illustrations appeared on social media, staging a series of oppositions: interior and exterior, domestic and public, secret and transparent, each of which attempts to designate the difference between enemy and friend (Figure 14).

One Instagram post depicted an Israeli flag hung over the rooftop of a home. Underneath the house, inside the bomb-shelter, two individuals embrace each other while out of harm's way. In a related image, on the rooftop of the second house a green Hamas flag dangles proudly. Yet, according to the IDF, this Palestinian house is sharply distinguished from the Israeli one; hidden in the underground shelter we see bombs concealed from the public eye. The idea of 'home' illustrated by the Israeli military is reframed by the dialectics between the two images. The image of the warm and sheltering Israeli home is contrasted with its Palestinian opposite: that which must be cast off. Here, the Israeli home is a subject that presupposes and produces a domain of agency from which it is

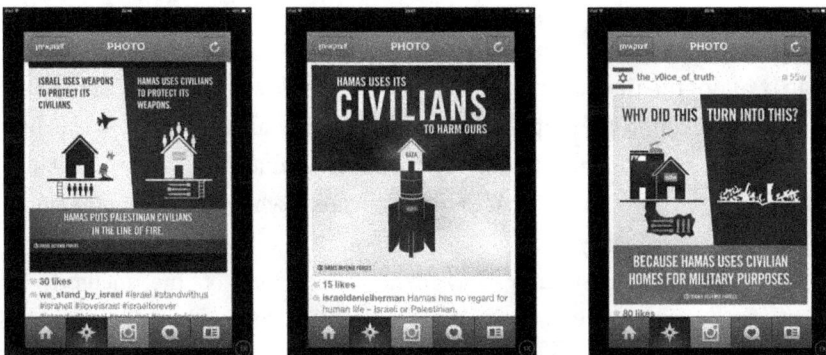

Figure 14 Screenshots from the IDF's official Instagram account, 2014.

differentiated, delineating that which does not belong to it, setting a border and securing it. Indeed, everything that disturbs this border is either the source of disgust or, as we see here, the 'Other'.

The illustrations capture what photographs and videos can never fully frame in one singular image: an idea that feeds a given community with fear about what must be kept outside of the home, but which nevertheless lingers and contaminates it from within. The dichotomies are made to communicate the idea that security itself is conditioned by access to the domestic, undergirded as the basic condition of sociability asserted by security, evoking the ancient dictum that conditions the freedom of an individual to her access to private property.

In another illustration, the difference between the positive and the negative formulation of domesticity is marked by the relationship between the inhabitants of the home and the structure itself, clearly predicating a vertical hierarchy between the dweller, the house and the technologies of security that protect it. This relation between the 'elements' forms a triangle that draws the model for both the Israeli and the Palestinian homes. On the Israeli side, the inhabitants are positioned under the house while the weapons are illustrated above it. This order of things, the image discloses, is projected as the normative and 'healthy' relation between inhabitants and homes. The icon of the house itself operates as a buffer between civilians and the military arms that protect them. On the Palestinian side, this vertical structure is turned on its head: the weapons are buried under the home while the civilians are positioned above, literally standing on the rooftops, consequently presenting the structure of the home an ammunition bunker devoid of human life. This illustration offers a structure through which the IDF signifies meanings in domestic spheres. This deeply convoluted model maps out a war that occurs between two homes in a direct and unmediated clash. The delimiting of the home as the space of security demonstrates that war becomes the general matrix of domination, a regime of bio-power, that is a form of rule aimed not only at controlling the population but controlling all aspects of social life. 'War brings death but also paradoxically, must produce life', wrote Hardt and Negri. This is also what the image above proclaims while delimiting the home as arena of such duality.

The Instagram posts not only demonstrate one of the methods of legitimizing the military force deployed by the IDF during the 2014 assault; it also characterizes the home itself as a weapon. Yet, another illustration in the same series presents the Palestinian home as the tip of a missile. By conflating the structure of the house and the concealed body of the bomb, the IDF explicitly proposes that the threat is encapsulated in the Palestinian home and in the life dwelling within. The dwellers in the home are claimed to be human shields for combatants.[25]

Producing secrecy

The graphic illustrations are of course abstractions. Such abstractions manipulate the inaccessibility of domestic spaces as a way of making homes the source of fear and illegal activity. No doubt, the limit of visibility is central for the production of this biopolitical split between the homes. The inability to fully see what occurs within the interiors of domestic spaces makes them a fertile ground for arousing the imagination, where affective relations such as closeness, affinity, fear and violence are found. Remaining invisible to the eyes of military intelligence, the Palestinian home is redesigned by the IDF as a sealed container for everything that comes to threaten life. It shares architectural elements with the military bunker, manifested not only through its protective function, but also its secretive character. Capturing the interiors of the home through photography and video therefore becomes an 'operative' military objective.

In August 2014, the short videos filmed by IDF soldiers were distributed by the Israeli Ministry of Foreign Affairs, together with shots taken by drones and satellites above the Gaza Strip. Cutting together the first-person videos with the aerial views, the document titled *IDF report: Hamas illegally used civilian infrastructure during Operation Protective Edge* appealed for what lies 'beyond representation'. Photographic images were essential for the claim made by Israel that private homes are used as launching pads. Videos of grainy footage taken by drones juxtaposed with mobile phone cameras that document the ammunition within suggest, in the words used in one video, that 'red dots represent more than just destruction' (Figure 15). If, implies the report, red dots usually represent destroyed homes, they also represent homes from which ammunition is fired. The illegibility and unintelligibility, it seems, serve to promote the idea that therein lies a secret.

Secrecy is the hallmark of walls and rooftops that no longer offer a temporary refuge from the potential violence of war but mark out the domain of violence itself. Secrecy implies an unreachable domain, always feeding itself, assuming a level of depth that subverts privacy in its very essence as it presumes the

Figure 15 Illustration produced by the Israeli of Foreign Affairs, 2015.

unknown and the unknowable. The secret is by definition unrepresentable. It can be seen, as Jacques Derrida conceived it, only once it is already on the way to getting lost. In the process of exposing what it seeks to hide, the hidden dissolves and can no longer be called secret. The secret ontologically negates the ability to capture an image; it is always other to itself – invisible. It is therefore extremely useful for the IDF. While the interiors of the home are repeatedly framed as the harbinger of a secret, the secret itself is always already elsewhere, not visualized by one image or another. More concretely, when planting the missiles within the home, the IDF plants a 'secret' inside the Palestinian household.

The IDF, the report claims, deployed cutting-edge technology to make the invisible visible. The presence of the military UAVs and satellites hovering around and above Gaza assumes that the surface of the roof of the home is a layer that conceals the object, whether that be a combatant or an ammunition storage. The aerial top shot of the roof contains a certain depth that is not actually represented in the image itself but nevertheless is imagined. Where the spaces of the home are invisible, this depth can extend indefinitely and contain the idea of unforeseen terror. The desire to expose what remains unseen not only contradicts the culturally loaded conception of domesticity as an enclosed and private domain but also marks the limitations of the photographic medium in its claim for visual evidence.[26]

According to another document distributed by the Israeli Ministry of Foreign Affairs published in May 2015, the 'IDF airborne forces faced residential homes containing military command centres, multi-story buildings housing pre-prepared surveillance positions, civilian structures extensively booby-trapped, and tunnel openings and infrastructure hidden in and under civilian areas.'[27] The document obstinately emphasized the exploitation of domestic spaces and direct involvement of Palestinian civilians in 'acts of terror'. This form of terror depended on imbuing a dangerous 'depth' to the interiors of the home that was rendered indistinguishable from the mundane everyday life, camouflaged as domestic routine.[28]

Soldier/Dweller

In May 2015, The NGO 'Breaking the Silence' published the oral testimonies of over 60 soldiers that took part in Operation 'Protective Edge'. In the document soldiers described in detail the nature of IDF operations in various combat zones. The testimonies describe the depth of involvement and extent of penetrations and intrusions into the private homes of civilians, based on first-person accounts. In reading these testimonies, one can get a sense of the fragility of the border that divides the war zone and the home – and furthermore – between military conduct and habitual behaviours. According to one anonymous soldier:

> When we entered for the first time, we didn't see a single person inside. We saw no enemy, and no [civilians] either. We went into houses, some of which were already riddled with holes. We broke down the door, entered, 'cleaned' the house with bullets; you walk in shooting. In the beginning you shoot anything that looks weird, you roll up carpets, move things around to make sure there's absolutely nothing there. The house was totally abandoned.[29]

Another testimony exposes the routine of being stationed in one of the homes. This is where the occupation of the homes becomes conflated with its quotidian functions, where suddenly the soldier becomes a dweller.

We slept on their mattresses. In the beginning when there was water, we used toilets, and after that we used sandbags. There was an intense argument over whether it's OK to use their kitchens or not. One guy was the first to go make black coffee and that led to lengthy deliberations: to drink or not to drink. The way I saw it, I pictured this family returning to their house and seeing it totally wrecked, the windows all broken, the floors torn up and the walls messed up by grenades and they say, 'The sons of bitches ate my cornflakes, I can't believe it.' No chance. They won't care if you used their cooking gas, if you used their kitchen. All this happened before we knew the houses would be blown up once we left them.

Several soldiers testified to the dilemma about domestic functions, asking themselves an existential question- 'to drink the coffee, or not to drink' – a question that captures how certain practices define a space, a deliberation emerging from the inability to fully 'clean' the presence of the inhabitant to whom the home belongs before it is turned into an army post. The soldier's practices in the occupied spaces cannot fully eradicate the domestic qualities that define it as a home.

After the ground operation in Gaza ended, the IDF distributed yet another Instagram image. This one was of a different kind. It showed a collage that merged the figure of a soldier and a returning son, fusing a tent with a house (Figure 16). The Instagram post targeted the Israeli society's susceptibility to identify with the transition of the IDF soldier back into a tender son. The right half of the image presents a man standing while he exits a typical home, perhaps his own. In the left half of the collage, the home is substituted by a tent, while the man momentarily pauses on the threshold of the dark interiors. This soldier/ dweller seems to be caught in an intermediary position between war and home, and between the secrecy of destruction and the privacy of the domestic realm. 'We salute the reserve soldier', says the caption beneath, wedding the obligation to home with a commitment to nationhood.

The double body of the solider/dweller relates to the same internal duality in the viral videos of the returning soldiers. Indeed, if I started this chapter by claiming that there are two homes, split and separated through a militarized imagination, this single body speaks to the inseparability of two roles, the two domestic interiors, and the two places – be it Gaza or Tel Aviv. In other words, the double body of the soldier/dweller implicitly captures the inseparability of the violence unleashed in Gaza and the protection granted by the home. No doubt, the original message of this Instagram post addresses the soldier as a beloved son, one that must be saluted. But another meaning sneaks into the collage, one

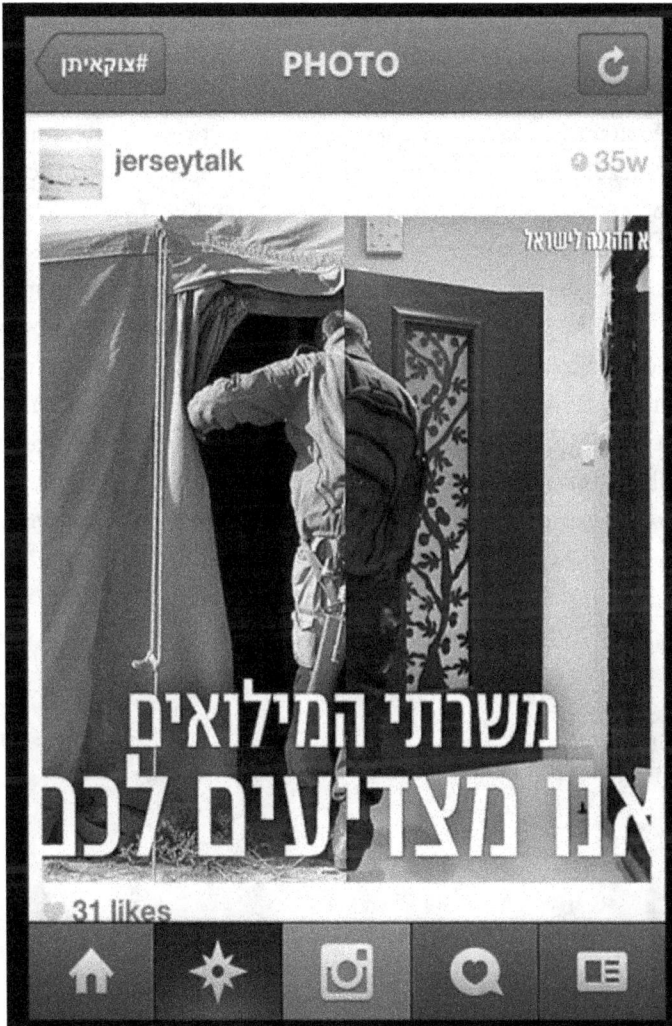

Figure 16 Half civilian, half soldier. An Instagram post distributed by the IDF, 2014.

that can potentially subvert the viral propaganda disseminated by Israel. This alternative meaning pertains to the merging of the civilian with the combatant, or the war zone with the home as two interdependent, indivisible and symbiotic parts of one whole. Such a reading would expose the deeply disturbing reliance of Israeli homeliness on the destruction and denial of the Palestinian home; on the *homing* of one space and the *unhoming* of the another.

This figure of the soldier/dweller also speaks to the rise of an active media user and its centrality for the media campaign waged by the IDF during, and after, the 2014 war. The collage captures the slippage of media practices, shaped initially by the everyday, before gradually being implemented in combat, and as a justification for invading, raiding and occupying. If initially considered as a risk to the IDF, after the massive operation, habitual practices of filming and sharing were more readily incorporated into the official strategies and media coverage.

Indeed, media practices are inseparable from that fissure between two domestic spaces, with radically different accesses to life. The pervasive use of media technologies traces the soldier's passage from the private realm of his or her home into the space of exception, conceived by the military as war zones and defined as hazardous by the military logic. The gradually intensifying usage of social media by soldiers meant that by the end of the 2014 war this passage was most visible, and part of a constructed imagination of what life at home is, and why it is central to Israel's security regime. Media practices, as I have demonstrated, were re-appropriated to produce uneven access to safety and life.

Saving face: Between uniformity and isolation

Herald: By command of His Most Merciful Excellency, your lives are to be
   spared. Slaves you were and slaves you remain. But the terrible penalty of
   crucifixion has been set aside on the single condition that you identify the
   body or the living person of the slave called Spartacus.
Antoninus: I'm Spartacus!
Slaves, one after the other: I'm Spartacus! I'm Spartacus! I'm Spartacus! I'm
   Spartacus! I'm Spartacus! I'm Spartacus! I'm Spartacus![1]

(Spartacus, 1960)

In August 2015, a Palestinian activist filmed a routine arrest carried out by Israeli
soldiers in the village of Nabi Saleh in the West Bank. Almost immediately, videos
of the incident were circulated widely on social media platforms. One such video
shows a masked soldier chasing down 12-year-old Mohammed Tamimi, who
had allegedly thrown a rock towards a nearby patrol. The soldier is wearing a
balaclava to cover his face (Figure 17). He grabs and tries to detain the boy,
who gasps for air under the weight of the soldier's body. Unwilling to abort the
arrest, the masked soldier struggles with the Palestinian activists surrounding
him, warning them against intervening. The activists ignore his warnings. They
reach into the entanglement of limbs and eventually tear off the soldier's mask
to reveal his face to the camera lens. The soldier suddenly looks bewildered like
an actor who has lost his costume in the midst of a theatrical scene. The lifting
of the mask, and the revelation of his face, is a tipping point, beyond which the
mission cannot continue.

The incident in Nabi Saleh was not an isolated event. On a number of occasions
in 2015, IDF and Israeli law enforcement officers were seen or photographed
wearing masks of various kinds, which were often improvised during regular
security exercises in the West Bank. 'A new phenomenon: Policemen in
Jerusalem wear masks in concern of being exposed on Facebook', one newspaper
headline ran.[2] Media commentators suggested that due to the omnipresence of
cameras, both border police and soldiers were becoming worried that their faces

Figure 17 Soldier trying to detain Mohammad Tamimi, age 11 (Source: Abbas Momani/AFP/ Getty Images, 2015).

could end up on social media and that, as a result, they might become targets for Palestinian reprisal. 'It's not an official instruction', one policeman explained. '[M]asks were usually worn only by special units for particular operations, but today it's essential for everyone.'[3] But such comments divert attention from a more pressing problem: the circulation of images of faces can potentially expose legally questionable military procedures. Once a camera captures the faces of a soldier engaged in such a procedure, his or her image is likely to circulate virally on social media and to force the soldier to confront the social and legal implications of his or her actions. What, in such a situation, does the hidden face have to hide? And why does its uncovering seem to pose a new threat to the Israeli military regime? How does the face – unlike the body – undermine authority?

In this chapter I argue that the human face has emerged as a new site of politics driven by the use of social media in warfare. While IDF soldiers have begun to hide their faces, the Israeli government has begun to track down the faces of Palestinians on social media platforms with increasing urgency. In

2015, the Israeli government and the IDF updated their surveillance tactics in accordance with growing social media usage. Supplementing their own advanced facial recognition technologies, the IDF began to exploit social media extensively to facilitate pre-emption strategies, including arrests of Palestinians. At the same time, Facebook has gradually become an online forum for public adjudication: videos of IDF soldiers and Israeli police officers killing or attempting to kill Palestinians are frequently uploaded to social media platforms for public discussion. Israeli leaders, meanwhile, have been quick to accuse social media of inciting violence.

As a result of the rapid co-option of everyday media technologies and practices into the military routine, the collective appearance of Israeli soldiers is gradually being replaced by an individuated appearance. Images of the faces, I argue below, can be singled out as a new Achilles' heel for a long-standing and highly media-conscious military regime. The state derives its power, in part, from the way its agents appear as a homogeneous whole and cohere into an undifferentiated group of representatives. Individuating soldiers through the exposure of their faces, therefore, constitute an inherent threat to this collective authority. The disclosure of images of the face undermines the military's attempt to present its agents as abstract figures. By maintaining the upper hand on visualization, the ruled subjects are prevented from shaping a collective political identity. Meanwhile, authority remains faceless while framing the faces of those subjugated to it. The facemask is thus a shield against a gaze that threatens to fragment and divide the military's homogeneous collective body and to penetrate the layers of impunity that protect the soldier as a representative of state authority.

Particularly in Israel-Palestine, where everyday life and habits are shaped by and inseparable from military and security routines, the face becomes a symptom of individuation. The term 'individuation' here refers to the rapid concentration of media attention on identifiable individuals. This process, accelerated by social media, is inextricably linked to two broader developments: first, the outsourcing of governance onto supra-national private companies such as Facebook, and second, the shifting of media focus from the collective to the individual.

Furthermore, where every soldier and civilian is likely to be holding a mobile phone, and with more than 1,700 security cameras installed in the West Bank and East Jerusalem alone, visibility is inevitable.[4] Vast networks of video cameras have been installed to facilitate the military rule in the West Bank and to capture the faces of Palestinians. Today, this system of surveillance is gradually being turned against the face of authority itself. In an unexpected boomerang effect, the technologies that were set up to govern and control are now being used to document the faces of soldiers.

The risks and political dynamics created by this constant visibility are shifting over time, rather than attempting to hide themselves altogether. Today IDF soldiers are more concerned with keeping their faces shielded from the cameras and, hence, from the social media algorithms that disseminate and individuate their uniformity. The dichotomy of visibility and invisibility turns increasingly around the face itself. This dichotomy, therefore, must be redefined against a new political context that emphasizes similitude and distinction, collectivity and individuality.

In the context of the Israeli occupation of the West Bank and the Gaza Strip, social media initially introduced a new threat to military practices before being adopted wholesale to extend the reach of the military itself. As I will argue, due to the military co-option of social media, the human face now constitutes a battlefield where collective groupings are atomized and personalized. The surface of the face lends itself to measurement and calculations that make it a central target for this kind of identification and individuation.

Examining photographs and videos that have gone viral on social media, I aim to make the often-invisible connection between disparate images tangible. The sources used here are compiled from available data shared on social media platforms – Facebook in particular. Following the connections made by social media algorithms can shed light on the ramifications of new media on the exercise of state power. By analysing photographs and videos produced and circulated by soldiers and civilians over the last three years, I attempt to rethink how such images function, both as representation – showing what happened at a particular place and time – and as information.

Looking back over the history of portrait photography, I contend that the photographic image of the face has long been torn between its representational mode and its biometric calculability. From 2015, this split function has been reinvigorated by social media and by facial recognition algorithms embedded into platforms' operating systems. To focus on the face is to frame it as both an image and a vehicle for communication and information. Sigrid Weigel reminds us of the wider historical significance of portraits by considering both what the images represent and how the faces operate as media. As Weigel explains, on one hand, '[T]he face has become a concentrated image of the human'; on the other, 'emotional codes and cultural technologies show the history of the face as first and foremost a history of media'.[5] For Emmanuel Levinas, the face is that which stands between the 'I' and an 'Other'. The human face, in his view, forces a confrontation with the Other, 'exceeding the idea of the other in me' where 'the face of the Other at each moment destroys and overflows the plastic image it leaves me'.[6] As Levinas notes, the face is a conduit precisely because it refuses to be fossilized into a picture – what he referred to as a plastic image. Hans Belting, on the other hand, approaches the visual history of the face through its masked counterpart. The expressions of the living face reveal and proclaim as much as they conceal and deceive. Whereas Levinas speaks of an unfathomable depth, Belting insists that the face is first and foremost a surface or a vehicle for an array of images, and an image in itself. 'The concept of the face as mask is ambiguous because it is not merely a face that resembles a mask', writes Belting, 'but also a face that creates its own masks when we react to, or engage with, other faces'.[7]

Theorists of digital media, meanwhile, have analysed the face as a surface subject to measurements and calculations. For Zach Blas, the face has become the target of numerous recording devices from CCTV cameras to mobile phones, which derive information from human bodies. Blas adopts Shoshana Magnet's conception of the 'information cage' to depict the way the face is recorded and held captive in information networks. 'The cage is always with us', writes Blas, 'hovering over the surface of our bodies – softly and virtually – awaiting activation'.[8] That cage, maintains Blas, disturbs the dichotomy between opacity and transparency, and with that disruption, the stakes of political action shift radically.

Such perspectives encompassing the history of the portrait, as well as the face in contemporary visual cultures, together shed light on the various tensions that surround images of faces on social media: between representation and quantification, depth and surface, and presence and absence. Such digital images both represent individuals and operate on them by activating automated protocols and algorithms through which the individual is singled out. To understand the significance of faces caught on camera in the context of highly charged political and military conflict, representation and quantification should be thought of together, both supporting and contradicting each other. It is this duality that makes the face a unique target within the context of the armed conflict between IDF soldiers and Palestinians.

Facing social media

With the rise of social media, the face has become a target of warfare. During the 2006 Lebanon War, the wide availability of mobile phones and digital cameras resulted in an unexpected surge of images taken by soldiers on the battlefield.[9] Soldiers, conscripts and reservists deployed in Lebanon took hundreds of photographs that substituted the official photographs and videos released by public affairs officers. Before the Lebanon War, Miri Regev, the IDF spokesperson at the time, dismissed the importance of online images, claiming that 'they pose no problem whatsoever to military conduct'.[10] Regev underestimated the unofficial channels soldiers would use to publicize their videos such as YouTube and Flickr. Together, these alternative channels painted a grim image of the IDF's incompetence during the war.

At the same time, Hezbollah, Israel's long-standing opponent in Lebanon, proved that its media strategy was superior. In comparison to the IDF, Hezbollah's flexibility and spontaneity allowed it to disseminate more images and at a much faster pace. Hezbollah operated a YouTube channel followed by thousands of users, while the IDF relied on traditional strategies of communication. To avoid being spotted by the Israeli army, reporters for Al-Manar, Hezbollah's broadcasting agency, disguised themselves as civilians, riding motorbikes and taking photos on the go.

As mentioned in the previous chapter, during the military operation in the Gaza Strip in 2008, Israel shifted its attention to social media. When the operation began, the IDF was already armed with its own YouTube channel, embracing wholesale the hype of self-promotional slogans from social media textbooks. In their book *War 2.0*, Thomas Rid and Marc Hecker show how the IDF embraced social media as a platform for its public affairs, continuing to run its YouTube channel even when it enforced a comprehensive press ban.[11] Two weeks after the operation in Gaza was launched, more than 40 videos were already uploaded, some showing footage recorded from drones of targeted killings of Hamas officials. In the end, however, the IDF relied too heavily on the spectacle of advanced technology, which seemed proof of its own technological superiority, and its social media strategy failed to recognize the importance of the bottom-up, amateurish media practices of soldiers on the ground. As I have shown in the last chapter, in addition to the military's venture into social media, the 2008–9 military operation was a moment of mass civilian engagement with new media technologies.

> In addition to the military's advance into social media, this was another moment of mass civilians conscription of new media technologies for militarized ends. But unlike the earlier cyberbattles, this conscription involved large number of ordinary civilians who were employing everyday social media tools as their vehicles, logging on from their home computers to argue the state's case before global online audiences.[12]

After the 2008–9 operation, the soldiers themselves were already enthralled by a new platform that encouraged them to share their own photos and selfies. Within the aftermath of the operation the IDF realized that Facebook unleashed a new and popular way to share photographs and videos that were captured by combatants in the Gaza Strip. Posting thousands of photographs on Facebook, soldiers documented their deployment in Gaza, presenting raids into houses, violent arrests, explosions and more than anything, their own faces.

Circulating on social media, snapshots provided a closer look at how soldiers were coping with their routine of combat, which often includes long hours of boredom. Evoking the imagery from domestic life, these photos were the outcome of conflated habits weaved from domestic leisure, play and invasive military procedures. Unsurprisingly, these digital images and the information attached to them stimulated anxiety within the military's top officers, who confronted increasing international critique. Avital Leibovich, who used to act as the head of the Israeli Defense Forces' foreign press branch, claimed: 'The blogosphere and new media are another war zone [...]. We have to be relevant there'. [13]

Coincidentally, in the same year, the German software company Betaface introduced an online facial recognition search engine called MyFaceID, which allows users to upload photos of faces and match them with others in the MyFaceID database. In Betaface's words, MyFaceID allows you to 'automatically process your photos, find all faces, help you tag them and let you search for similar people'. [14] The company was immediately contracted by Facebook, which began to actively encourage users to tag faces and names, and to search for resemblances between them. This shift turned the face into a pivotal site of identification, not only for governments and institutions attempting to monitor and control populations but also for social media users themselves. The face became a means of self-branding through which users could maintain and personalize their online personas. A new database of faces was in the making, fed by what Mark Andrejevic calls 'lateral surveillance', which pertains to the two-fold process through which users follow and search for one another, while tagging and assisting the processes of identification. [15]

> The proliferation of uncertainty serves as one marketing strategy for the offloading of verification strategies onto members of the general populace. In keeping with the so-called interactive revolution, individuals are invited not just to participate in the forms of entertainment they consume (interactive television) and in the

production of the goods and services they consume (mass customization), but in formerly centralized forms of surveillance and verification.[16]

Lateral surveillance, as I will suggest below, would gather force and dictate new modes of self-control and monitoring, displacing more direct, top-down forms of administration with strategies that govern indirectly. While soldiers use social media for their own self-expression, their adoption of this technology also serves broader institutional aims. By tagging and naming pictures of themselves, IDF soldiers unknowingly maintain and feed the algorithms that connect geographic locations, identities and real bodies, making it increasingly easy for the algorithm to identify faces and link additional personal information. Social media turns IDF soldiers into constant contributors to a multifaceted database of images, which in the future might be used as incriminating evidence of military actions in Palestine.

In 2010, more than a year after the operation in Gaza concluded, the head of information security for the IDF, Lieutenant Ami Weissberg, sent a warning to high-ranking commanders. The subject line read 'regarding your own personal safety and the information you disclose on the internet'. The memo contained a cautionary request against sharing images and data on social media: 'Your pictures, together with additional personal information on social media, will allow the enemy to locate your home address'.[17] The letter was strongly worded and expressed grave concerns about the circulation of images on social media and the ease with which the personal identities of soldiers can be extracted from them.

Anxiety about the use of new media was aggravated further when an anonymous source published a list of 200 Israeli soldiers who had participated in the assault on the Gaza Strip. This came against the backdrop of the United Nations (UN) verdict on the war, declaring it a potential violation of international law. The list, which came to be known within the IDF as the '200 List', included a compilation of selfies that had been shared on social media by the soldiers themselves or tagged by their friends (Figure 18). From these images, it was possible to trace the identities of the soldiers and to attach them to names, military units and even home addresses.[18] An inversion of a typical 'most wanted' terrorist list, the 200 List was comprised of faces of alleged accomplices in a military campaign that took the lives of 1,385 Palestinians, of which 960 were civilians.[19] Combining photographs of soldiers taken during both family events and military operations, the list marked a shift in the traditional role of the mug shot in juridical and policing procedures. That is to say, given that

Israeli army condemns publication of Gaza 'war criminals'

Names, photographs and addresses of soldiers said to have taken part in Gaza offensive put on website

Figure 18 Media report on the '200 List' in November, 2010 (Source: AP).

image aggregation has been developed by state institutions to monitor governed populations, the 200 List showed that social media can flip the cameras onto the faces of soldiers and reverse the processes of control. Facebook algorithms, in allowing users to pin down specific individuals, briefly turned social media into an open-source counter-surveillance system, which could be used to identify those responsible for the outcomes of war.

In 2011, the year that saw the Arab Spring in Egypt propelled by Facebook users, Palestinian dissidents also used Facebook as a key instrument for investigating and demanding accountability for the unlawful actions of IDF soldiers in the West Bank. In December of that year, one of the weekly demonstrations in Nabi Saleh ended with the violent killing of a Palestinian activist. A mobile phone documented an IDF soldier shooting a gas canister at 28-year-old Mustafa Tamimi and directly striking his head.[20] A frame extracted from the video, showing the tip of a rifle poking out of a military jeep, caught the exact moment the IDF soldier fired the canister, milliseconds before it hit Tamimi. This frame, which included both the weapon and Tamimi, was the catalyst of a Facebook page titled 'Who Killed Mustafa Tamimi?' devoted to unveiling the identity of the rogue soldier. The Facebook campaign was initiated by residents of Nabi Saleh and Israeli activists, who together conducted an independent investigation into the unlawful killing of Tamimi. While the soldier's face was not exposed in the frame, the viral campaign allowed users to explore social media databases and to narrow down the number of soldiers who might have fired the deadly shot. Following a trail of links and hashtags, users eventually arrived at the perpetrator's Facebook profile, where he openly boasted about his actions (Figure 19). The soldier, whose name is Aviram Boniel, actually facilitated the investigation by uploading numerous selfies to his profile, linking them to specific times and locations.[21] The identification of his face marked the success of the investigation, which had taken full advantage of the digital footprint left by the soldier's habitual practices of photographing, tagging and sharing.

The 'Who Killed Mustafa Tamimi?' Facebook campaign utilized social media algorithms to zero in on the individual behind the killing. Such algorithms accelerate the process of individuation and maintain direct links between selfies and embodied subjects. Facial recognition technologies today are deeply embedded in social media platforms but too easily ignored. The influx of

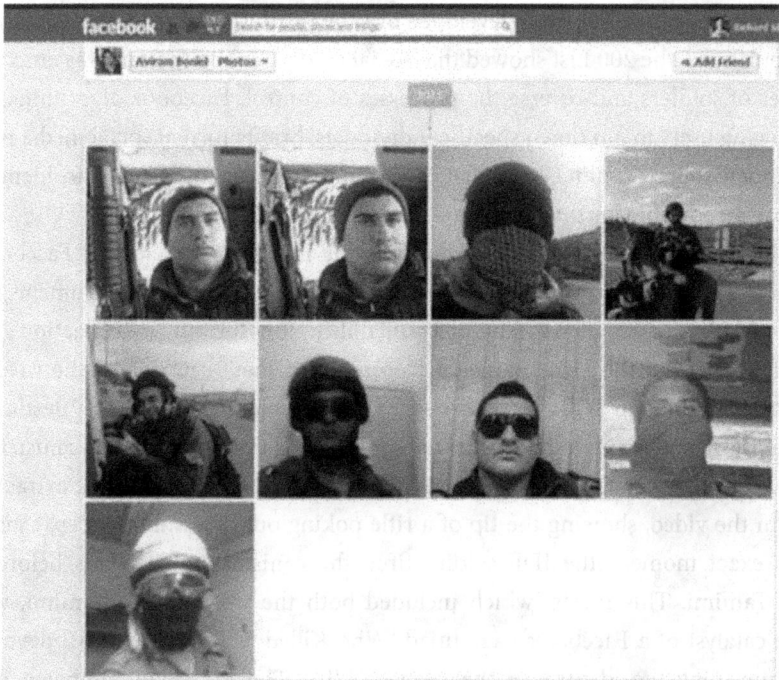

Figure 19 Aviram Boniel, Facebook, 2011 (Source: Who Killed Tamimi Campaign).

media into everyday life brings with it constant self-identification: capturing, uploading, tagging, updating, sharing and linking. As a ubiquitous self-detection instrument, Facebook contributes to the splitting up and atomizing of a military network into its individual agents, the soldiers themselves.

Facial recognition technologies use various procedures to convert the image of a face into a 'facial template'. This template contains a compressed amount of data that can be compared to existing images stored in a database. The digitization of the face is only one step within the multiple procedures performed by an algorithm: faces are detected in images and then extracted from the background, torn from their context, before being standardized to fit a given format. Using this condensed template as an index, facial recognition systems aim to link an image to a real and embodied person.

State actors most often use facial recognition technologies for security and surveillance. Today, however, not only public spaces are surveyed, but also everyday patterns of communication predicated on the use of mobile phone cameras and social media, which automatically track and record. More importantly still, whereas technologies of state surveillance often spark debates around privacy and extra-juridical actions, it is rarely taken into consideration that the ubiquity of social media proliferates the use of algorithms that capture, analyse and detect individuals in everyday life. And it is rarely taken into account that these procedures require the active participation of users, who willingly tag images and, thus, expand the databases that algorithms search and analyse.

In *Black Matters: On Surveillance and Blackness*, Simone Browne proposes a compelling argument that resists the temptation of the 'new' in the surveillance technologies used to govern the lives of black subjects.[22] For Browne, surveillance is embedded in how Otherness is imagined within a predominantly white visual culture. The technological innovation underpinning capacity to identify faces and bodies is a symptom of existing racial biases that organize a much vaster hierarchy of bodies. Rather than seeing surveillance as something inaugurated by new technologies, Browne excavates the origins of automated facial recognition, to see it as ongoing and to insist that 'we factor in how racism undergirds and sustains the intersecting surveillances of our present order'.[23] Browne draws on the field of surveillance studies to question how personal data, privacy, and security intersect and coalesce as techniques to manage everyday life. Browne writes that:

> Since its emergence, surveillance studies have been primarily concerned with how and why populations are tracked, profiled, policed, and governed at state

borders, in cities, at airports, in public and private spaces, through biometrics, telecommunications technology, CCTV, identification documents, and more recently by way of Internet-based social network sites such as Twitter and Facebook. Also of focus are the ways that those who are often subject to surveillance subvert, adopt, endorse, resist, innovate, limit, comply with, and monitor that very surveillance.[24]

Drawing on David Lyon's work on surveillance, Browne asserts that vital and positive end-goals such as participation, welfare and safety are advocated, leaving social control 'seldom a motivation for installing surveillance systems even though that may be an unintended or secondary consequence of their deployment'.[25]

David Lyon has argued that the 'surveillance society' as a concept might be misleading, for it suggests 'a total, homogeneous situation of being under surveillance' rather than a more nuanced understanding of the sometimes discreet and varying ways that surveillance operates.[26] Lyon highlights the necessity to underline 'sites of surveillance' such as the military or the state in order to come to an understanding of the commonalities that exist at these various sites.[27] A more nuanced understanding of surveillance is urgent in the process of understanding how it operates. Key to the operation of surveillance is the dual function of identifying a particular subject, while at the same time including that someone in a much broader category based on race, ethnicity and gender. The isolation of a face or a body is rapidly advanced due to everyday use of technologies by individuals who 'voluntarily' share their information online.

In *Undercover: Police Surveillance in America*, Gary Marx isolates the core difference between the new and emerging forms of surveillance from the older and institutionalized modes of control.[28] What makes 'the new surveillance' substantially distinct from older and more traditional forms of social control is laid out by Marx in a set of characteristics that new technologies, practices and forms of surveillance share to varying degrees. First, such technologies no longer require physical borders and structures such as fences and walls, but rather operate by receding to the background of the everyday. Second, the capacity to share and store data allows surveillance to remain undetected, facilitating practices of data collection and aggregation by states and companies without the consent of users. A mode of self-surveillance becomes the most common and ubiquitous form of auto-monitoring in which one 'frames' him or herself. Third, new surveillance opens the possibility of monitoring while reducing the labour invested into detection and investigation.[29] The military, or NGO organizations can effectively utilize social media as research tools to detect and incriminate a soldier or a Palestinian activist.

Crucially, practices of self-monitoring, or what Marx has called 'new technologies of surveillance', are best situated as part of an economy of well-being, whereby habits are cultivated around technologies that allow a close monitoring of oneself. Face recognition technologies used as part of an everyday practice of tagging friends on social media are part of a wider category of technological operations that measure, calculate and assess the body. Deborah Lupton refers to such practices as self-tracking, alluding to the ways in which people knowingly and purposively collect information about themselves.[30] Self-tracking differs, she argues, from covert surveillance or means of collecting information on people that result in data sets to which the subjects of monitoring do not have access. Self-tracking is a key element of a 'quantified self', that 'can be interpreted more broadly as an ethos and apparatus of practices that has gathered momentum in this era of mobile and wearable digital devices and of increasingly sensor-saturated physical environments'.[31] As a broad category that includes the voluntary contribution of information by users and the myriad ways in which companies and states capitalize on such information, 'dataveillance' need not involve digital technologies. Nevertheless, one form of it occurs when digital data are collected on any interaction that people may have with internet-connected activities that generate information – either automatically, for instance when people use search engines, or intentionally, when they upload images or texts to internet sites such as social media platforms. As Lupton observes:

> Digitised dataveillance is a participant in the vitality of digital data and in the dispersal of digital technologies of watching, from sensor-embedded environments to sensor-embedded wearable technologies. It therefore differs from earlier modes of panoptic surveillance in that there is no centralised location from which people are watched.[32]

The distributed feature of dataveillance is emphasized in the joint work of sociologist Zygmunt Bauman and David Lyon.[33] The two use the phrase 'liquid surveillance' to describe the ceaseless monitoring of citizens with the help of digital technologies across a range of sites and for a variety of purposes. Not only is personal information gathered via the use of digital surveillance technologies, but individuals can easily be grouped or sorted into discrete categories and classes on the basis of this information and then subjected to assessments on the basis of prior assumptions or inferences.[34] While dataveillance facilitates the individual targeting of singular users, it is equally a categorizing force that ties multiple users and bodies to imagined groups. Facial recognition technologies operate on that logic, isolating while forming mass identities, based on ethnicity, race, class and lifestyle. This tug and pull is a pervasive force that reshapes the operation of military power, and indeed, the political assembly formed to resist it.

Mass individuation

Facial recognition technologies have historically depended on the ability to capture in photographs the data that identify a face, while excluding the particular variations in facial expression that have a significant role in face-to-face communication. In the 1960s, technologies of facial recognition were developed to address growing concerns around the problem of 'disembodied identities', a term used by Kelly A. Gates to refer to individuals that exist and circulate only as visual and textual representations, independently of real bodies.[35] Disembodied identities, writes Gates, are produced by 'visual and textual representations of individuals that circulate independent of their physical bodies'.[36] In other words, the 'disembodiment of identities' results from floods of images that detach embodied individuals from their physical presences, culminating in what Frederic Myers, as far back as 1886, coined 'phantasms of the living'.[37] 'What men and women in the late nineteenth century faced with alarm', writes John Durham Peters, 'is something we have had over a century to get used to: a superabundance of phantasms of the living appearing in various media'.[38] Whereas such replicas are today embedded within the fabric of everyday life, social media platforms have intensified image circulation and with it the issue of how to reconnect images to embodied individuals return with a new urgency.

Facial recognition algorithms aim both to automate the procedure of connecting faces to identities and to allow the sharing of those identities across computer networks, leading to a regime of mass individuation. The idea of mass individuation, surely an oxymoron, points to a long-standing ambiguity in the photography of faces: on one hand, photographs of faces represent particular individuals; on the other, photography from its early days envisaged categories or types of human faces, sharing natural and physiognomic qualities. Kelly Gates historicizes the term as a technique central to the emergence of a liberal form of governance in the nineteenth century, whereby individuals were converted into images. Drawing on John Tagg, Gates underlines the process of collecting portrait photography, which in turn, could be meticulously examined one by one and categorized in filing systems and archives.[39] Mass individuation pertains to the procedure of subjecting entire populations to scrutiny, dealing with each specific case according to pre-existing categories. This process is augmented by computerization and the advent of networked databases. 'Mass individuation' is a governmental tactic for population management that operates by collecting and filing the precise details of each of the individuals of a given populace, according to hierarchies of race, nationality, class, gender and political agency. By producing a new group, weaved from disparate individuals, 'mass individuation' can become modular, flexibly shifting between the 'masses' and the 'individual', either pin-pointing singular members within a collective or hiding them deep within that collectivity to protect them against this isolating capacity. This last aspect, as I will argue in the next section, turns 'mass individuation' into a particularly useful weapon for the Israeli military.

To individuate is to collapse together the specific and the generic. Alexander Galloway and Eugene Thacker stress that networks deindividuate as much as they individuate. Networks separate and individuate within themselves, stratifying different types of nodes, users and social actors. 'But these processes of individuation are always supplemented by processes of deindividuation', write Galloway and Thacker, 'for each individuation is always encompassed by the "mass" and aggregate quality of networks as a whole, everything broken down into stable, generic nodes and discrete, quantifiable edges'.[40] Social media and facial recognition algorithms represent the culmination of mass individuation, which has expanded from state-controlled social regulation to omnipresent social media platforms. While facial recognition technologies were initially developed for military purposes, like many other technologies they are by now part of everyday communication.[41] The habituation of facial recognition technologies implies that the detection of the face and the subsequent identification of the individual have been co-opted into a network that no longer distinguishes between military prerogatives and the habits of everyday communication. The embedding of facial recognition into everyday communication is facilitated predominantly by social media, which has become a new site of social regulation and governance, where users offer their personal information as a means of communicating with friends and other interested parties, while similarly partaking in the monitoring of other users online.

Hiding in photographs

The significance of the human face as a site of incriminating information is deeply rooted in the history of portrait photography, used as a tool for classification and identification. The notion that portrait photography can be used to produce vast archives of potential criminals and prevent unruly behaviour by individualizing the collective dates back to scientific, medical and epistemological shifts during the mid-nineteenth century. In parallel with these shifts, photography became adopted as a new instrument for scientific studies of the human body, and in particular the human face. The fundamental assumption underlying studies in physiognomy and phrenology was that faces, once compared, juxtaposed and superimposed, reveal similarities and likenesses from which categories of classification can be produced. These studies sought to demonstrate that the face not only marks the individuality of the person but also exposes natural connections that tie groups together through shared characteristics.

As Allan Sekula notes, 'from 1860 photography produced a system of representation capable of functioning both honorifically and repressively'.[42] On the one hand, Sekula argues, the photographic portrait is inseparable from a cultural tradition of portraiture in which the image of the face provides a 'ceremonial presentation of the bourgeois self'.[43] That is to say, photography marked the face as an icon of social class and familial heritage, which celebrated individuality. On the other hand, photographs also lent themselves to anatomical illustration of organic life. What connected these two modes of portraiture was not merely the face as a site of identity but the assumption that an image of a face can tip over from its socially individuating function to its mere indexical use for identification.

By the 1880s, photography was accepted as having juridical reliability. The use of photography for juridical purposes can be seen in the way it was used to categorize and archive populations on the basis of class types. In turning the new objectifying lens towards socially excluded and out-cast 'types', a new form of degenerate 'social body' was posited. The human face was arrested in order to 'read' criminal states of mind in its features. An archival process was undertaken to subordinate and territorialize faces into predefined social roles, categorizing them by different criminal propensities.[44]

The idea of a typology of human behaviour arose from the assumption that ideal or representative 'types' could be deduced from the physiological characteristics of individuals, as though by superimposing photographs upon one another, a new face emerges that combines all other faces, illuminating the generic image of the criminal.[45] The very notion of human type – the idea of a physiological mean in which the ideal would be deduced from the observation of the ordinary – was made possible by the sociologist Adolphe Quetelet. The author, in his *Treatise of Man and the Development of His Faculties*, articulated the traits of a generalized human being comprised from multiple others.[46] 'This was the reversal of the classical, Neoplatonic notion of type based on the ideal', writes Georges Teyssot to describe the desire for abstraction, even of the human body.[47] The physiognomy of the face provided a site in which art and the emerging bio-social sciences intersected during the mid-nineteenth century. 'Proof' was attaining a double-sense, as both proof connecting a portrait to its referent and proof connecting the singular man to a multiplicity of archived bodies.

This technique was explored in the summer of 1877 by the Victorian biologist, anatomist and physician Francis Galton who presented his new findings in photography and portraiture to the Royal Anthropological Institute.[48] Galton began his research by collecting hundreds of photographs of prisoners. Through multiple exposures, he then developed a technique of superimposing one image upon another, creating a combination of multiple portraits consolidated into a single face; in this way, he created an ideal type that both concealed the individuals and revealed an imaginary typology. Galton first published his research in *Nature* in 1878, where he wrote:

> The photographic process enables us to obtain with mechanical precision a generalised picture; one that represents no man in particular, but portrays an imaginary figure, possessing the average features of any given group of men.[49]

One of Galton's more zealous followers adapted this technique to produce an image of the ideal soldier. A professor of physiology at Harvard University in 1876, Henry Pickering Bowditch, was particularly interested in identifying resemblances among soldiers, merging the faces together to detect the 'average soldier'.[50] The ideal-type soldier was deduced from this process, clearly identifiable in the resultant image and simultaneously hidden within it. This composite image supported the idea that soldiers were merely nodes that together formed the ideal face of authority. Put together, the soldiers projected an imaginary figure of authority, which then materialized as a singular generic face, belonging to no one and to everyone (Figure 20). In 1894 Bowditch wrote:

> For our amateur photographers, who are constantly seeking new worlds to conquer, the opportunity of doing useful work in developing the possibilities of composite photography ought to be very welcome. Not only will the science of ethnology profit by their labours, but by making composites of persons nearly

Figure 20 Wend soldier composite, Bowditch, 1894 (Source: Harvard Archive).

related to each other, new and very interesting kind of family portrait may be produced. The effect of occupation on the physiognomy may also be studied in this way.[51]

Bowditch's experiment supports the view that the perfectly generic face is another kind of mask. It conceals individuality and as such plays a crucial military role in shielding individuals underneath a cloak of generality. Where bodies appear to be uniform, the soldier is partially hidden; this is a long-standing principle of military concealment based on uniformity among the men. In fact, military uniform itself forms a visual insignia that connects subjects together under the same banner; it is precisely this shared costume, or disguise, that allows the military to cohere as a whole. The word uniform is a derivation from the Latin *uniformis*, meaning 'having only one form or shape'. The word is comprised of *una* (one) and *forma* (form), which merges the heterogeneous into one homogeneous entity by rendering the average image in the manner prescribed by Bowditch.

From the early twentieth century, the standardization of soldiers' uniforms was inseparable from various techniques of concealment, which were developed as visual media and became integrated into combat. How the soldier disappeared was, thus, indivisible from the technologies that made him visible. In 1914, the French general and artist Lucien-Victor Guirand de Scévola coined the term 'camouflage' to refer to systematic dissimulation to avoid photographic detection.[52] The better the enemy could see with the aid of optical technologies, the better and more precise camouflage needed to be. As Hanna Rose Shell emphasizes, techniques of camouflage reveal much more than military tactics; they form part of political imagery and articulate indirectly what a given state wants to keep hidden. Military concealment always seeks to incorporate the enemy's mechanized gaze and to envision the battle through the enemy's eyes. While the extension of the human eye through visual technologies allowed armies to perceive the battlefield more clearly and to take control of it, such technologies at the same time exposed soldiers to the camera.

In 1896, Abbott Thayer, an American portrait painter and a pioneer of camouflage, introduced the principle of 'snapshot invisibility'.[53] The idea took inspiration from how animals conceal themselves in a moment of danger. Thayer suggested that a camera's snapshot presents exactly the same kind of danger to the combatant (Figure 21). With camouflage, he explained, the twentieth-century soldier could find a way to 'hide in photographs' through an alteration in his or her dress, just as the primitive warrior once hid in the undergrowth, and just as animals adapt to their natural environment.[54]

The conditions of visibility when policing dense urban areas are hardly similar to those of trench warfare. Nevertheless, the historical origins of military camouflage shed light on how visual technologies dictate the way authority 'appears' in the eyes of others. The masked face is part of the history that links concealment both to the photographic medium and to the increased threshold of visibility that photography introduced. Meanwhile, the resolution and proximity of visual technologies have radically increased, and as a result, the face has become a focal point of individuation and distinction. The history of camouflage reveals the conditions of visibility and invisibility, pointing to a desire to dissolve and disintegrate into the environment by shedding personal traits. Camouflage was once used to mimic the environment; now the masked face is used to dissolve, not into

Figure 21 Abbot Thayer, 1896, Snapshot invisibility, Abbott Thayer and Background-Picturing.

the environment but into the group, that is, into an average face that can dodge the algorithms. Consequently, soldiers no longer hide their location or actions but their singular identities, not their bodies but their faces, not their existence but their individuality.

Camouflage is a phenomenological articulation of what the psychiatrist Roger Caillois called 'depersonalization'.[55] In his essay 'Mimicry and Legendary Psychasthenia', Caillois conceived of mimicry as a kind of blurring of singularity of the individual by dissolving into space. 'From whatever side one approaches things', he writes, 'the ultimate problem turns out in the final analysis to be that of distinction [...], Among distinctions there is assuredly none more clear-cut than that between the organism and its surroundings'.[56] In Caillois's view, distinctions are identified and delineated by a gaze that seeks to distinguish the body from its surroundings. Providing numerous examples from animal life, Caillois contends that mimicry allows animals to diminish the distinction between themselves and their environments, so that they begin to resemble the very spaces they inhabit. This 'depersonalization by assimilation to space', as Caillois puts it, requires the animal or the human being to eradicate the visual attributes that mark them out from their surroundings. Rather than defining camouflage in terms of exposure and concealment, Caillois proposes the alternative dichotomy of distinction and resemblance. The act of blending in, for him, requires the erasure of the self and what he calls the 'pathological evacuation' of identity. In Caillois's terms, then, the act of hiding the face becomes an extension of military camouflage, the aim of which is not so much disappearance as the erasure of personality.

Collective selfie

As I have argued, visual technologies define the tactics of concealment. Accordingly, where the presence of the camera is a given, the line between visibility and invisibility increasingly hinges on markers of personal distinction, such as the human face. The ubiquity of mobile phones and social media, which increasingly substitute traditional forms of military reconnaissance, reintroduces the traditional notion of camouflage. The face mask enables the combatant to 'depersonalize' his or her appearance, and hence, hide his or her face from algorithms. In this way, the soldier protects his or her impunity through depersonalization and uniformity. Thus, with the face mask, the age-old question of *how not to be seen* is replaced with a new one: *how not to be isolated*? Or, better yet, *how to obfuscate the always already visible*?

The omnipresence of capture devices within the West Bank and East Jerusalem compels the IDF to look for new tactics of obfuscation. The word 'obfuscation', notes Helen Nissenbaum, suggests bewilderment and ambiguity; in this way, it differs from disappearance and erasure. 'Obfuscation assumes that the signal can be spotted in some way and adds a plethora of related, similar, and pertinent signals – a crowd in which an individual can mix, mingle, and, if only for a short time, hide'.[57] To illustrate this point, Nissenbaum refers to one of the simplest and most memorable examples of obfuscation during a scene in the film *Spartacus* in which the rebel slaves are asked by Roman soldiers to identify their leader for crucifixion. As Kirk Douglas, who plays Spartacus, is about to speak, one by one the others around him stand up and proclaim, 'I am Spartacus!' until the entire crowd is on its feet.[58] By becoming identical, the rebels save the true Spartacus from detection and crucifixion. I will return to the notion of obfuscation in the next chapter. For now, I want to focus on the division between the similitude and the distinction as a technique of obfuscation, which culminate around the face.

One particular incident vividly exemplifies this conflict between similitude and distinction. In April 2014, an IDF soldier was caught on camera, cocking his weapon and threatening to kill a young Palestinian man who refused to follow his orders while passing through a checkpoint in the Palestinian city of Hebron. The video, which clearly showed the soldier, whose name was David Adamov, grossly abusing his authority, was uploaded to YouTube and circulated on social media.[59] Following the public controversy that the video sparked, Adamov was arrested and tried in a military court. After the release of this video, IDF soldiers initiated a spontaneous Facebook campaign trying to justify Adamov's behaviour. As part of this campaign, which slowly went viral, the soldiers released photos of themselves, all covering their faces (Figure 22). They also displayed a sign with the slogan 'We Are All David Adamov', deliberately and ironically echoing the title of the well-known Facebook page 'We Are All Khaled Said', which spearheaded the Egyptian revolution.[60] The juxtaposition of the hidden faces and a slogan that directly articulated a speech act of identification aimed to construe the rogue soldier as a kind of 'everyman'.

By taking these self-portraits, which nonetheless hid their faces, the soldiers produced selfless selfies. The removal of the self from the selfie invokes, once again, Caillois's notion of mimicry as a technique of self-evacuation. Implicitly, this gesture also expresses a refusal to be subjected to the individuating force of social media. If Facebook contributes to the mass individuation of its users,

Figure 22 'We Are All David Adamov' Facebook campaign, 2014 (Source: Facebook).

the repeated gesture of hiding the face aims at 'de-individuation' in order to counteract the algorithms that lock faces to individuals.

The succession of concealed faces sought to pull Adamov back into the shadows of generality. Although Adamov's face was caught in the net of visual media, the campaign was intended to reinstate his impunity. 'I am Adamov!' says each soldier to save the real Adamov from crucifixion by algorithms.

Weaponizing habit

While IDF soldiers gradually implemented the new demand to hide their own faces, in 2015 the Israeli government and the security services found new urgency in probing for the faces of Palestinians via social media platforms. Indeed, it was not until 2015 that the Israeli army compensated for lost time and updated their surveillance tactics in accordance with social media and the various algorithms operating within. Supplementing advanced technologies of facial recognition, social media were now weaponized by the IDF to facilitate strategies of pre-emption and accelerate the immediate arrest of individual Palestinians seen as posing a threat to security. Carefully following Palestinian users online and easily plucking them out from the Palestinian population when the time came was adopted as a valuable addition to the existing technologies of 'mass individuation'.

By 2015, the desperation of Palestinians under Israeli military rule escalated into what various sources referred to as the 'Intifada of Individuals'. Unlike those in 1987 (The First Intifada) and 2000 (The al-Aqsa Intifada), Israeli security forces could not detect any centralized leadership behind the Palestinian uprising. Palestinian youth '[w]ere not acting on anyone's orders but rather motivated to act based on feelings of national, economic and personal deprivation'.[61] A somewhat sinister paradox, the 'Intifada of Individuals' combines two contradicting signifiers that, put together, short-circuit the essence of civil uprising. 'Intifada', which means 'shaking off' and alludes to a collective struggle to end the Israeli occupation by the Palestinian people, was now absorbing what can potentially disarm its political potency: the separation, segregation and isolation of individual Palestinians, often bound to their private spaces in prolonged house arrests. The individual – at the heart of the 'Intifada of Individuals' – reflected a new resolution calibrated by both security and social media platforms. This new resolution latched onto the faces of Palestinians.

One headline in the Israeli newspaper *Haaretz* ran: 'East Jerusalem's Leading Role in Terror Attacks Catches Israel Off Guard'.[62] What began as a single incident in the Old City of Jerusalem quickly escalated into a spree of sporadic violence; Palestinians attempted to stab Israelis using whatever sharp instruments they could lay their hands on. While the Israeli mainstream media speculated about the origins of the violence and debated whether a third intifada was on its way, it became clear that this was not a single event or a planned insurgency but rather a series of uncoordinated actions stemming from an extended period of enforced segregation and deep control of all forms of life under occupation.[63]

It is precisely the apparent spontaneity of these isolated assaults by solitary Palestinian men and women that disoriented the Israeli mainstream media. Short video clips and snapshots caught on security and smartphone cameras were distributed on social media, showing Palestinian individuals in the act of stabbing, or trying to stab, policemen and civilians. The clips also documented the deaths of Palestinians by Israeli gunfire. The violence was made visible through numerous pixelated and ambiguous video clips depicting events taking place in public spaces: a busy crossroad, a central bus station, a main street. The fingers of Israeli soldiers, police and in some cases civilians were quick on their triggers, ready to shoot down anyone displaying the 'symptoms' of terror, which often meant covered faces.

The concealed face of the Palestinian dissident, once the iconic image of the Palestinian Intifada, is considered to be a signature of terror by Israel's security services and the society at large, not only because it is linked to how radical Islam is imagined to appear, but also because it thwarts identification and individuation. The hidden face summons the lost collective political spaces that the Israeli state desires to depoliticize. Indeed, in the First Palestinian Intifada, which erupted in 1987, the concealed faces of Palestinian enabled multiple individuals to be identified as one collective. The Palestinian '*keffiyeh*' – the black-and-white chequered scarf – originally used by Palestinian farmers to shield against the scorching sun, was re-appropriated as a collective symbol of Palestinian national determination. Inspired by the leader of the Palestinian Liberation Organization, Yasser Arafat, who wore the scarf and therefore became identified by it from the 1970s, Palestinians covered their faces before confronting Israeli soldiers en masse in public spaces.[64]

In 2015, Israeli police and military warned Palestinians in the West Bank and East Jerusalem that every veiled face would attract suspicion and might lead to fatal mistakes. The IDF, therefore, urged all civilians to allow the authorities to clearly see their faces at all times. In September, a young woman wearing a niqab approached a checkpoint at the old Palestinian city of Hebron: the 18-year-old Hadeel al-Hashlamoun veered off the route leading into the old town and slowly approached one of the IDF military posts (Figure 23). Immediately, Israeli soldiers began shouting, ordering her to turn around and leave. But Hadeel al-Hashlamoun did not comply. Seconds later, a first bullet was fired into her left leg, after which a second was fired into her right leg. While lying still on the ground, one of the soldiers approached her injured body and fired seven additional shots into her upper body, killing her on the spot.

Two weeks later, a young Palestinian woman, veiled in a green hijab, stood still in the middle of a busy bus station holding a kitchen knife in her hand, before being shot and injured by a local security man (Figure 24). Preliminary

Figure 23 Image of Hadeel al-Hashlamoun at a checkpoint in Hebron (Source: *Haaretz*).

Figure 24 Isra'a Abed presenting a knife while wearing a hijab (Source: *Haaretz*).

investigations suggested that Isra'a Abed had intended to carry out an attack, but as the full details of the event were revealed, it was concluded by an Israeli court that, in fact, she had intended to elicit a violent response from the authorities and get herself killed. Israeli media claimed it was an attempt at suicide, after which the case was closed. Indeed, the video clip itself could attest to such conclusions. Standing still, kitchen knife in hand, Abed enacted a drama—stepping forward as the image of terror—that would likely lead to her immediate death. Covering her face, holding the kitchen knife and stretching out her arm, Abed's body became instantly visible, drawing the attention of all cameras and eyes around her. In bright green hijab that hid her face, her body was already marked out, spectacularly visible, even as it fell to the asphalt below.

Following these events, the Israeli police circulated photographs of weapons that were found next to the bodies of Palestinian assailants on the streets of Israeli cities. These taxonomic-forensic images presented a catalogue of kitchen knives, potato peelers and screwdrivers placed one next to the other (Figure 25). As the IDF or police traced these weapons back to their supposed place of origin, the path took them to private realms, conceived by the Israeli authorities as the source of terror. The habitus of domestic life was often perceived by the Israeli security forces an extension of the body of the terrorist. These acts of 'breaking routine' with the aid of a kitchen knife or a pair of scissors became the restaging of a domestic gesture as political action. Domestic arrest and the confinement to the private sphere were 'publicized', exteriorizing habit and transforming it into an expression of pain – no longer in isolation. It made procedures of segregation

Figure 25 The Israeli police presenting the various domestic tools used as weapons (Source: *Haaretz*).

and confinement visible. The 2015 'Knife Intifada', as it was also dubbed by the Israeli media, should perhaps be renamed the 'Kitchen Cupboard Intifada', bearing in mind the knives, scissors, potato peelers and screwdrivers that the attackers used as weapons.[65]

The 'Intifada of Individuals' alluded to a shift in perspective that oriented security agencies towards the resolution of the individual person who was suspected to be a terrorist due to the mere fact of being Palestinian. Faces of Palestinians were cropping up on Facebook to be scrutinized under the suspicious eye of authority. In her essay titled 'The Resolution of the Suspect', Ariella Azoulay addresses the fluctuating 'ways of seeing' that enable the Israeli security forces to focus their investigations on specific faces that are deemed to be unruly by virtue of being Palestinian in a particular time and place. 'Under an enduring occupation, in which Palestinians are depicted a priori as the incarnation or a political persona such as "suspect" or "terrorist"', writes Azoulay, 'the portrait emerges as an image of life-or-death struggle.'[66]

While security forces used Facebook to monitor the Palestinian populations, Israeli leaders were quick to blame social media for inciting further rage and violence. Prime Minister Benjamin Netanyahu went so far as to describe Facebook as the platform where 'Osama bin Laden meets Mark Zuckerberg'.[67] Israel's minister of interior affairs, Gilad Ardan, implied that 'the blood of the murdered is on Zuckerberg's hands', attempting to force Facebook to curb political dissent on the platform. Facebook's headquarters in Israel were vandalized with graffiti that said: 'the blood is on your hands'.[68]

Indeed, between 2015 and 2017, more than 70 Palestinians were arrested due to social media posting and selfies uploaded to Facebook. An official agreement between the Israeli government and Facebook was reached in late 2016 after which the platform was officially integrated as a monitoring device. By the end of that year Israel submitted 158 requests to Facebook to assist them with locating the identities of inciting materials and another 13 requests to YouTube, almost all approved by both companies.[69]

Israel's claim that Facebook was a key catalyst in the mobilization of the 2015 'Intifada of Individuals' is partially true, but for the wrong reasons. Rather than simply fuelling Palestinian aggression towards Israel and catering to hatemongers, the platform contributes to the division and separation of collective political mobilization, isolating individuals who are easily located by the security apparatus. The 'Intifada of Individuals' should thus be seen as the outcome of the splicing and dividing of a group that seeks to cohere as one solid unit. More than anything Facebook allows Israeli security institutions to follow the expression, movement and behaviour of individuals to pre-empt any kind of organized political mobilization, violent or not. The 'Intifada of Individuals' is therefore an outcome of divided spaces that are today inseparable from the mediascape, confining each user on social media into its own cage.

The potential of social media to restrain state authority and empower Palestinians is turned inside out. While soldiers hide their faces to maintain the unity of the military group, Israeli authorities capture and identify the faces of Palestinians, even before they are politically mobilized. After a decade of online activism during which social media has opened new windows for political mobilization and counter-visualities, today this window of opportunity appears to be quickly closing. State authorities are co-opting what initially posed a challenge to their seamless operation, as social media and everyday practices are appropriated to cater to security needs, while individuation is used as a weapon to single out activists from wider political groupings.

Unlike modern camouflage tactics, which protect the body of the soldier from both cameras and gunfire, the concealment of the face is essentially an inoculation against accountability; it is a shield against the ethical demands of the face-to-face encounter. Not being seen no longer means becoming invisible; instead, it means becoming indistinguishable from others. Today, soldiers themselves recognize that their faces have become sites of contestation due to the way images are circulated and operate on social media. These technologies, thoroughly embedded in everyday life, are now increasingly integrated into military routines and practices.

As I have argued in this chapter, the image of the face is torn between its representative value and the operation that it triggers. On the one hand, portrait photographs are inextricably tied to the individuals they represent; on the other, the image of the face is a mere surface that lends itself to automated calculations and algorithms. As such, the face defines what is at stake for state authority: a fine slicing and dissecting of the body politic into the sum of its individualized parts. In other words, the soldier's personal use of media technologies and intimate engagement with social media decentralize and individualize authority. The image of the soldier's face is the visual expression of this individuation; the algorithms that distribute and identify such images deprive the soldier of an impunity rooted in the facelessness of sovereignty. The masked face, however, preserves the uniformity and generality exemplified in Bowditch's 'average appearance'. But while Bowditch's ideal face is the construct of national imagery, its equivalent today is the erasure of the face altogether, counteracting the individualizing effects of social media to shield soldiers from accountability.

5

The Azaria Case: The selective enforcement of the visual

In a world in which individuals who are naturally at risk confront each other in a competition whose stakes are power and prestige, the only way to avoid a catastrophic outcome is to institute among them sufficient distance so as to immunise each other from everyone else [...]. From here the need arises for strategies and control apparatuses that allow men and women to live next to one another without touching, and therefore to enlarge the sphere of individual self-sufficiency by using 'masks' or 'armor' that defend them from undesired and insidious contact with the other.[1]

On 24 March 2016, an incident was caught on camera that would quickly spark an international controversy. That morning, Imad Abu Shamsia, a Palestinian resident in Hebron, heard gunshots outside his home located near the Jewish settlement at the heart of the Palestinian city. Abu-Shamsia had been filming the daily frictions between IDF soldiers and the Palestinian residents of Hebron for years. 'I live just ten meters from the place', Abu-Shamsia later testified, 'I heard gunshots and immediately rushed outside with the camera in hand'.[2] Familiar with the task, Abu Shamsia was quick to find a position from which to film the unfolding events in the junction below. Minutes before Abu Shamsia's camera started recording the event, the assailant – Abed Fatah al-Sharif – attacked an Israeli soldier with a knife and injured him. Fatah al-Sharif was then shot with six live bullets. Gravely wounded, Fatah al-Sharif was still alive when the Israeli soldiers, together with local Jewish settlers, huddled around his body, unsure how to proceed. It was then that the incident took an unexpected turn: one of the soldiers on the scene – a sergeant by the name of Elor Azaria – took matters into his own hands. After assisting with the evacuation of the wounded soldier, Azaria handed his helmet over to a nearby soldier, approached Fatah al-Sharif, cocked his rifle and shot him in the head at point-blank range. He died on the spot.

Figure 26 The killing of Abed Fatah al-Sharif, Hebron, 2016 (Source: B'Tselem).

Hours later, the three-minute video was already circulating on social media platforms. Instantly going viral, the killing was there for all to see (Figure 26). The rapid circulation of the video was the fuel that instigated the legal action taken by the IDF military police against the soldier. Once the video was out there – posted, shared and reshared – nothing could have restrained its rapid circulation. Abu Shamsia later explained his decision to send the camera's memory card to B'Tselem, an Israeli NGO devoted to documenting violations of human rights in Israel-Palestine, as a way of ensuring that the original file would not be immediately discredited.[3] Anticipating the IDF's incentive to foil the distribution of the video and scrutinize its credibility by any means, B'Tselem released the video within hours.

Various media outlets stressed that the recording of the extrajudicial killing in Hebron reaffirmed the capacity of photographic images to expose abuses of power by IDF soldiers that otherwise could have been kept hidden. Undoubtedly, the video provides a solid example of the utility of filmed evidence in the procedure of demanding accountability for grave violations of human rights against the Palestinian population in the West Bank. However, this function of visual media is often overemphasized, occluding other less perceptible operations that complicate the agency of visual media. Rather than asking how visual media are appropriated by colonized subjects, I want to shed light onto economies of image circulation that determine which images can threaten the modus operandi of the state, and which merely sustain its prevailing code of conduct. In what might seem counter-intuitive, I suggest that the video, and the process of incriminating the seemingly 'rogue soldier', speaks less of the ethico-legal assertions made possible through media, and more to the myriad of ways in which the military protects itself from the increasingly mediatized space of the occupied territories. Focusing on the video of the extrajudicial killing and the trial that followed, the question of how the Israeli state protects itself from dissident media in a hyper-visible space resurfaces with new urgency. It seems that the age-old tactics of image containment, such as restricting the use of cameras or censoring images, are no longer adequate. Particularly in the Occupied Palestinian Territories, where soldiers are tasked with policing the civil population, and with the sheer ubiquity of mobile phone cameras and social media, visibility is inevitable. In such circumstances, the very dichotomy of visibility and invisibility should be thoroughly reconsidered by taking into consideration the excess of image-data and the deluge of images that appear on our screens.

Surfacing from the video of the killing in Hebron is an unlikely question that pertains to the capacity of visual technologies not merely to mobilize legal accountability, but also to eclipse it. Whereas the video of the killing in Hebron accentuates the crucial role of cameras held by Palestinians as disfranchised subjects, I argue here that it should be thought of within a wider context of data circulation and the solid stream of information that saturates our databases and screens, which in turn, destabilizes the binary logic that separates between the emancipatory potential of visual media and their repressive, regulatory and containing ends.

The overabundance of visual documents of armed conflict has been long considered as another form of obfuscation. In his seminal essay 'Mobilising Shame', Thomas Keenan unpacks the role of shaming where the law is suspended or absent as a tactic used by international human right movements.[4] Mobilizing shame, for Keenan, means deploying affectivity visual evidence where legal accountability does not hold. This belief in the power of photographs and oral testimonies, however, can lead to an impasse, particularly in certain conflicts in which violent acts are no longer hidden and obscured. Turning the power of representations of violence inside out, Keenan suggests that exposure could in fact operate to erase

> The dark side of revelation is overexposure. Sometimes we call it voyeurism, sometimes compassion fatigue, sometimes the obscenity of images or 'disaster pornography'. If shame is about the revelation of what is or ought to be covered, then the absence or failure of shaming is not only traceable to the success of perpetrators at remaining clothed or hidden in the dark. Today, all too

often, there is more than enough light, and yet its subjects exhibit themselves shamelessly, brazenly, and openly.[5]

The very category of shame, for Keenan, is inadequate in thinking about the role of media in contemporary armed conflicts. The invocation of shame relies on the problematic notion that if the perpetrators are 'caught in the act', shame might be their final punishment. What if, asks Keenan, the so-called shameful act performed by soldiers or police is routinized – no longer considered by them as something worth hiding? Or, asked differently, what if shame is mobilized by the perpetrators themselves to isolate particular incidents, excluding certain acts as extreme, and in so doing, allowing the routine to continue uninterrupted? What if, due to the sheer excess of images and data, confusion takes over and the ability to see and point a finger at the shameful moment becomes severely hampered?

I argue here that reconsidering the ability of representations to mobilize shame, and indeed accountability, requires a closer look into the media practices utilized to document armed conflict. While images circulate rapidly via social media platforms, the circumstances of their production and the economy of their reach are rarely considered. Once we move beyond what the video frames and the fine details within, we inevitably pass into a realm governed by a patchwork of forces that together determine what is revealed, and what remains obscure, what is exceptional and what is utterly mundane. It seems as though images are merely the sharp edges of a more expansive constellation that merges bodies, technologies and modes of circulation. Unlike the affective quality of one particular video, such constellations can potentially expose how media can either demand personal liability for abuses of power by state actors, or in other cases, sustain their uninterrupted continuation. The video of the killing of Abed Fatah al-Sharif necessitates that we answer two urgent questions: what kinds of political impunity are erected against visual documents? Can a single image reveal a more endemic structural violence, and if not, how can this violence be made apparent?

Selective enforcement

These questions are not merely a theoretical exercise; they were in fact implicitly articulated by the soldier's defence lawyers during his controversial trial. By May of 2016, the soldier's trial had begun, and, alongside it, a deep division of the Israeli public into two camps had emerged. The first, consisting of 30 per cent of the public, deemed his act unlawful and condemned it wholeheartedly. But the second camp, to which more than 47 per cent of the Israeli public belonged, supported Azaria and justified his extreme measures.[6] By refusing to accept the soldier's act as a crime, numbness and indifference among the bystanders were sustained and, simultaneously, an avoidance of guilt was made possible. When an IDF military policeman presented the footage to Azaria during an internal enquiry, he instinctively stated: 'I do not believe what I see'.[7] Dormant in his statement is not only a desperate attempt to shake off his personal accountability, but a reliance on the deep suspicion towards images as truth-claims. Although obscene, Azaria's dismissal of the video is worth exploring, not so much as an indictment of the video's authenticity, but as a statement targeted at the inherent limitation of representations.

According to the protocols of the court ruling, the video was submitted as evidence under the scrutiny of the soldier's defence, which took the effort to discredit it as unreliable and deceptive.[8] Following a forensic examination, an expert confirmed that the video was not tampered with in any way. Frame by frame, the footage was dissected with the purpose of exposing the fine details of the incident. From the analysis of the video it was evident that Abed Fatah al-Sharif, the injured assailant, did not pose any threat to the soldiers around, and therefore was already incapacitated when Azaria shot him at point-blank range. The claim that Azaria sensed immediate danger and therefore shot Al-Sharif to thwart a potential attack was simply unfounded. One after the other, the arguments presented by the soldier's defence were deflated by a careful examination of the visual document. Come January 2017, Azaria was convicted of manslaughter by the military court and sentenced to 18 months in prison.[9]

But the controversy was far from over. The defence attorneys were quick to appeal the conviction before the Israeli Supreme Court. Led by attorney Yoram Sheftel, the team collected evidence that pertained to other events, during which an IDF soldier had shot and killed a Palestinian man.[10] These cases, Sheftel argued, presented similar circumstances to the killing in Hebron. The purpose of the appeal was thus to show that other soldiers were not tried or convicted for their acts. Azaria, claimed the defence, was selected deliberately to be accountable for what others are routinely exempt from. 'Other incidents are as severe as the case in question', claimed the defence: 'In all cases, either the incident was not investigated in the first place, or the soldier was never charged with criminal prosecution'.[11]

The defence appealed for *selective enforcement*, a legal clause that addresses a situation in which the official enforcing the law selectively chooses to arrest an individual for acts performed by others alike.[12] Contrary to uniform enforcement, where all violators caught are charged, selective enforcement is used when an individual is singled out from the public to face allegations that others routinely evade. The logic of the appeal was predicated on the argument that the case was far from exceptional. Selectively, the defence attorneys argued, the trial had become a facade that sought to demonstrate the military's attempt to display values that are regularly disregarded by the IDF. By presenting this argument, the soldier's defence unleashed a direct attack against the military establishment: rather than focusing on the minute details of the incident, the defence diverted the attention away from the singularity of the incident and onto other similar events that presented comparable circumstances, during which an IDF soldier shot and killed an unarmed Palestinian man. Elor Azaria, the defence insinuated, should not carry the burden and legal liability for the code of conduct embedded into the system.

Peculiarly, the evidence submitted to the court was based on a collection of articles compiled by an activist who sought to expose the permissiveness of 'Open Fire Regulations' in the West Bank and the numerous killings exercised by the IDF, which were never investigated.[13] According to Jon Brown, 97 per cent of internal investigations in the IDF are left unresolved. Beginning with the eruption of the al-Aqsa intifada in 2000 and until 2016, 9,250 Palestinians were killed by IDF fire, 262 of which were investigated by the military police, but only one soldier was convicted of manslaughter.[14] Jon Brown was hired by Azaria's defence and was put in charge of collecting sufficient evidence of other cases that present similar circumstances. For a brief moment, the soldier's defence found a common interest with an activist devoted to exposing the abuse of power by the Israeli state. Together, they intended to prove that this particular incident was compatible with a broader pattern of structural violence.

Brown prepared a file that contained 14 different cases, almost all of which were never documented by any camera. When the files were submitted to the court in May 2017, they were immediately rejected, mostly due to the lack of visual documents that could support a selective enforcement procedure. Pictures, the court insisted, are the linchpins of incrimination. Or more significantly, if the Israeli court had accepted the argument that the soldier acted according to a normative code of conduct, it would have been forced to admit that the Israeli state exercises extrajudicial killings as part of its military rule in the West Bank. The military court was thus effectively compelled to treat the soldier as a bad apple. Amputating the gangrenous limb would save the body.

By diverting the attention from the singularity of the video to other similar incidents that were never caught on camera, Azaria's defence lawyers shrewdly invited the public to critically reflect on the role of images in how accountability is sought and ascertained. Deflecting the gaze elsewhere, they implicitly invoked an interrogation into the dominant position of representations in legal procedures of incrimination. The shot executed by Azaria, they argued, should be compared, juxtaposed, superimposed and imagined against other incidents, even those that lack representation altogether. Although intended to save the murderous soldier from prison, the defence's argument invited a critical inquest into the ontological status of visual media.

The selective enforcement of the visual

Pursuing the argument of Azaria's attorneys means accepting that while visual media are commonly conceived through their ability to reveal and expose, they can also erase and obfuscate. This duality may seem contradictory, as we rarely think about the existence and circulation of images and data as obstacles for truth-claims, nor take into consideration the significance of circulation itself as a threat to the potential evidentiary status of an image. Instead, we tend to look at an image, focusing on the content and detail within the frame, from which we can extract our narratives. At stake in this urgency to *see*, decipher and forensically analyse, is a legal scopophilia that diffuses the substantial role of circulation in defining a threshold between what can be evidentiary and what will be automatically dismissed. It is these stakes that the defence latched onto during the Azaria trial. Thus, for a brief moment, a single visual document of unlawful killing was used in concert with numerous other violent incidents that were never caught on camera. In the argument of the military court the singularity of the event is conflated between its exceptionality and its availability as a document. In construing the event as 'exceptional', the court blurs the deeper patterns of violence that together emerge in less visible forms. Focusing on a spectacular outburst of rage manifested in the split second of a gunshot could thus be complicit with obfuscating the longer, imperceptible persistence of suspended violence that bleeds from the edges of the frame. 'Spectacle', suggest Jared Sexton and Steve Marinot, 'is a form of camouflage'.[15]

The frame, writes Judith Butler, '[d]oes not simply exhibit reality, but actively participates in a strategy of containment, selectively producing and enforcing what will count as reality'.[16] In this way, Butler also employs the vocabulary of 'selection' and 'enforcement' to formulate her critique of images of atrocities. The primacy of the visual document, stresses Bulter, not only represents but also shapes the very reality that it captures.[17] 'The frame is always throwing something away', argues Butler, 'always keeping something out, always de-realizing and de-legitimating alternative versions of reality, discarded negatives of the official version'.[18] The process of selection inherent in framing a photograph, suggests Butler, is itself a mode of violence. Images are always already more than a represented scene since by virtue of having a frame, and of being framed, the photograph or video implicitly suggests that there is an outside, an exteriority, ever so slightly beyond our vision. Is that not what Azaria's attorneys intended by igniting the imagination to compensate for a lack of images rendering similar incidents visible? Could Butler's cautionary critique amount to a warning against a visual selective enforcement that elevates a singular image, without delicately examining the structural lacks and lacunae that complicate the relationship between a given representation and the circumstances of its production? Not unlike the strategy adopted by the soldier's legal team, Butler redirects our inquiry to the periphery, to articulate an appeal against the selective enforcement of a singular image. Against the selective enforcement of images, the meaning of an image should be redefined by repositioning it within a broader assemblage of data. From this assemblage, the economy of circulation that separates the extraordinary and the mundane, the exception and the norm, is gradually put to question.

Partial images

In the files prepared by Jon Brown for the court, the defence team stated:

> The Israeli Army censored the records we obtained. The names of the soldiers were erased from it, and in some of the cases, the locations of the killings were left out. This list is not meant to imprison those who have killed. The real blame is placed on the system. The essence is not the individual soldier, but the establishment.[19]

The argument posed by the defence elicits the dichotomy conjured by the tension between the singular and multiple. The individual soldier, excommunicated due to his unruly behaviour against the establishment, is a body politic composed of the many. But does the same spectrum apply to the visual realm? Gathering and comparing documents, juxtaposing different incidents, the defence team of

Azaria sought to appeal to a new logic that stems from a montage comprised of partial images.

Georges Didi-Huberman argues that montage can potentially move the gaze away from a given representation and probe into the significance of an absence, in this case the lack of evidence or a coherent narrative that could shed light into the procedures employed by the IDF. 'The knowledge value could not be intrinsic to one image alone', writes Didi-Huberman, 'on the contrary, it is a question of putting the multiple in motion, isolating nothing, showing the hiatuses and analogies, the inter-determinations and the over-determinations'.[20] Didi-Huberman aims to respond to what he sees as the brutality of reducing history to singularities, to a single document that speaks of a certain violence. 'We must respond to this perceptual brutality', he writes, 'by pointing out that the image is neither nothing nor one, nor all, precisely because it offers multiple singularities always perceptible to differences'.[21] Drawing on Didi-Huberman's argument, one could say that images of atrocities appear with a seductive nature that imbues them with a power to show, and *tell*, with an aura of truth. But this seeming power must be critically examined. A totalizing conception of an image is bound to fail by either *seeing too much* – what Didi-Huberman calls an 'all-image', which stems from a belief that the image can show you everything – or by censoring it altogether, dismissing it as a treacherous copy of the event.[22]

The military institution was invested in convicting Azaria precisely to turn the images of his killing into an exceptional *all-image*. The motive behind the Israeli army's insistence on bringing Azaria to court and convicting him of manslaughter was not only to turn his trial into a showcase, but also to isolate the video that caught him red-handed. In this example the IDF can afford the admission of a singular violent act in order to spare the system itself. The video that catches Azaria 'in the act', could be absorbed by the military complex via labelling the video and the killing it documents as an isolated incident.

Nevertheless, it is crucial to recognize that the isolation of the video/image/ event is not the only one way in which the IDF can contain the condemning quality of images. After all, there are other strategies to curb the capacity of images to incriminate that which often escapes the eye. Appealing against such isolation essentially means considering the proliferation of sources from which images emanate. The single, incriminating image, is gradually replaced with an abundance, which undermines the traditional agency of one visual document. At the core of this strategy is a move from representation to circulation, which for Andrew Hoskins and Ben O'Loghlin, is innate to digital media and their capacity to be shared and circulated online. What Hoskins and O'Loghlin call the *mediality of images* – or the focus on conditions of distribution rather than their specific content – directly affects their power to mobilize reaction and to propel investigation while, at the same time, weakening the impact of a single photograph or video.[23] Mediality refers to how media texts are interwoven into everyday lives, how the continuity and familiarity of these representations interact with everyday media practices.[24]

Against the potential of videos and photographs to expose violations of human rights, the IDF has gradually recognized that the most efficient strategy to defuse the contaminating capacity of viral images is to produce and circulate more image-data to swamp and drown out the impact of any single and particularly incriminating image. The shield against exceptional images is made out of numerous other images that together amount to a 'scale armour' comprised of various documents. If Didi-Huberman addressed the scarcity of visual images in specific cases where photographs and films could not have been produced due to censorship, confronting the documentation of the armed conflict in Israel-Palestine means replacing scarcity with overabundance.

A counter-counter visuality

A closer look at the media strategies employed by the IDF exposes a gradual shift from image censorship to image inundation. In the last decade, the IDF began realizing that the flood of images, emerging from the habitual use of mobile technologies and social media, could in fact operate as another mode of visual containment, and even concealment. The IDF gradually adopted techniques of obfuscation as responses to the organized use of visual media by colonized subjects. Practices of filmmaking emerged from modes of non-violent resistance aimed at gathering international support for the Palestinian struggle towards self-determination.[25] Such practices, cultivated to render life under occupation visible, stem from the unique form of occupation that Israel exercises and the dilemmas that emerge from it. The extension of its sovereignty to the West Bank would confer citizenship on, or at least provide the choice of citizenship to, its Palestinian population and thus would diminish the Jewish majority of Israel. The ongoing expropriation of Palestinian land – both public and private – for the benefit of the Jewish settler population, as well as the neglect and indifference of the Israeli police and military to abuses and attacks on Palestinians by settlers, highlights the duality of the legal and practical circumstances under which Palestinians live in the Occupied Territories.[26]

Filmmaking was thus practised, not only to document events and incidents that take place within that space of exception, but also to compensate for the lack of protection that the law confers on individual Palestinians. This is also the impetus behind Abu Shamsia's practice of filmmaking. Living in Hebron, Abu Shamsia began collaborating with the NGO B'Tselem, with the purpose of collecting visual evidence.

A decade ago, B'Tselem initiated an organized project, oriented towards the documentation of life under military rule. In January 2007, the NGO launched its camera distribution project as a video advocacy project focusing on the West Bank and East Jerusalem.[27] The project was devoted to allocating video cameras to Palestinians living in high-conflict areas. One of the core strategies of the project was to distribute cameras to civilians rather than known activists (Figure 27). The purpose of the initiative was to 'bring the reality of Palestinians' to the attention of the Israeli and international public, exposing and seeking redress for violations of human rights.

In 2007, the presence of cameras in high-conflict areas presented a new dimension of visibility not known before. Oren Yakobovich, then the director of B'Tselem's video department, focused on power and transparency:

> It's giving power. You know, this word is called 'empowerment'. I don't like this word so much, but I will use it. It's the children, and the kids [who] are filming. It's helping to mobilise communities. In Hebron, where the community was

Figure 27 Volunteers participating in the 'Shooting Back' project of B'Tselem (Source: B'Tselem).

destroyed, suddenly they're filming, and they have some interest in seeing the videos, talking about it. And what I hope to achieve, that everything is going to be filmed, at least [that]... there's going to be a feeling that everything is being filmed, nothing is being done in the dark.[28]

The technological utopianism and the emancipatory tone embraced by B'Tselem in the first years of the project materialized from the firm belief that cameras counterbalance the lack of democratic governance and eventually empower Palestinians. The metaphor of darkness and illumination, employed by the director of the project, is endemic of the agency imbued to visual documents and the perception that sunlight is the best disinfectant.

But where sunlight is bound to expose, it can potentially also burn the eyes. Gradually, the IDF began to experiment with visual strategies that were tailor-made to limit the viral potency of the videos produced by Palestinians, in collaboration with B'Tselem. The partial success of the videos to stimulate the awareness of the international sphere convinced the IDF that the best possible way is to mimic dissident practices.

From 2011, for instance, IDF soldiers were actively encouraged to document the daily encounters with Palestinian resistance in the West Bank. A specially designed project was inaugurated by the IDF to mirror the B'Tselem initiative. The project titled 'Documenting Warrior' allocated 30 cameras to soldiers deployed in the West Bank. The private Israeli company El-Sight 'designed special cameras units for IDF soldiers who confront the various cameras held by the enemy'.[29] Providing to each of the 30 soldiers a 'documentary camera unit', El-Sight announced:

> The IDF long understood that the war in the media arena is no less than that conducted in the field [...]. The IDF is looking for a comprehensive offering, combining small tactical hardware and advanced state of the art software, which will provide the operational tools to create fast video broadcasting clips from raw video feeds, arriving from the different units, spread across the field.[30]

The emphasis on advanced technologies and technological superiority overlooks the crucial fact that daily habits and practices of image-making could be appropriated for operational needs. In other words, while the IDF initially attempted to mirror the 'Shooting Back' project, the superiority of their technologies was rendered superfluous when confronted with the force of habits. The acknowledgement that soldiers carry mobile phone cameras with them as part of their everyday routine was quickly implemented and weaponized by the IDF, replacing a concerted institutional media strategy. By imitating grassroots media, soldiers attempt to defuse the contagious potency of images. Using their own mobile phones as army-issued cameras, soldiers incorporate what initially posed a risk to the authority they enforce.

By 2011, various new practices were adopted by IDF soldiers to challenge the use of cameras by Palestinians. At the time, soldiers had to cope with cameras that were recording their routine procedures of raiding and searching homes in the West Bank. Subjected to frequent search by soldiers, Palestinians in the West Bank were prepared to film with their own cameras in case their home was to be raided. To mirror the persistent practices of filmmaking undertaken by civilians, soldiers cultivated a new procedure codenamed 'mapping'. Mapping involves collecting information during nightly raids into Palestinian homes and gathering visible evidence about the lives and living environments of families in dense urban spaces in East Jerusalem, Hebron, Ramallah and Jenin.[31] Waking up the family members in the dead of night, lining them up in their pyjamas, the soldiers take out a lightweight camera or a smartphone to snap photographs of the inhabitants' faces. The stated purpose of mapping is to deter individuals from taking political action. The logic is such that if one's face is captured as a photograph, he or she is then easily identified by surveillance technologies that frame public spaces and record any suspicious behaviour or illegal action such as throwing rocks or demonstrating. 'Often', one soldier recalls, 'we erase the files by the end of the day'.[32] Whether surveillance systems actually probe faces from existing archives remains unclear. Nevertheless, deleting images does not erase the potential of information to trace back particular subjects and to incriminate the inhabitants of a given household. The influx of image-data accumulating in the military hard drives is meant to disseminate smokescreens of visual data – photographs and videos – that would obscure a single 'problematic' video.[33]

Whereas the Palestinians initially began the concerted practice of filmmaking to challenge Israel's visuality and to collect evidence for judicial purposes, the IDF developed a sort of 'counter-counter-visuality' shaped by the attempt to claim back authority and to nourish 'data-fatigue'. To eclipse the potency of dissident media practices, the state gradually began parroting these practices. Increasingly, the organized efforts of both Palestinians and IDF soldiers were replaced by habits of image production and circulation, inscribed by technologies such as mobile phones and social media. Imperatives were quickly replaced with a chaotic exchange of recording devices. The more Palestinians appropriate their cameras and mobile phones to document soldiers, the more soldiers are prone to do the same.

Media mimicry

Media mimicry is adopted when more traditional strategies of banning images and censorship can no longer suffice to ensure (at least partial) discretion around events and incidents. It is a tactic of obfuscation that recognizes the futile attempt to maintain secrecy in a highly visible environment in which visual media no longer pertains to technological superiority.[34] Media mimicry emerges when the ruling power begins to imitate the ways in which dissidents employ filmmaking to document and distribute what the state desires to keep obscured.

This obfuscating strategy is demonstrated by another image that was recorded in Hebron, this time by an IDF soldier. In May 2015, exactly a year before Elor Azaria shot Fatah al-Sharif in Hebron, a much less spectacular incident unfolded at the very same junction, on the border with the Jewish settlement in the heart of the city. Abu-Haya, a Palestinian resident in the city, was having his lunch at home when he noticed a group of 40 soldiers climbing up towards the rooftop of his house.[35] Accustomed to filming everyday life in Hebron, Abu-Haya picked up his video camera and began filming the bewildering situation. What looked like a typical raid, took an unexpected twist when it turned out that the sole purpose of the sudden intrusion was to snap a photo on the rooftop of the house. One after the other, the Israeli soldiers climbed the stone steps around the house and congregated on the roof. All the while, Abu-Haya was recording their unsolicited activities and their unlikely meeting on his house. While posing for a group photograph, one soldier stepped forward with his mobile phone and snapped a single image: a group photograph.

Resentful towards Abu-Haya's practice of filmmaking and his collaboration with B'Tselem, the soldiers were there to claim back the mediascape and to demonstrate their authority and dominance over it. The snapshot taken by the soldiers is thus not the typical trophy photograph taken by soldiers who wish to boast about their superior power. Unlike many other cases in which the trophy is the snapshot itself, here the claim over mediated space is a performance of domination over the cluster of gazes and visual media. This gesture, which concludes with a single and superfluous file, demonstrates the capacity to obfuscate the material produced by Abu-Haya, who aims his camera towards them. This gesture of snapping an image is aimed at defying the evidentiary mode of representation through conjuring multiple additional images that complicate, obscure and fog a given document. 'Obfuscation', writes Helen Nissenbaum, 'assumes that the signal can be spotted in some way and adds a plethora of related, similar, and pertinent signals – a crowd which an individual can mix, mingle, and, if only for a short time, hide.[36] Dispensing with the representative value of the image itself, through this incident we enter into the realm of pure mediality, where images become data produced to blur and disorient.

Immunizing itself, the military must incorporate the substance that initially threatens its upper hand and control over visualization. This auto-immunitary process adopts the aesthetics of dissent to render them hollow. Israeli soldiers with mobile phones, for instance, rapidly produce low-resolution images, not merely to visually obfuscate (as I have mentioned already) but also as means of neutralizing the aesthetics of resistance, often conceived through grainy, pixelated and shaky footage. This approach resonates with the Third Cinema manifesto 'For an Imperfect Cinema', in which Juan García Espinosa calls for a blurring of roles and positions between consumer and producer, audience and author, high and low resolutions of images.[37] Hito Steyerl, in her celebrated essay 'In Defence of the Poor Image', draws a link between the low-resolution data-images that circulate online and the political impetus of Third Cinema.[38] On the one hand, Steyerl stressed, those low-resolution images that drift astray online have a certain kinship to the emancipation promised by Third Cinema, and on the other, the excess of data opens up new avenues to exercise power and eventually to centralize it. 'The networks in which poor images circulate', writes Steyerl, 'constitute both a platform for a fragile new common interest and a battleground for commercial and national agendas'.[39] In this light, Steyerl redefines the value of the image, not only through resolution and exchange value, but also, and more crucially, by 'velocity, intensity, and spread'.[40] As they migrate and travel, the meaning of images shifts and gets displaced by their dematerialization and fluidity – a capacity today used and abused by the state actors.

Between the exceptional and the redundant

Finally, the militarized 'family portrait' snapped in Hebron alludes to these non-representational aspects of the image as data – made to circulate freely somewhere, perhaps never to resurface. This snapshot also brings me back to the video of the extrajudicial killing. Placed side by side, both media exemplify two distinct procedures aimed at diffusing the capacity of images to expose abuses of power by the state. On the one hand, the video of the killing in Hebron is isolated by the military as a potentially contaminating depiction of violence. By marking the video exceptional and the solider as unruly, the IDF sought to inoculate the military institution against contracting accountability. Shame, to use Thomas

Keenan terms, is only a way of individualizing a structural criminal act, thus saving the system. On the other hand, the snapshot grabbed on the rooftop – more than a vandalizing provocation against the inhabitants of the occupied city of Hebron – is a symptom of an unofficial tactic of visual obfuscation that adds noise and confusion into the already flooded archives and databases. While the video of the killing in Hebron can blur the wider patterns of violence, which are less spectacular, the snapshot taken by the soldiers on the rooftop is about deflecting the attention and adding noise to an already saturated visual field.

The comparison between the two media – the video and the snapshot – sheds light on the ramification of ubiquitous media on everyday life in Israel-Palestine. The snapshot is produced as a reaction to the ever-expanding pervasiveness of media that threatens the continuation of specific military procedures, while the video is the ultimate example of that threat. Both, however, appear on the same spectrum that stretches between the singularity an event (the killing) and the inherent proliferation of media as part of the everyday in the Palestinian West Bank (the group photo). By gliding on this spectrum, the IDF can either deem a particularly unfavourable image as a singular instance or increase the circulation of images to suffocate the incriminating potential within the bottomless pool of poor images. Both, however, are used flexibly to immunize the military system against visual evidence and to conceal the prevalent and indeed daily, abuse of power underneath a cloak of images and data.

6

The regime of the self: Between the one and the many

In April 2018, a video appeared online and sparked an immediate outrage (Figure 28). Shot by a mobile phone, the audio-visual clip depicts an Israeli sniper shooting an unarmed Palestinian man standing in the vicinity of the Gaza-Israel border fence. At a distance, the man can be seen visibly hit by the long-range bullet and collapsing to the ground. The short clip, which was widely shared on social media and shown on Israeli prime-time television, appears to have been

Figure 28 Israeli sniper on the Gaza fence, CNN, April 11 2018. Available here: https://edition.cnn.com/2018/04/10/middleeast/video-israeli-sniper-intl/index.html, video distributed in April 2018 (unverified recording time).

filmed through the telescopic lens attached to a sniper's rifle. 'Do you have a bullet in the barrel?', asks someone from behind the camera. But the shot is fired and hits its target. 'Wow, what a video. Yes! Son of a bitch!', another person yells while, on the other side of the fence, others run towards the injured man to help. 'Wow. They hit someone in the head', says an off-camera voice.

The grainy mobile phone video came after weeks of daily protest on the Israel-Gaza border expressing anger over the inauguration of the US Embassy in Jerusalem by Donald Trump and his allies. Coinciding with the 70th anniversary of Israel's founding, Trump's daughter Ivanka, her husband Jared Kushner and the US Treasury Secretary Steven Mnuchin attended an opening ceremony in the former consulate building in Jerusalem. Moving the embassy to Jerusalem sent a clear and strong message: Jerusalem will not become Palestine's capital.

The embassy's inauguration in Jerusalem unfolded while Israeli soldiers occupied military positions on the Gaza-Israel fence from which to observe, deter and shoot Palestinian demonstrators approaching the barrier. Men, women and children gathered by the border to express their rage against the historical injustice and to participate in the weekly 'Great March of Return' demonstrations, calling for the Palestinian right of return and the end of the Israeli blockade on Gaza. While most protestors were peaceful, some attempted to damage the fence, burn tires and throw stones and Molotov cocktails towards Israeli forces. In response, Israeli forces deployed snipers, fatally shooting more than two dozen people and wounding hundreds. According to the United Nations Office for the Coordination of Humanitarian Affairs, 'between 30 March 2018 and 22 March 2019, 195 Palestinians, including 41 children, were killed by Israeli forces in the "Great March of Return" demonstrations, including during the weekly protests near the perimeter fence, protests against the naval blockade at the beach, and the night activities near the perimeter fence' (Figure 29).[1]

Extraordinarily, the video above documents the sniper's bullet hitting the body of an unarmed man, while at the same time, visualizing the personal point of view of the sniper himself. On the level of representation, it clearly and explicitly captures the shot. It also, incidentally, records the embodied presence of the sniper, his long breaths before pulling the trigger and taking the 'money shot', before the excitement of the hit, which isn't shown directly, but is clearly audible.

Meanwhile, on the other side of the fence, in Gaza, Palestinian civilians, activists and journalists recorded videos that clearly depict IDF soldiers standing side by side as one unit, faces covered, holding their guns. 'They are

Figure 29 'IDF soldiers lined up as firing squad' (Source: Associated Press).

essentially a firing squad', as one activist suggested.[2] But the Israeli sniper's point of view breaks that unity. The obscenity of the video lies precisely in the way it presents a personal point of view vis-à-vis a military procedure. It disturbs the idealized military fantasy according to which bullets are fired by a highly professional unit that takes a concerted and calculated choice to shoot and kill. The tension between the single soldier and the unit becomes volatile, and once again, evokes the distinction between the *one* and the *many*, and with it, modes of exposure and concealment.

No doubt, the shot exposes a grave abuse of power. Yet, it is not the killing itself that I would like to position at the centre of this final chapter, but the politics of exposure and concealment that it captures. This point-of-view shot summons the various ways in which media can individuate state violence and undo the uniformity of the military. In this case, the video captures the two poles of weaponized visual media: on one end, the Palestinian body, and on the other, an IDF soldier.

The sniper and the firing squad

From the Gazan side of the fence, IDF snipers essentially function as a firing squad, as one demonstrator has suggested. The firing squad was developed as a technique of execution during the First World War under martial law. The scene is familiar: the prisoner would either stand or sit against a brick wall, or some other heavy barrier. Five or more soldiers stand in a line several feet away from the prisoner's body, each aiming his firearm directly at the captive's heart.[3] Upon hearing a cue called out by a senior officer, all of the gunmen fire simultaneously. In most cases, so the story goes, the prisoner will be blindfolded when placed before the firing squad, often as much for the benefit of the executioners as it is for the prisoner. When the condemned person can look directly at the members of the firing squad, the executioners' anonymity is greatly reduced, creating a more stressful situation for those simply fulfilling their duty.

Although each squad member must fire, between one and three of the gunmen usually receive a gun with a blank. This bullet is known as the 'conscience round' and promotes diffusion of responsibility among the executioners, ensuring that no one in the group can know for sure which one of them fired the fatal round. By firing together as one concerted machine, the killing of the prisoner is more easily imagined as a death sentence commuted by an abstract entity – the military or the state. The individual shooter becomes enmeshed into the group, permitting the killing to be delivered by the body-politic, and not the single soldier that serves it, while the burden of guilt need not lie on the shoulders of any particular subject. Together, the gunmen are able to preserve opacity. The blank bullet of the firing squad allows soldiers to show themselves and perform the execution in the name of the law (usually martial law). Thus, the killing is imagined to be a 'joint effort'.

But something happens once the gunmen start to shoot separately, each of his own volition. Each firing separately, the squad gradually loses its concerted action and effectively converts into a group of individual snipers. To maintain the opacity achieved through the synchronized fire, other ways of remaining opaque become pertinent, because now each of the gunmen can be easily singled out as the one shooting the deadly bullet.

This dichotomy corresponds to *ways of seeing* and *being seen,* wherein the sniper and the gunman stand in for two kinds of spectators. 'Seeing like a firing squad', to paraphrase James C. Scott, is seeing through the eyes of the military establishment, through the amalgamation of numerous points of view, which produce an image that obscures individual responsibility within a collective or a group action. Seeing like a firing squad is looking at an image made from a patchwork of gazes that together neutralizes the agency that produces it and blurs the traces that might lead to one single gunman/spectator. Instigating cinema's idealized spectator, the firing squad's way of seeing can allow a degree of impartiality, remaining external to the unfolding event, producing an abstracted spectator.

The sniper, on the other hand, performs the killing by himself and from a hidden location. Replace the rifle with a camera, and you will get a single film-maker, carefully framing the body in the viewfinder. The iris that closes in on the target implies a single gaze. But to maintain the abstraction of military power, and to deflect accountably, the sniper hides. He is essentially a voyeur.

There is a media archaeological link between the sniper and the filmmaker. It was Friedrich Kittler who pointed out the lineage between the camera and the colt rifle as two devices with which one aims and shoots. One of the very first prototypes for the motion picture camera, Kittler notes, was Etienne-Jules Marey's *'fusil photographique'* (photographic rifle), a device fashioned in 1882 and modelled upon the revolving rifle able to 'shoot' 12 photographs per second in rapid succession. Shooting and aiming like a gunman, Marey would shoot a sequence of images.[4] Film scholar Elisa Lebow addresses this relation between the camera and the gun to suggest that,

> 'the framing and tracing of movement through the "viewfinder" of a gun, along with the mechanisms supporting its agility and efficiency, are eventually mimed by the cinematic apparatus, further nourished by the vast investments in the development of weaponry that is guided by, and/or monitored through, the lens of a camera'.[5]

The two ways of looking are flexibly used by the military to either injure bodies or to shoot them with cameras, while also outlining two modes of appearance that stand in for the tension between individuality and collectivity, the gamut that I attempted to draw and employ throughout this book.

The *firing squad* and the *sniper* are the two figures that appear at two poles of a continuum that allows the IDF to flexibly disband the military unit into isolated actors. But the essential difference here is not between the army and the individual, but between two ways of seeing that have been co-opted into the IDF's arsenal of weapons. If Israel needs the firing squad to diffuse responsibility horizontally, it also obligates the sniper to bear accountability, vertically. As we have seen with the Eleor Azaria case, the military can isolate the individual soldier and detach him from the system. The IDF therefore finds this highly personal perspective risky, as well as beneficial when shedding responsibility for the acts that it routinely performs becomes indispensable. This video visualizes the disintegration of state authority into individual viewpoints: a firing squad broken down into single agents that no longer hide in their posts. Clearly distinguished from the video shot by Abu Shamsia in the Azaria case, the shooting of bullets and audio-visual documents are here merged as one auto-documentation of a killing, where both the gun and the camera are finally one. From the sniper and the firing squad, a more pervasive politics can be extrapolated that returns to the tension between the group and the liberal individual, which correspond with the community, and immunity measures implanted to protect it.

As I will suggest in the next section, individuality – the essence of what the video of the killing inadvertently exposes – not merely facilitates the contraction of accountability, but is also the source of the violence itself. That is, violence erupts when a collection of individuals, afflicted by the fear of over-proximity to the Other, is out to reinstate borders and divisions. The fence that separates the sniper and the demonstrator in the video above seems like another military technology of enclosure and indeed it is. But it also illustrates the model of the defensive Self that kills an Other (too far to become specific) who comes too close; an Other imagined as an absolute threat, one that should be entrapped in a fence and killed if needed. This defensive, insular and militarized Self is where the violence stems from. While in this video it is clearly made visible through a simple sniper, it can also become the core of a community and a crowd. Below, I will explain what that might mean. For this, I want to address another documented event.

The lynching

In May 2021, an attempted lynching of a young Palestinian Israeli was broadcast live on Israeli news media. Said Musa was driving through the city of Bat Yam, just south of Tel Aviv, when he found himself surrounded by a raging mob of Jewish Israelis out to vandalize Palestinian-owned shops. Musa was asked whether he was an Arab and he said yes. He was then dragged out of his car, pulled down to the asphalt and beaten repeatedly. Fully exposed to the eyes of hundreds of bystanders, the attempted lynching was a sudden eruption of racial violence. The deadly blows meted out by Jewish Israeli civilians served as an extraordinary reminder that even though some Palestinians became Israeli citizens after the 1948 war, they are rarely held as equal citizens, nor are they protected against expressions of hate that the civil contract is meant to deflect.

No doubt, the attempted lynching should be perceived as part of a longer chain reaction to the political void left intentionally by the government at the end of Benjamin Netanyahu's reign. Right-wing Jewish militias got a free pass to take part in policing the Arab population in Israeli cities. The attempted lynching was also the culmination of rapidly escalating provocations by Jewish settlers in Palestinian villages and towns and in East Jerusalem. Only days before, a few hundred members of an extreme-right Jewish group, 'Lehava', marched through central Jerusalem, chanting 'death to Arabs' and attacking Palestinian passers-by. A group of Jews were filmed attacking a Palestinian home, and others assaulted drivers who were perceived to be Palestinian. And of course, there was Gaza. According to the Israeli Air Force, Hamas, the militant group that rules the Gaza Strip, has fired more than 3,300 rockets towards Israeli cities and towns, killing at least 12 people. Israeli forces have struck homes, refugee camps, medical facilities and other buildings killing 260 people, including at least 61 children, according to local health authorities, drawing international condemnation. Nevertheless, any attempt to bracket the event into the condensed timelines of May 2021 is a failure to recognize that the violence of dispossession and separation continues to linger as a structural repression and to persist as a social, economic and cultural divide between Jews and Arabs in Israel-Palestine.

Considering the gathering of people on the main street, it is no surprise that recordings of the attempted lynching were shared by numerous users and sources, including by a local journalist (for KAN news) who aired live on Israeli television. The video footage clearly depicts the singling out of Musa's body from the chaotic, unrestrained, almost festive crowd of people. Objects are being thrust at him; the pole of an Israeli flag is wielded as a weapon to beat him over the head. Looking closely at the video, it is difficult to make out who exactly partakes in the beating and who watches obliviously from a 'safe' distance. From the commotion in the frame, the tension between the distinctiveness of Musa's body and the many hands and feet that injure him emerges as a stark contrast between the single and many.

One thing can be easily established: the video records an event that unfolds before many eyes. Where violence takes place out in the open, and in front of the cameras, it hides in plain sight. Seemingly, by performing acts of violence brazenly and openly in the middle of the street, the perpetrators should be deterred from potential exposure that could lead to their arrest. While I have discussed several ways in which soldiers conceal themselves in broad daylight, here civilians seem to hide in the crowd, or more accurately, become a crowd. Between the uniformity of this mass, and the threatening individuality that this crowd attempts to destroy, the video recording – not unlike the video of the sniper with which I started – captures the tension between the singular and multiple, and with it, different degrees of opacity and transparency.

The ability to expose the perpetrators in the video is diminished through the degree of obscurity produced by the crowd. It is difficult to see who exactly is striking Musa. But this difficultly is not simply a question of seeing and detecting details in the frames. The blending in the crowd, the ability to dissolve in it, should be understood here as both the condition that feeds the violence, and the impunity to perform it without facing immediate consequences. Understanding what has happened that night thus requires much more than picking through the video and extracting frames that expose the faces of responsible individuals from the crowd. It requires exposing the mechanism of immunity granted to the *community*, to the violence of a community predicated on racial and ethnic ties. On the one hand, the singling out of an individual as an Arab unleashes a violent response directed at one body, which for them, stands in for the Palestinian collective. The victim is cast into the role of the Other, which contains the multiplicity of the Palestinian people. On the other hand, the raging crowd that attempts the lynching hides under the cloak of sameness, and which provides a sense of immunity in the heat of the moment, is built on that fictional figure of the single individual.

Looking closer at this video and at the violence driven by this crowd, it is tempting to conclude that the mass is more prone to become violent because it diffuses the individual voices (an observation that has become so commonplace it is trite). If, as I have argued through this book, the individual is a constructed figure that both extends sovereignty through liberated selves and protects the state from contracting ethical responsibility for state violence, this crowd is not the opposite of the Self but its very expansion (this expansion, as I argued in the first and third chapters, is the expansion of the household into the political realm). The uniformity in this raging mass is rooted in a sense of community made up from defensive Selves that become a group, a crowd and a community that permit lynching as way of diminishing the Other.

In her recent book titled *The Force of Nonviolence*, Judith Butler returns to the individual in politics as a fictional figure produced by liberal political theory. This singular unit fragments the community into selves as means of setting clear boundaries between subjects. According to this model, most famously drawn by Thomas Hobbes, a degree of separation must divide individuals to protect them from chaos, referred to as the 'state of nature'. The Hobbesian view, which in many ways is the foundational one in political thought, tells us that individuals are pitted one against each other in a violent competition, and that individuals must fight each other to make their claim and gain social dominion. But this violent state of nature has always been a fictive world, and according to literary critic Jean Starobinski, one that validates a narrow conception of the individual: 'self-sufficient, without dependency, saturated in self-love yet without any need for another'. Butler draws on that model to argue that the group, the mass and the nation state, could be the extension of this defensive self at the heart of liberal democracy. Butler writes: 'Such a "self" can function as a kind of *regime*, including as part of its extended self all those who bear similitude to one's color, class, and privilege, thus expelling from the regime of the self all those marked by difference within that economy'.[6]

The violence that the crowd unleashed that night is nothing but the violence inherent in the figuration of the *individual*. Drawing on Roberto Esposito's notion of immunization, community is not based on the shared experience of the common, but rather on the impossibility of its realization. Esposito writes that '[...] we need community because it is the very locus, or better, the transcendental condition of our existence, given that we have always existed in common'.[7] By lacking a shared object and prohibiting the possibility of a stable and closed identity, the community produces fear. Against that fear of losing oneself in a community, Esposito offers his 'immunization paradigm'. The immunization paradigm is about planting in the body the seeds of their future possible annihilation so that the living body might actually be able to fight off those future threats: 'In a world in which individuals who are naturally at risk confront one another in a competition whose stakes are power and prestige, the only way to avoid a catastrophic outcome is to institute among them sufficient distance so as to immunize each from everyone else'.[8] He goes on to emphasize that immunization not only affects individuals; it also concerns collectives and the masses. To protect itself from what threatens to destroy it, the protective community shields itself by building walls and fortifying its borders. Yet, according to this paradigm of immunization, the crowd is not the opposite of the individual, but its very extension. It follows that the attempted lynching of Said Musa is not the expression of ideology, nor is it the failure to imagine a common or a community that can include a Palestinian individuality. On the contrary, it is the expression of a community based on sameness which is established on what Butler refers to as the regime of the self. But how is this notion of self and community, which inherently includes others, not a contradiction?

In his book on the politics of fear, Corey Robin returns to the tension between individuality and collectivity to address the role of anxiety in perpetuating state violence.[9] He addresses the rise of what Alexis de Tocqueville, in *Democracy in America*, called 'the lonely crowd' to refer to the culmination of homogeneity and sameness between people, the very sameness that allows individuals to come together as one raging mass. For Tocqueville, notes Robin, this faith in the mass had nothing to do with its ideology or power. It arises from an inner and personal impulse, connected to the material conditions of equality. 'The nearer men are to a common level of uniformity', the 'readier' they are 'to trust the mass', wrote Tocqueville. 'In times of equality men, being so like each other, have no confidence in others, but this same likeness leads them to place almost unlimited confidence in the judgment of the public'.[10] Contrary to the distribution of power in democracy where the sovereign is instated to govern individuals, contends Robin, this combination of sameness, a sense of uncertainty and fear lead men and women to grant authority to the fluctuating crowd. 'However powers within a democracy are organized and weighted', Tocqueville wrote, 'it will always be very difficult for a man to believe what the mass rejects and to profess what it condemns'.[11] The mass, in other words, is an expression of an amplified individuality, and a protective and parochial one at that.

According to Tocqueville, it is the individual's constant and inescapable feeling of loneliness that prompts the gathering of the crowd. In a secular society, each person is 'forever thrown back on himself alone', while being 'shut up in solitude of his own heart', an absence of authority, the most anxiety-inducing experience of all.[12] 'When there is no authority in religion or in politics, men are soon frightened by the limitless independence with which they are faced'. Tocqueville here alludes to what would come to be known as the fear of freedom, the vertigo that is supposed to afflict anyone forced to make a choice without the comfort of established foundations and authority, where all are 'frightened of their own free will', 'afraid of themselves'. In claiming that anxiety did not have to be crafted, that it was a constitutive feature of the democratic self and its culture, Tocqueville suggested that danger came from within, that the enemy was a psychological fifth column lurking in the heart of every man and woman. As he wrote in a notebook, 'This time the barbarians will not come from the frozen North; they will rise in the bosom of our countryside and in the midst of our cities'.[13] Tocqueville turned people's attention inward, towards the quotidian betrayals of liberty inside their anxious psyches. If there was an object to be feared, it was the self's penchant for violence. 'From now on', writes Robin to conclude his discussion of Tocqueville, 'individuals would have to be on guard against themselves, vigilantly policing the boundaries separating them from the mass'.[14]

Weeks after the attempted lynching of Said Musa, the Israeli police returned to the videos shot that night and began dissecting them, freezing frames and zooming in, a process of fragmentation that was meant to incriminate individuals. The news report that was broadcast live immediately turned into evidence. The video functions here as a map with which to undo the mass, and to lead to the arrest of those who took part in the heavy beating. In the *Haaretz* newspaper, a series of frames from the video depicted blurred faces of those who clearly participated. Sometimes the motion of the assault appears as a strobe. The newspaper zooms in to the crowd to extract from it partially masked faces and sometimes names of the particular individuals who are known to the police. *Haaretz* rightly questions why it is that the police failed to arrest most of those vigilantes, although their faces are very clearly exposed. Some are standing around the injured Musa and filming with their mobile phones (Figure 30).

As *Haaretz* clearly notes, this procedure of pinpointing faces and identifying individuals is undoubtedly crucial. But it also requires editing out the crowd. The forensic procedure performed for the sake of accountability and potential incrimination is oriented by the need to individuate this crowd into the realm of jurisdiction, which inherently demands isolating perpetrators. Indeed, this protective individuality that orients the violence is not one that can be captured in an image. With this procedure, we are led back to the role of images in the procedure of seeking justice, or more accurately, to their limitation in doing so.

The tendency to latch onto the face, as I have argued in the fourth chapter, is inseparable for this so-called *regime of the self*. The urge to see the face in the

Figure 30 Illustration marking out the faces of the Jewish protestors, from Peleg and Appelbaum, *Haaretz* news paper, published 24 May 2021.

crowd blinds us to the need to bear witness to the faceless individuality at the heart of violence in a liberal society. It seems that the scopophilia of pinpointing serves to obfuscate the violence endemic to a mass organized around the figure of the Self, one that is threatened by over proximity of an Other.

Of course, singling out perpetrators is extremely important and urgent. Nevertheless, the image of the 'lonely crowd' can only be seen from the 'in between': in between the multiplicity of images that surged in May 2021, in between the bodies congregating around the injured Musa, in between single events and eruptions of spectacular violence. It is there, in the interconnection between the events that took place in numerous places, in Gaza or Israel, that the violence is located, performed by individuals who move together against individual bodies that embody threat. Capturing the images of the many requires unseeing the distinct and separated subjects to sense the violence coming from the community itself. Those who hold up their cameras and mobile phones to document the event are absent from the frames, but are nonetheless complicit in this violence, which emerges from the sense of kinship produced by separate protective selves.

Conclusion

I have argued in this book that the intensification of the security regime in Israel-Palestine and the increasingly personal use of media technologies by soldiers and civilians are deeply entangled. What initially transpired as two separate paradigm shifts, which culminated together from the 1990s, has been formulating as a co-constitutive condition, shaped by a symbiotic relationship between the ongoing military occupation of the West Bank and the Gaza Strip, and the ubiquitous use of media technologies. I have argued that while practices of media are directly shaped by the notion of security, which affects all aspects of life, the sheer ubiquity of media technologies has fundamentally restructured the exercise of military power in Israel-Palestine.

Parallel to the capacity of media to expose abuses of power by the state and to reveal grave violations of human rights throughout the West Bank and the Gaza Strip, other and less tangible functions of images are permeating into the mesh of media and security. Instead of examining representations that can bear witness to the Israeli occupation, I have focused my inquiry on the often-overlooked practices and habits of mediation that are co-opted into warfare. This focus on media practices has stemmed from the perception that the significance of visual media in warfare is determined not only by images but also and perhaps more significantly, by the capacity to activate disparate soldiers as dependent and self-oriented agents of state power. My emphasis has been on media habits and their integration into procedures of policing within the West Bank, East Jerusalem and the Gaza Strip.

Through habits, the division between the civil and the military spheres in Israel becomes increasingly blurred. Habits of mediation, contracted over long periods of time, are both an old threat and a new opportunity for state authority. The round-the-clock use of media routinely exposes situations and actions, such as illegal arrests or unlawful killings, that can a spotlight into the structural violence of the occupation. At the same time, habits can also immunize the military body against legal and ethical accountability. By incorporating the very substance that can potentially expose violence, the IDF sought to confront the increasing competence of Palestinians to document everyday life by creating smokescreens of information and data that might diffuse the incriminating potential of media. Rather than containing or restricting the media practices imported from the habitus of everyday life, the IDF gradually learnt to employ and re-appropriate such practices for military ends. Three main tactics through which media immunizes the military establishment were explored in this study: *individuation, circulation* and *habituation*. In way of conclusion, I want to briefly address these three distinct yet interwoven concepts by recapitulating how each emerges from the different case studies mentioned.

Individuation, as I attempted to define it in this study, pertains to both the personal engagement of individuals with media technologies and the capacity of media to isolate the individual soldier from a group or a military unit. Where every soldier carries a smartphone alongside his army issued rifle, the figure of the individual re-emerges, not as the object of disciplinary power, but as an active agent oriented by personal interests. For instance, soldiers produce numerous selfies and group snapshots during their routine deployment. Such images are symptoms of the self-promotional values embedded into social media that permeate a routine of policing. At the same time, as I have argued, soldiers hide their faces from cameras and algorithms to remain inseparable from the military group and evade identification. Rather than understanding these two seemingly contradictory practices as separate, I have aimed to examine them as two operations that enclose on the individual soldier as a central figure of power. If the selfie is endemic to the productive biopolitical dispositif that reaffirms the soldier's vitality through connections with friends and family, the masked face is turned against the perceived enemy as the selfie's necropolitical flipside, allowing the soldier to perform, and at times even abuse his authority.

Meanwhile, state authority has mutated into a combination of various agencies that together exert a fragmenting force. The complicity of private companies such as Motorola, Celcom and Facebook in the occupation of Palestine has elevated the position of the individual as a user of media, while at times, diminishing collective political action by Palestinians. Due to the personal engagement with media, the uniformity of soldiers is dissected into isolated individuals with a degree of liberty to act according to their own instincts. This liberty, given to the Israeli citizen and soldier to actively communicate, snap images and share material online, was addressed in the second chapter as a by-product of liberal governance. I used the term individual to shed light on the liberal values coerced into the unique power formation of the Israeli occupation, whereby soldiers are imbricated not merely as abstracted nodes within a war machine, but as members of an extended family.

Individualism, as I have argued in the first chapter, is deeply rooted in the Israeli perception of defence. Focusing on Israel's Civil Defense Regulations, I have shown that Israel's defence strategy is predicated on the ability to activate citizens individually when the state apparatus fails to operate. Lying dormant in Civil Defense Regulations is liberal governance that operates by positioning the individual at the core of security. By elevating self-interest, and conflating between the private home and the homeland, the state is able to exude a soft power, characterized by the leeway it relegates to its citizens.

It is these liberal roots that in the early 1990s suddenly turned, for the first time, into practices of filmmaking aimed at capturing what the military could not. With the looming threat of an impending chemical attack and the eruption of the First Gulf War, the Israeli army encouraged civilians to document the incoming missiles from Iraq. Beginning with the early 1990s, the escalating fear that leaked into the habitat of Israeli civilians coincided with the domestication of media technologies and the ability to appropriate daily practices of filmmaking towards defensive purposes. What surfaced from this mesh, I have shown, is a militarized user that appropriates habitual media practices to expand the state's visuality.

I have further suggested that a crucial component in the process of activating the individual is risk. Risk mobilizes otherwise docile citizens and urges them to partake in strategies of self-defence. The escalating risk that has infiltrated deep into mundane life is thus inseparable from the rapid habituation of media technologies. By unpacking the rarely examined clauses of Israel's Civil Defense Regulations from 1951, I have explored the notion of self-defence as a model of communication galvanized by risk and fear. The escalating fear triggered by Saddam Hussein's threats was a momentous opportunity for the Israeli state to tie together the relationship between defence and media practices. By making this link, I underlined the role of emergency routines in shaping new habits of filmmaking, based on individual use of technologies and the shifting scales between the home and the homeland.

Drawing on Wendy Chun, I have suggested that habitual media thrive on perpetual emergency. In her book *Update to Remain the Same: Habitual New Media*, Chun argues that habitual media is sustained by the constant and repetitive engagement of users on the one hand, and a permanent crisis perpetuated by the never-ending necessity to recalibrate practices of media on the other. This, at first glance, is a contradiction. 'Crises', writes Chun, 'cut through the constant stream of information, differentiating the temporally and temporarily valuable from the mundane, offering its users a taste of real-time responsibility and empowerment'.[1] Confronted with the dynamic mediascape, and the demand to update technologies, users are stimulated to remain always alert, updating their media practices according to new technologies. Habitual media, for Chun, are inseparable from the perpetual crisis of the new, which constantly interrupts acquired knowledge and past experience that produce habits. This logic of crisis, maintains Chun, depends on what seems to be its opposites. Chun's counter-intuitive observation, seeking to define habit through change and adaptability, is particularly productive in unpacking how fear and risk sustain habitual media and shape practices of defence.

Where Chun questions the activating force of economic crisis in the neo-liberal condition, in the first chapter I have suggested that in Israel the distribution of fear and insecurity operates in a similar vein. Permanent emergency interrupts habits by requiring immediate responses, actions and reactions. Effectively, an environment permeated by a permanent emergency, which requires alertness and responsive actions, produces dynamic habits that can be altered and transformed according to security needs. Habits, as I addressed them in this study, are not the outcome of passive or docile existence. Rather, as Elizabeth Grosz has argued, habits are creative forces that allow the possibility for change. The IDF, an authority that struggles to keep up with the pace of change, adopts this crucial aspect of habit to become modular and adaptable.

Since the 2000s, the hinge linking self-defence and habitual media has turned into a unique weapon. The more media technologies have been integrated into vital patterns of life, the more intimately individual soldiers have become integrated into the maintenance of security. In the second chapter I have shown that the rapid fragmentation of collective modes of participation accelerated due to the transforming notion of security in Israel. With the failure of the peace talks in 2000 and the intensification of the violent clashes between the military and the Palestinian populace, the scale and resolution of security changed, shifting from the population as a whole to the individual suspect. The slicing of territories in the West Bank and the rise of the separation principle were reflected not only in the infrastructure of the military occupation, but also by the proliferation of media sources that acted as an equally fragmenting presence. Aligned with the al-Aqsa Palestinian Intifada of 2000, mobile technologies and handheld cameras introduced a degree of visibility that the IDF could not yet control. Videos recorded by Palestinians, such as the controversial video of the killing of al-Durrah in the Gaza Strip, caught Israel unprepared for the mounting criticism coming from the international sphere. The establishment of the International Criminal Court in 2002 and the coming into effect of the Rome Statute opened a legal frontline that Israel hardly pre-empted. Therefore, the Palestinian uprising and the military operation that followed required a new understanding of what media is or can be.

The military film unit, usually tasked with collecting and carefully selecting images for the public's eye, was debilitated due to the omnipresence of cameras and mobile phones held by both journalists and civilians. While deploying professionally trained soldiers to gather high-quality, edited and carefully censored videos, the IDF consistently failed to grasp the impetus of habitual media. As mentioned in the second chapter, after a professional military cameraman from the military spokesperson had been shot and killed in Gaza, it became apparent that traditional media coverage was no longer suitable for combat taking place in the heart of cities, villages and refugee camps. The technological superiority of Israel, which has been part of the military ethos for years, was challenged by low-resolution images produced with small cameras and their rapid distribution.

During the first years of the new millennia, the IDF clumsily attempted to keep up with rapid technological progress. Reimagined as flexible nodes within a 'netwar', the role and figure of the singular soldier were slowly changing. Military think tanks in the IDF conceitedly latched on to what they envisioned as a revolutionary perception of media, based on network formations. Borrowing from theoretical concepts shaped by the Revolution of Military Affairs, the Operational Theory Research Institute (OTRI) envisioned a small and flexible IDF force that could easily move within urban spaces as a network and grab images on the go. However, dispelled by the violence on the ground and the escalating death toll, such theoretical models of communication were found to be inadequate.

From the haze of this confusion, an unlikely media strategy was taking shape in the aftermath of operation 'Defensive Shield' in 2003. My findings show that throughout the first decade of the twenty-first century the IDF gradually transitioned from a perception of new media as an immediate threat, to a careful adaptation to, and adoption of, habitual media. Relaxing the restrictions on the use of cameras, mobile phones and social media by soldiers, new tactics allowed the military to flexibly transform its strategy according to the rapidly shifting media ecology. The training schemes at the IDF film unit were replaced with crash courses for combatants, devoted to explicating how already existing practices of media could and should be redirected for military ends.

If in the early 2000s the IDF was still attempting to censor images produced by both soldiers and Palestinians, by the time of the invasion into the Gaza Strip in 2008–9 the military was already armed with its own YouTube and Facebook pages, to which soldiers were invited to post photographs. Snapping hundreds of photographs during the military deployment in Gaza, the soldiers' media practices were gradually leading the way to a new understanding of media. Pushing further Rebecca Stein's argument that images of leisure and pastime produced by soldiers during military operations in Israel-Palestine indicate the entrenchment of the normalized military occupation, my aim in this discussion was to demonstrate how habitual media inscribe a degree of resilience that allows state authority to cope with the increasing visibility of its code of conduct. In other words, instead of looking at such images as symptoms of a militarized society, or yet another expression of a deeply rooted civil-military complex, I proposed to think of them as the outcome of practices that are by now an integral element of warfare. What is at stake is more than a new way for Israel to normalize violence; rather, it is a scale of technology that comes to absorb functions of the state and the work of governance.

By activating individual soldiers and civilians as media users, I have suggested that the IDF gained three main advantages. The first is the capacity to replace representation with tactics of visual obfuscation. The surge of images, originating from the ubiquity of visual media, could potentially diminish the singular and incriminating potential of representations that directly capture the abuse of power by soldiers. Overabundance of images and data can disorient and confuse, adding more noise into the already clustered visual archive of armed conflict. In the second and fourth chapters, I have shown that, parallel to the capacity of images to bear witness, rapid circulation of images and data alludes to the shifting function of images in conflict. Circulation is not about the quality of the image, or what it can show, but about the quantity and multiplication of images that might together obscure certain acts performed by IDF soldiers.

The second is what I called media mimicry. In the fourth chapter, I explicated how, beginning in 2007, a concerted effort was made by Palestinians to document everyday life under Israeli military rule for the purpose of both collecting potential evidence for legal violations of rights, and deterring soldiers from harassing, violating and colluding with Jewish settlers. Practices of filmmaking were spreading quickly after the NGO B'Tselem inaugurated its 'Shooting Back' project, which allocated cameras to Palestinians who live under particularly intense military presence. Partially paralysed by the presence of cameras, IDF soldiers intuitively began to mimic dissident media practices as a way of containing them. Procedures such as 'mapping', during which soldiers take snapshots of Palestinian civilians, often in their homes, stemmed from the attempt to disarm the singularity of a visual document. Habits of media, I have shown, are shaped by mimicking practices of resistance as a way of neutralizing them. This second advantage encourages IDF soldiers to use their everyday practices to collect information about Palestinian subjects and to monitor them individually.

The third advantage of habitual media in and as warfare brings me back to the core argument of this study. Throughout the book I have traced how the personal engagement of soldiers with media technologies fragments the formally homogenous military group into disparate and isolated soldiers. In the third chapter I have shown that the soldier's face became a site of identification that is inextricably linked to accountability. This isolating and incriminating quality amplifies due to the automatic operation of algorithms embedded in social media platforms. Much more than merely pictures, images can link soldiers to identities, locations and names, and are thus exposing authority to an individualizing force that looms around zones of conflict. The face becomes an emblem of a new spectrum that stretches between the singular and multiple. By exposing the face, the singular soldier attracts to herself the responsibility for acts perpetrated as a representative of state authority. This last outcome of habitual media allows the military to transfer accountability to singular actors as a way to save the institution from ethical and legal responsibility.

After exploring the various case studies in this book and assessing how they are weaved together, this spectrum that stretches between the singular and multiple emerges as the most pervasive outcome of habitual media *in* and *as* warfare. This spectrum culminates from the intersection of security and media. Diffusing the political urgency of collective participation, habitual media assist in the recruitment of disparate selves as active agents of state power, while at the same time disarming Palestinian-organized political mobilization by targeting and dissecting the collective into isolated users. Defining this looming force of individuation required a close examination of archival materials, military protocols and most significantly, images and data shared and reshaped by IDF soldiers on social media. From the sources used in this study, the inseparability of bodies and media technologies continuously alluded to the tension between the individual and the institution as one that can be incorporated as a new form of power.

At various stages of writing, I asked myself whether an in-depth examination of how habitual media affect Palestinian resistance should be explicated.[2] Although this question is equally pressing, my intention was to provide a detailed account of how media shapes state authority from within. Through habits, initially produced as somatic and embodied knowledge, I aimed to move from the micro of the singular soldier or civilian to the macro of the state. The modes of power exerted through habits underline the internal values, social formations and embedded perceptions within Israel, which are at the root of the military occupation. Whereas extensive scholarly work has been done around the civic and emancipatory potential of media, or the representation of violence in Israel-Palestine, little attention has been given to the question of how state power surfaces from within the social fabric in Israel and is gradually reshaped by the all-consuming presence of media.

I find urgency in probing into the intricate ways in which citizens of Israel can live in complicity with a violent history of Palestinian expulsion, that persists today through the varying degrees of control over approximately four and a half million Palestinians in the West Bank and Gaza. Indeed, to live alongside the Gaza Strip and within a society that supports and justifies the ongoing blockade requires more than a collective denial. Sustaining the enduring military occupation is a deep separation principle that intensifies with time, one that reaches far beyond architectural, infrastructural and legal seizures that cut between populations with unequal access to life. Rather, it is maintained by an aesthetic divide, which subdues the capacity of representations to affect the Israeli national community. This aesthetic divide pertains to perceptions that enable the Israeli public to dismiss images of grave abuses of power as nothing but bloody edges of a much wider picture. To understand this visual paranoia, a more attuned inquiry must focus on how certain defensive practises are habituated into the fabric of the Israeli state.

The heavily monitored fence that separates Israel from Gaza is a border that underlines a perpetual fissure policing the senses, sustained by the refusal to imagine co-existence, shared spaces and eventually a kinship between 'us' and 'them'. On the Israeli-Gaza border, where IDF soldiers fire live ammunition at Palestinians who demonstrate, this divide manifests itself as the 'right to kill with impunity'. But to find the sources of what justifies such killings, and to potentially expose them, one should search elsewhere, far from the line of fire. Instead of looking directly into the violence perpetrated against Palestinians in Gaza, I propose to turn around and face the embedded perceptions within Israel that drive and feed it. Through the notion of habit, maybe we can glimpse the invisible forces that fuel the permanent state of exception and also conceive of them as potentially malleable, open-ended and ever-changing. By tracing the acquired habits of civilians and soldiers, and defining them through their constant transformation and change, I have attempted to think beyond the concept of normalization and with the transformations that habits invite, that could, if rewired, change everything.

Notes

Introduction

1 Grosz, Elizabeth. Habit Today: Ravaisson, Bergson, Deleuze and Us. Body & Society. 19 (2&3) 221. Sage, 2013.

2 Flusser, Vilém. *Into the Universe of the Technical Image* (Minnesota Press (third edition), 1985): 52.

3 Arkin, Dan. 'As Close as it Gets to Enemy Territory', 26 January 2020. Available at: https://www.israeldefense.co.il/en/node/41556.

4 Amir Granot, head of Bagira Systems' Intelligence & Training Division, explains the principles of simulator training: 'There is a virtual enemy opposite whom I produce a scenario relying on a database'. It is a combination of training on the ground and training on the simulator, and the trainee experiences all of the stages and activities, including the debriefing after the training session. Everything is documented and recorded, and the training session may be replayed – 'learn from your mistakes and do it again' (ibid.).

5 Colonima, Beatriz. *Domesticity at War* (MIT Press, 1991): 324.

6 In the 1990s, Vilém Flusser talked about a telematic society in which our flesh and blood presence is replaced by our interactive telepresence, perhaps anticipating the expansion of a network that would connect users to one global nervous system. Telepresence is the feeling of being present at a remote location by means of real-time telecommunications devices. Roy Ascott later saw our age as one that includes an art of interactivity, involving the human use of computerized communication and electronic telepresence. He believed this approach carries great potential and hope for our emergence into the next millennium as caring, cooperative and creative human beings.

7 Peters, John Durham. *Speaking into the Air: A History of the Idea of Communication* (University of Chicago Press, 1999): 140–1.

8 According to Esposito, the notion of community contains the very lack of what constitutes a community, so much so that community is made up of those who do not have a community. Invoking the original meaning of community, Esposito suggests that it is founded by a boundless exchange between human beings and is therefore haunted by the potential violence that can erupt from over-proximity; the blurring between inside and an outside, and between an 'I' and an 'Other'. For Esposito, community and violence are inherently related through the risk of over

proximity and competition between individuals. He stresses that without a degree of distancing between individuals, a community cannot survive, because what frightens human beings is a lack of boundaries that places them in direct contact with others who are so similar to them. *Journal of Theoretical Humanities*, Volume 18, 2013: 45.

9 Zyliska J. and Kember S. *Life after New Media* (MIT Press, 2012): 21.

10 Ibid., 45.

11 Peters, John Durham. *The Marvellous Clouds: Toward a Philosophy of Elemental Media* (University of Chicago Press, 2016).

12 According to Massumi, 'Soft power is how you act militarily in waiting, when you are not yet tangibly acting. It is a way of preventing the wait itself from being an attrition, or even a way of turning it to advantage. In the condition of nonbattle, when you have nothing on which to act tangibly, there is still one thing you can do: act on that condition. Act to change the conditions in which you wait. After all, it is from these same conditions that any action to come will have emerged'. Massumi, Brian. *Ontopower: War, Powers, and the State of Perception* (Duke University Press, 2016): 69.

13 Chun, Wendy Hui Kyong. *Updating to Remain the Same: Habitual New Media* (MIT Press, 2016): 65.

14 Ibid., 3.

15 Bratton, Benjamin. *The Stack: On Software and Sovereignty* (MIT Press, 2016).

16 This definition of habit in turn recalls the dualism postulated by Immanuel Kant, between spirit and nature, where spirit lends human beings their reason and autonomy, and nature is causal and mechanical. Malabou, Catherine, Addiction and Grace: Preface to Félix Ravaisson's on Habit', in *Of Habit*, Ed. Felix Ravaisson (Continuum Press): vii.

17 Ibid., 23.

18 Grosz. 'Elizabeth Habit Today: Ravaisson, Bergson, Deleuze and Us', *Body and Society*, Volume 19, Number 2&3 (2013): 217–39, 221.

19 Chun, Wendy Hui Kyong. *Update to Remain the Same: Habitual New Media*, 2.

20 Rebecca Stein and Adi Kuntsman. *Digital Militarism: Israel's Occupation in the Social Media Age* (Stanford Press, 2016).

21 See Roadstrum Moffett, Martha. *Perpetual Emergency: A Legal Analysis of Israel's Use of the British Defence (Emergency) Regulations, 1946, in the Occupied Territories* (Al-Haq, 1989): 1–2.

22 Loevy, Karin. *Emergencies in Public Law the Legal Politics of Containment* (Cambridge University, 2016)

23 Hardt, Michael and Antonio Negri, *Multitude* (Penguin Press, 2005): 20.

24 Ibid., 34.

25 Karin. *Emergencies in Public Law.*

26 Lovink, G., *Social Media Abyss: Critical Internet Cultures and the Force of Negation* (Amsterdam Press, 2016): 35.

27 Ibid., 64.

28 Blum, Gabriella, 'The Individualization of War: From War to Policing in the Regulation of Armed Conflicts', in *Law and War*. Ed. Austin Sarat, Lawrence Douglas and Martha Merrill Umphrey (Stanford Press, 2014): 57.

29 Kotef notes that for us to understand colonial violence in Israel-Palestine, we must revisit the figure of the individual in liberal thought, and its reliance on property. As I will suggest in the first chapter, the home and the habitus of the home are significant in shaping the militarized user of media. For Kotef, the home, both in its concrete and political meanings, expands to absorb the traditionally public sphere of politics. Kotef, Hagar. *The Colonizing Self* (Duke, 2020).

30 Snowdon, Peter. *The People Are Not an Image: Vernacular Video After the Arab Spring* (Verso, 2020).

31 Hochberg, Gil. *Visual Occupations: Violence and Visibility in a Conflict Zone* (Duke University Press, 2016): 6.

32 Ibid., 6.

33 Benjamin H. The Stack.

34 Birchall, C. *Shareveillance: The Dangers of Openly Sharing and Covertly Collecting Data* (Minnesota Press, 2017).

35 Birchall proposes that we interrupt shareveillant subjectivity by claiming, not a right to access more and more data or a right to privacy, but a 'right to opacity'. Birchall imagines this right as 'the demand not to be reduced to, and interact with, data in ways delimited by the state – to resist the terms of engagement set by the two faces of shareveillance (i.e., sharing data with the state and monitoring shared data)'. Indeed, if the dominant discourse celebrates this economy for its entrepreneurial ability to share ideas, sceptics focus on the neo-liberal erosion of labour rights and the commercialization of communitarianism.

36 Ibid.

37 Galloway, Alexander. *Protocol: How Control Exists after Decentralization* (MIT Press, 2004): 4.

38 Ibid., 8.

39 Ibid., 35.

40 Galloway, A. *The Interface Effect. Are Some Things Unrepresentable?* (MIT Press, 2004): 90.

41 Fallon, K. 'Data Visualization and Documentary's (In)visible Frontiers', in *Documentary across Disciplines*. Ed. Erika Balsom and Hila Peleg (MIT Press, 2016): 296.

42 Gabriella Blum addresses the gradual shift in the legal framework of international law from the collective to the individual. Blum argues that 'wartime regulation has evolved from a predominantly state-oriented set of obligations – which view war as an inter-collective effort – to a more individual focused regime'. While the regulation of war through law has always divided the collective from the singular individual, Blum argues that the former is gradually giving way to the individual. This shift from the collective to the individual marks the replacement of military strategy with a policing that individuals who are responsible for their acts. Blum, *The Individualization of War*, 53.

43 B'Tselem. 'About B'Tselem video Project', 19 November 2017. Available at: https://www.btselem.org/video/about-btselem-video.

44 Nissenbaum, Helen. *Obfuscation: A User's Guide for Privacy and Protest* (MIT Press, 2015).

45 Ibid., 56.

Chapter 1

1 Colomina, Beatriz. *Domestication at War* (MIT Press, 1991): 4.

2 Ibid., 61.

3 Bonen, Ze'ev. 'The Missiles Are Coming', *Haaretz Newspaper*, 4 February 1991: 3b.

4 Cohen. 'The Collapse of the Public Shelter', *Al Hamishmar Newspaper* [in Hebrew], 25 February 1991.

5 Switzer. 'Private Homes Would be the First Destination of Chemical Warheads: Security Experts Claim', *Haaretz Newspaper* [in Hebrew], 10 February 1991: 1b.

6 Farkash, Zeev. 'Preparedness of the Civil Front at Times of War'. Ed. Meir Elran, *Research Report*, 1 June 2009, Institute for National Security Studies.

7 Foucault, M., 'The Subject of Power', *Critical Inquiry*, Volume 8, Number 4, Summer, 1982: 777–95.

8 'The Civil Defense Law', according to Ruth Levush, 'regulates various procedures for defending Israel's civilian population from any attack or a threat thereof'. According to an amendment from 2011, 'an attack' includes an aerial bombardment, artillery or missile shelling, and any other long-range shooting by the 'enemy', as well as any other attempt to inflict harm by an army of 'an enemy state'. Civil Defense Law, 5711–1951 [in Hebrew], (5711–1950/51).

9 IDF Archives. 'The Fundamentals of Home Front Command' (Ministry of Defence, 2009): 100.

10 Ibid., 49.

11 Yaniv, Avner. 'A Question of Survival: The Military and Politics under Siege', in *National Security and Democracy in Israel*. Ed. Avner Yaniv (Lynne Rienner Publishing, 1993): 88.

12 Ibid.

13 Lissak, Moshe. 'Civil Components in the National Security Doctrine', in *The National Security and Democracy in Israel*. Ed. Avniv Yaniv (Los Angeles Press, 1993): 66–8.

14 According to Guy Oaks, American civil defence 'was chosen to convince the American people to pay the price for the failure of deterrence. America would accept the risks of nuclear war (with the Soviet Union) only if they could be assured that a nuclear attack would not be too costly [… The] civil defense programs of the 1950s represented an attempt to produce this demonstration by persuading Americans that they could be trained to protect themselves against nuclear attacks' Oaks, Guy. *The Imaginary War: Civil Defense and American Cold War Culture* (Oxford University Press, 1994): 6–9.

15 McEnaney, Elaine. *Civil Defense Begins at Home Militarization Meets Everyday Life in the Fifties*' (Princeton University Press, 2000): 121–31.

16 Ibid., 3.

17 Ibid., 4.

18 Masco, Joseph. *The Theater of Operations: National Security Affect from the Cold War to the War on Terror* (Duke University Press, 2014): 47–50.

19 Ibid., 48.

20 Ibid., 51.

21 Ibid., 49.

22 Orr, Jackie. *Panic Diaries: A Genealogy of Panic Disorder* (Duke University Press, 2006): 43–55.

23 Christison, Kathleen. *Perceptions of Palestine: Their Influence on U.S. Middle East Policy* (UC Berkley Press, 1999): 61–2.

24 From Mordechai Nimza-Bi to Yadin, 10 August 1948, IDFA 2384/50/40.

25 Sluzky, Yehuda. *A Short History of the Hagana* [in Hebrew] (The Israeli Defense Ministry Publishing, 1986): 163–4.

26 IDF Archives. 1948, IDFA 481/49/43.

27 IDF Archives. 'The Danger of Aerial Bombardment', 4 April 1948, IDFA 481/49/43.

28 Krämer, Gedrun. *A History of Palestine: From the Ottoman Conquest to the Founding of the State of Israel* (Princeton University Press, 2008): 156.

29 IDF Archives. 'The Danger of Aerial Bombardment', 4 April 1948, IDFA 481/49/43.

30 IDF Archives. 'The Fundamentals of Home Front Command' (Ministry of Defence, 2009).

31 Balibar, Etienne. *Identity and Difference: John Locke and the Invention of Consciousness*. Trans. Warren Montag (Verso, 2013): 127.

32 In the *Human Condition*, Arendt attributes the transformation and decadence of the political realm in modern societies to the very primacy of natural life over biological action. Arendt argues that the 'household life exists for the sake of the "good life" in the polis', the polis understood as the locus of political action. According to Arendt, the 'private realm' of the *oikos* is where one is isolated and excluded from any political action. In describing the private realm Arendt emphasizes the 'privative' character of the *oikos*, arguing that 'to live an entirely private life means above all to be deprived of things essential to a truly human life' (Human Condition, 58). The subject confined to the 'household', in her terms the *animal laborans,* is bound to necessity, not appearing to others, therefore unable to communicate experience: 'it is as though he did not exist' (Human Condition, 58). s

33 (Foucault 1980, 142–3).

34 Technology of security is summed up as a technology that 'aims at the mass phenomena characteristic of a population as biological entity. The instruments applied here are regulation of control, rather that discipline and supervision' (Lemke, 37).

35 Wendy, Brown. *Undoing the Demos: Neoliberalism's Stealth Revolution* (MIT Press, 2016).

36 Foucault, Michel. *The Birth of the Biopolitics Lectures at the Collage de France 1978–79.* Trans. Graham Burchell (Palgrave Macmillan, 2008).

37 Foucault goes so far as to say that, 'In practice, the stake in all neo-liberal analysis is the replacement every time of *homo oeconomicus* as a partner of exchange with *homo oeconomicus* as entrepreneur of himself, being for himself his own capital, being for himself his own producer, being for himself the source of [his] earnings' (ibid., 226). Foucault, *The Birth of the Biopolitics*, 252–3.

38 To understand oneself as a subject, writes Foucault in the third volume of *History of Sexuality*, the individual draws upon certain techniques that: 'Technologies of the Self permits individuals to effect by their own means or with the help of others a certain number of operations on their own bodies and souls, thought conduct and way of being, so as to transform themselves in order to attain a certain state of happiness, purity, wisdom, perfection or immortality' (1988:16).

39 Lemke, Thomas. 'The Birth of Bio-politics': Michel Foucault's Lecture at the Collège de France on Neo-Liberal Governmentality', *Economy and Society*, Volume 30, Number 2, May 2001: 190–207.

40 IDF Archives. IDFA 481/53/10 (1953), extracted July 2017.

41 Ibid., 9b.

42 Ibid.

43 Ibid.

44 Beck, Ulrich. 'Living in a World Risk Society', *Economy and Society*, Volume 35, Number 3, August 2006: 329–45.

45 Shaul. 'If You Must, Record Everything', *Davar Newspaper* [in Hebrew] 21 January 1991: 3c.

46 Baudrillard, Jean. *The Gulf War Did Not Take Place*. Trans. Paul Patton (Indiana University Press, 1995): 45.

47 Virilio, Paul. *Desert Screen: War at the Speed of Light*, First published in 1991 (The Anthole Press, 2002).

48 Ann Doane, Marry. *Information, Crisis, Catastrophe, in the Historical Film: History and Memory in Media*. Ed. Marcia Landy (The Athlone Press, 2001): 276.

49 Ibid., 283.

50 Ibid., 284.

51 Ibid., 262.

52 Chun, Hui Kyong Wendy, 'Crisis, Crisis, Crisis, or Sovereignty and Networks', *Theory, Culture and Society*, Volume 28, Number 91, 2011.

53 BITNET is an early version of the internet used domestically from the late 1980s. According to Robert Calliahu: 'BITNET's development in the US was facilitated by an IBM grant in July 1984 which provided initial funding for the establishment of centralized network support services. At its peak in 1991–2, this network connected millions of users in more than 1,400 organizations in 49 countries, for the electronic non-commercial exchange of information in support of research and education. In this truly cooperative network, each participating organization contributed communications lines, intermediate storage, and the computer processing necessary to make its part of the network function'. In Calliahu, *How the Web Was Born: The Story of the World Wide Web* (Oxford Press, 2000).

54 Werman. *Notes from a Sealed Room: An Israel View of the Gulf War* (Southern Illinois University Press, 2004): 14.

55 *Haaretz* Newspaper. 'The Schur Family'. November 1990 (Source: News Archive Tel Aviv).

Chapter 2

1 Dziga Vertov. 'The Council of Three (1923)', in *Kino-Eye: The Writings of Dziga Vertov*. Ed. Annette Michelson (The University of California Press, 1984): 14–21, here 17f.

2 Shiloni and Frish. *Ynet*, available at: https://www.ynet.co.il/articles/0,7340,L-2576013,00.html.

3 Quoted in Ben Shaul, Nitzan. *A Violent World: TV News Images of Middle Eastern Terror and War* (Rowman & Littlefield, 2006): 98.

4 Rees, Matt. 'Streets Red with Blood', *Time Magazine*, 18 March 2002.

5   Editorial, BBC News. Tuesday, 8 February, 2005. Available at: http://news.bbc.co.uk/1/hi/world/middle_east/3694350.stm.

6   Landsberg. 'The Military Frontline in Today the Television, and the IDF is Failing the Battle. Imagine 500 Cameramen Documenting the War', *Maarachot -Mabat Ishi* [in Hebrew], 2003.

7   Arie Kramp has argued that the gradual liberalization of Israeli society during the 1990s marks the beginning of a seemingly contradictory process whereby neo-liberal forces gradually gather momentum, while Israel is also becoming more nationalistic. What seems like a contradiction on first sight is a unique condition that characterized Israel as a society. In Kramp, Arie, *The Israeli Path to Neoliberalism: The State, Continuity and Change* (Oxford Press, 2018): 32–4.

8   Shavit, Michal, *Media Strategy and Military Operations in the 21st Century: Mediatizing the Israel Defence Forces* (Taylor and Francis: Contemporary Security Studies, 2017): 23.

9   Basic Laws by the Knesset – the Human Dignity and Liberty Basic Law (1992) and the Freedom of Occupation Basic Law (1994) – characterized the 'constitutional revolution' in Israel. These laws wrought a fundamental change in the rights of the individual and broadened the authority of the Israel Supreme Court over the Knesset and the government. In Barzilai, Gad. 'War, Democracy and Internal Conflict: Israel in a Comparative Perspective', *Comparative Politics*, Volume 31, Number 3, 1999: 317–36.

10 On the liberalization of Israel, see Yadgar, Yaacov, *Our Story: National Narratives in the Israeli Press* (Haifa University Press, 2004): 189.

11 On July, 2000, Bill Clinton hosted Ehud Barak and Yasser Arafat at Camp David for final status negotiations on core issues pertaining the conflict. Barak insisted there would be no withdrawal to the border of 1967, no division of Jerusalem and no evacuation of settlement. Due to the reluctance of Israel to grant these fundamental request, Yasser Arafat was unwilling to proceed with the talks (Mitchell, 2016:85).

12 Michal. *Media Strategy and Military Operations in the 21st Century*, 37.

13 Gordon, Neve. *Israel's Occupation* (University of California Press, 2008): 197.

14 In Cordersman, Anthony. *Arab-Israeli Military Forces in an Era of Asymmetric Wars* (Stanford Press, 2008).

15 Despite Israel initially admitting that the bullets had 'apparently' come from their positions, and apologizing for the incident in what the report describes as the 'fog of war', lobbyists have long argued that the footage was staged. In Dawber. 'The Killing of 12-year-old Mohammed al-Durrah in Gaza became the Defining Image of the Second Intifada. Only Israel Claims it was All a Fake'. *The Independent*, 2000. Available at https://www.independent.co.uk/news/world/middle-east/the-killing-of-12-year-old-mohammed-al-durrah-in-gaza-became-the-defining-image-of-the-second-8624311.html (accessed April 2017).

16　Rid, Thomas and Hecker, Mark. *War 2.0: Irregular Warfare in the Information Age* (Praeger Security International, 2009): 56–8.

17　Ibid.

18　Ibid., 202.

19　Weizman, Eyal. *Hollow Land: Israel's Architecture of Occupation* (Verso, 2007): 117.

20　Brown, Wendy. *Walled Stated, Waning Sovereignty* (MIT Press, 2010): 29.

21　Ibid.

22　Ziv A. 'Israel's Defense Ministry Signs Deal for Military-grade Smartphones', *Haaretz*, 3 January 2014. Available at: https://www.haaretz.com/.premium-idf-smartphones-on-the-way-1.5307579 (accessed February 2016).

23　According to Tawil-Souri, by 2000 Israel was one of only two countries to have passed the 100 per cent cellular penetration rate threshold. From 1994, private telecommunication companies were reaching out to Israeli settlements, allowing the basic infrastructure to mark a certain settlement as legitimate in the eyes of the state. In Tawil-Souri, Helga. *Signal Traffic: Critical Studies of Media Infrastructures (The Geopolitics of Information)*. Ed. Lisa Parks and Nicole Starosielski (University of Illinois Press, 2015): 156.

24　Ibid., 157–8.

25　Ibid., 176.

26　Doner, S. 'Celcom Recruits Soldiers', *Ynet Online* [in Hebrew], 2005. Available at: https://www.ynet.co.il/articles/0,7340,L-3093481,00.html (accessed March 2017).

27　Ibid.

28　Bain Lobovich. 'Celcom's Military Training', *Ynet Online* [in Hebrew], 2013. Available at: https://www.globes.co.il/news/article.aspx?did=1000884706 (accessed June 2017).

29　(Kittler, 1998b: 56).

30　Catignani, Sergio. 'The Strategic Impasse in Low-Intensity Conflicts: The Gap between Israeli Counter-Insurgency Strategy and Tactics During the Al-Aqsa Intifada', *Journal of Strategic Studies*, Volume 28, (2005).

31　Dima Adamsky. *The Culture of Military Innovation* (Stanford University Press, 2010): 101.

32　Ibid., 99–102.

33　Ibid., 107.

34　Chris Demchak notes that the dominant model for a 'modern' military emerged with the US military's 'Revolution in Military Affairs' (RMA). But the 'revolution' is ill defined, emerging as a rough social consensus on what constitutes a modern military: 'The US Department of Defense's Office of Net Assessments defines RMA as 'a major change in the nature of warfare brought about by the innovative application of technologies which, combined with dramatic changes in military doctrine and operational concepts, fundamentally alters the character and conduct of operations' See Demchak, C. 'Technology's Knowledge Burden, the RMA and the IDF: Organizing the Hypertext Organization for Future "Wars of Disruption"?' *Journal of Strategic Studies*, Volume 24, (2001).

35 Arquilla, J. and Ronfeld, D. *Networks and Netwars: The Future of Terror, Crime, and Militancy* (Rand Publications, 1999).

36 Ibid., 2.

37 Ibid., 13.

38 Weber, Samuel. *Targets of Opportunity: On the Militarization of Thinking* (Fordham Press, 2005): 90–190.

39 Ibid., 12.

40 Visualizing is conceived to be the role of state authority. Visuality, in Nicholas Mirzoeff's terms, is waged and determined on the ability to make spaces and bodies within a given territory visible and intelligible. Visuality, which is distinctly different from the more common visibility, is not merely predicated on perception or the ability to made visible, but also and more fundamentally, on the construction of historical narratives that emerge as by-products of what is rendered visible. Mirzoeff notes that visualizing is the distinctly military objective of overseeing a given battlefield or territory, the authority to visualize is given to he who is able to envision the landscape in his mind.

41 Cooksey, J. *The Vest Pocket Kodak & the First World War: Camera & Conflict* (Ammonite Press, 2017): 13.

42 Amnesty, 'Israel\Gaza: Operation 'cast lead: 22 Days of Death and Destruction', *Amnesty International*, 2 July 2009. Available at: https://www.amnesty.org/download/Documents/48000/mde150212009eng.pdf.

43 Briner. 'Mobile Phone Cameras? No in Our Bases'. *Walla Online*. Published 21 July 2008. Available at: https://news.walla.co.il/item/1316618 (accessed 13 April 2018).

44 Ibid.

45 Sher. *The Land Division Military Journal*, Number 34. Published 14 March 2020. IDF Publishing.

46 Sivan. 'Documentation at War', *Maarachot Journal* [in Hebrew], Number 18, 25 December 2013.

47 Ibid.

48 Ibid.

49 Ibid.

50 Lupton, Deborah. *The Quantified Self: A Sociology of Self Tracking*, Kindle Edition (Polity Press, 2016): 38–9.

Chapter 3

1   Flusser, Vilém. *The Freedom of Migrant: Objection to Nationalism*. Originally published 1994 (University of Illinois Press, 2003): 56.

2   From the report released by 'Breaking the Silence': "This is How We Fought in Gaza, 2015.

3   Quoted in Gordon and Perugini. 'The Politics of Human Shielding: On the Resignification of Space and the Constitution of Civilians as Shields in Liberal Wars', *Society and Space* 2015: 8.

4   Ishizuka, Karen I. and Zimmermann, Patricia R. *Mining the Home Movie: Excavations in Histories and Memories* (UC Press, 2007): 8.

5   De Certeau, Michel. *The Practice of Everyday Life*. Trans. Steven Rendall (UC Press, 1984): 117.

6   Human dignity holds a central place in IHRL as well, from its initial inclusion in the Universal Declaration of Human Rights (UDHR). It serves as a supreme value and the core of all other universal human rights. In the context of the right to privacy, the UDHR states that: 'No one shall be subjected to arbitrary interference with his privacy, family, home or correspondence, nor to attacks upon his honour and reputation. Everyone has the right to the protection of the law against such interference or attacks.' Quoted from 'Exposed Life', 2020, 24.

7   Teyssot, Georges. *A Topology of Everyday Constellations* (Princeton Press, 2016): 6. Teyssot explains that structuralists such as Levi-Strauss and Bourdieu noted a connotation to the term of *Habitus*, as referring to social status, style, and uses or practices that revolve around everyday life at home. See Bourdieu, Pierre. *Outline of a Theory of Practice* (Cambridge University Press, 1977). Mauss, Marcel. 'Technics of the Body', *Journal de Psychologie* 32, 1934: (3–4). Reprinted in Mauss, *Sociologie et anthropologie* (PUF, 1936): 6.

8   This notion of habitation is based on the structuralist theory of the habitat which historically meant to construct something found in the 'practices' of everyday life of the inhabitants (or any other agent in a society). What Pierre Bourdieu called *Habitus* refers to social status, style, and uses or practices, and is formed by habi-, which comes from *habere*, to have or to hold, and -tus, the suffix of verbal action. The archaic meaning of Habitus referred to the action of dwelling in, which explains why the Latin *habitare*, the frequentative of *habere*, refers to inhabiting.

9   Kotef, Hagar. *The Colonizing Self* (Duke, 2020), 8–9.

10 Amnesty. 'Israel\Gaza: Operation Cast Lead: 22 Days of Death and Destruction', *Amnesty International*, 2 July 2009. Available at: https://www.amnesty.org/download/Documents/48000/mde150212009eng.pdf.

11 Briner. 'Mobile Phone Cameras? No in Our Bases'. *Walla Online*. Published 21 July 2008. Available at: https://news.walla.co.il/item/1316618 (accessed 13 April 2018).

12 Ibid.

13 Hazroni. 'In at the Military Base: Selfie Stand for Soldiers', *Mako Online* [in Hebrew]. First published in December 2015. Available at: https://www.mako.co.il/news-military/security-q4_2015/Article-99e4a4314f16151004.htm (accessed 10 April 2018).

14 Kuntsman and Stein. *Digital Militarism*, 72.

15 Ibid.

16 Ibid., 81.

17 The notion of media domestication was coined by British media studies in the 1990s to address the 'taming of technologies' and integration into the home. David Morley, for instance, argued that for technologies to become imbed into everyday routines, it should be domesticated through their introduction into the household. Berker, Hartmann, Punie and Ward. *Domestication of Media and Technology* (Open University Press, 2006).

18 Gaza, 2014. Findings of an independent medical fact-finding mission, Executive Summary, 8.

19 Gaza Emergency Situation Report. United Nations Office for the Coordination of Humanitarian Affairs: Occupied Palestinian Territory. 3 August 2014.

20 Amnesty International. "Unlawful and Deadly". First published in March 2015.

21 Vidler, A, 167.

22 Rancière, J. *Dis-agreement. Politics and philosophy* (University of Minnesota Press, 1999), 78.

23 Rancière wishes to 'reserve the term politics for an extremely determined activity antagonistic to policing: whatever breaks with the tangible configuration whereby parties and parts or lack of them are defined by a presupposition that, by definition, has no place in that configuration – that of the part of those who have no part'.6 Quoted in Väliaho, Pasi. *Biopolitical Screens: Image, Power, and the Neoliberal Brain* (MIT Press, 2017).

24 Tawil-Souri, Helga.

25 The legal phrase 'human shield' became one of the central tropes promulgated by Israel during the Gaza war because, on the one hand, the categorization of civilians as human shields helps conceal the fact that 'pin point strikes' and 'surgical capabilities' can neither predict nor guarantee discrimination, while on the other hand, it helps Israel justify the large proportion of civilian deaths and the destruction of civilian spaces in Gaza. The normative argument became part of 'semiotic warfare' aimed at legitimizing Israel's military campaign.8 Hence, in order to understand how the phrase operated during Israel's war on Gaza it is vital to develop a critique of human shielding that is concomitantly a critique of both military and semiotic violence. Perugni and Gordon. 'The Politics of Human Shielding: On the Resignification of Space and the Constitution of Civilians as Shields in Liberal Wars', *Society & Space*, Volume 34, Number 1, 2015.

26 Shawn Michelle Smith has challenged the dominant histories that tend to empower the medium with the inescapable vision. She considers the degree of blindness in photography and that which remains unseen under the camera's inspecting lenses. Smith writes: 'Photography expanded the realm of the visible, but it also exposed its limits, both physiological and technological. Enabling one to see more, it simultaneously demonstrated how little is ordinarily visible, giving one the unnerving sense of living in a world only partially perceived'. In her book *At the Edge of Sight*, Smith investigates both photography's capacity and limitation to make visible. See: Smith, Shawn Michelle. *At the Edge of Sight* (Duke University Press, 2013).

27 'The Gaza Conflict: Factual Aspects' report (May 2015) was distributed by the Israeli Ministry of Foreign Affairs with the stated aim of providing information 'so that others may reach an informed understanding for the reasons of the conflict and the actions of the parties thereto'.

28 The document directly addressed the use of domestic spaces to claim that homes were intentionally included by Hamas leadership as a constituent in the armed struggle by promoting three main goals summarized by the Israeli government as such: '(1) *The activity of hiding weapons in homes needs to be done with secrecy and should not have a military character. (2) Placing equipment in residential areas needs to be done with household items. (3) Use residents of the area in order place the equipment inside.*' If the felonious is disguised by the mundane, then the environment of the home can become the most threatening battleground.

29 'Breaking the Silence' published the oral testimonies of over 60 soldiers that took part in Operation 'Protective Edge'. 2015, 84.

Chapter 4

1 Stanley Kubrick, *Spartacus*, Universal Studios, 1960.

2 Eli, Y. 'The Loner's Intifada', *Walla News*, [in Hebrew], 15 October 2015. Available at: https://news.walla.co.il/item/2897602#!/wallahistory (accessed 20 September 2017).

3 Ibid.

4 Harel, A. 'Israel Speeds Up Camera Placements in West Bank in Effort to Deter Terrorism', *Haaretz*, 22 June 2017. Available at: https://www.haaretz.com/israel-news/.premium-idf-speeds-up-camera-placements-in-w-bank-in-effort-to-deter-terrorism-1.5485764 (accessed 12 March 2018).

5 Quoted in Belting, Hans. *The Face and the Mask*. Trans. S. T. Hansen, A. J. Hansen (Princeton University Press, 2016): 26.

6 Levinas, Emmanuel. *Ethics and Infinity*. Trans. Cohen, R. A. (Duquesne University Press, 1985): 50–1.

7   Belting. *The Face and the Mask*, 6.

8   Blas, Zach. 'A Cage of Information', or, 'What Is a Biometric Diagram?' in *Documentary across Disciplines*. Ed. Balsom, E. and Peleg, H. (MIT Press, 2016): 80–90.

9   Shavit, Michal. *Media Strategy and Military Operations in the 21st Century: Mediatizing the Israeli Defense Forces* (Routledge, 2016).

10   Rid and Hecker. *War 2.0*, 82.

11   Ibid.

12   Kuntsman and Stein. *Digital Militarism*, 27.

13   Quoted in Hodge, Nathan. 'YouTube, Twitter: Weapons in Israel's info War', *Wired Magazine*, 30 December 2008. Available at: https://www.wired.com/2008/12/israels-info-wa/.

14   Quoted in Gates, Kelly. *Our Biometric Future: Facial Recognition Technology and the Culture of Surveillance* (New York University Press, 2011): 138.

15   Andrejevic, Mark. 'The Work of Watching One Another: Lateral Surveillance, Risk, and Governance', *Society & Surveillance*, Volume 2, Number 4, 2002: 479–97.

16   Ibid., 488.

17   Buchbutt. 'The IDF Declared War on Social Media', *NRG News*, 23 December 2010 [in Hebrew]. Available at: http://www.nrg.co.il/online/1/ART2/192/452.html (accessed 20 September 2017).

18   Associated Press. 'Israeli army condemns publication of Gaza "war criminals"', *The Guardian*, 19 November 2010. Available at: https://www.theguardian.com/world/2010/nov/19/israeli-army-condemns-gaza-list (accessed 20 September 2017).

19   B'tselem. 'A year to cast lead', Report (B'tselem 2009 Israel).

20   Rahman, Omar. 'Nabi Saleh Protester Hit by Tear Gas Canister Dies from Wounds', *+972 Magazine*, 9 December 2011. Available at: https://972mag.com/nabi-saleh-palestinian-shot-in-head-with-tear-gas-canister/29317/.

21   Cohen. 'Israeli Military Closes Probe into Death of Palestinian Protester Mustafa Tamimi', *Haaretz*, 5 December 2013. Available at: https://www.haaretz.com/. premium-probe-into-palestinian-protester-s-death-closed-1.5297524 (accessed 12 March 2018).

22   Browne, Simone. *Dark Matters: On the Surveillance of Blackness* (Duke University Press, 2015), 9.

23   Ibid., 8–9.

24   Ibid., 31.

25   Lyon. *Surveillance Studies*, 25.

26   Ibid., 26.

27   Ibid., 26–7.

28   Marx, G. *Undercover, Police Surveillance in America* (Berkeley Press, 1988): 206.

29 Ibid.

30 Lupton. *The Quantified Self.*

31 Ibid., 2–4.

32 Ibid., 60.

33 Bauman and Lyon. *Liquid Surveillance: A Conversation* (Polity, 2013).

34 Lupton. *The Quantified Self,* 60.

35 Gates. *Our Biometric Future.*

36 Ibid., 12.

37 Peters, John Durham. *Speaking into the Air: A History of the Idea of Communication* (University of Chicago Press, 1999): 140–1. Quoted in Gates, *Our Biometric Future,* 204.

38 Ibid., 141.

39 Ibid., 138.

40 Galloway and Thacker. *The Exploit: A Theory of Networks* (Electronic Mediations: University of Minnesota Press, 2007): 39.

41 On the role of the US military in the development of computers, see Manuel De Landa. *War in the Age of Intelligent Machines* (New York: Zone Books, 1991); Edwards, Paul N. *The Closed World: Computers and the Politics of Discourse in Cold War America* (MIT Press, 1996); Norberg and O'Neil. *Transforming Computer Technology.*

42 Sekula, Allan. 'The Body and the Archive', *October* 39, Winter 1985: 3–64.

43 Ibid., 6.

44 See Tagg, John. *The Burden of Representation: Essays on Photographies and Histories* (University of Minnesota Press, 1993).

45 Alphonse Bertillon, a Paris police official, was the first to harness photography to a defined system of *criminal identification.* First, he combined photographic portraiture, anthropometric description and short descriptions that fill in the gaps, where the images seemingly lacked details. Second, he organized these cards within a comprehensive, statistically based filing system. Bertillon was not the first to use photography within a juridical system, but he insisted that by taking mugshots of delinquents and filing them by categories of crimes, one could 'keep track' of them.

46 Quatelet, Lambert and Adolphe Jacques, *Treatise of Man and the Development of His Faculties,* First published in French in 1835 (Cambridge Press, 2013).

47 Teyssot, Georges. *A Topology of Everyday Constellations* (MIT Press, 2013): 51.

48 Gillham, NW. *A Life of Sir Francis Galton: From African Exploration to the Birth of Eugenics: From African Exploration to the Birth of Eugenics* (Oxford: Oxford University Press, 2001).

49 Ibid., 97.

50 Bowditch, Henry Pickering. 'Are Composite Photographs Typical Pictures?' *McClure's Magazine,* 1894.

51 Ibid., 342.

52 Rose Shell, Hanna. *Hide and Seek: Camouflage, Photography, and the Media of Reconnaissance* (MIT Press, 2012): 14.

53 Ibid., 25.

54 Ibid., 64.

55 Caillois, Roger. *Mimicry and Legendary Psychasthenia*. Trans. Shepley (MIT Press, 1984).

56 Ibid., 54.

57 Nissenbaum. *Obfuscation,* 47.

58 Ibid., 21.

59 Rotner, Rachel. 'The David Hanachlawi Facebook campaign', *Walla Tech* [in Hebrew]. 1 May 2014. Available at: https://tech.walla.co.il/item/2742383 (accessed 20 September 2017).

60 According to Linda Herrera, the Facebook fan page titled 'We Are All Khaled Said' began in June 2010 in honour of its namesake, a young man allegedly killed at the hands of plainclothes police and then blossomed into Egypt's most active and consequential anti-torture-campaign-turned-youth-movement in over half a century. This social media phenomenon crystallized a new kind of politics that was supposedly leaderless, horizontal and networked, and that operated on a principle of online to offline mobilization. By January 2011, the page had grown to 390,000 members, 70 per cent of whom were under twenty-four years old, and over 40 per cent of whom were young women, in Herrera, Linda. *Revolution in the Age of Social Media* (Verso, 2016): 102.

61 Cohen, Gili. 'Feelings of Discrimination Driving Palestinian Youth to Terror', *Haaretz*, 11 November 2015. Available at: http://www.haaretz.com/israel-news/. premium-1.685485 (accessed 12 June 2018).

62 Harel, Amos. 'East Jerusalem's Leading Role in Terror Attacks Catches Israel Off Guard', *Haaretz*, 17 October 2015. Available at: https://www.haaretz.com/. premium-e-jerusalem-terror-attacks-catch-israel-off-guard-1.5409887 (accessed 12 June 2018).

63 Throughout October 2015, the IDF recorded seventy-five terror attacks against Israelis in both Israel and Palestine. Most of the attacks were failed attempts that ended with an immediate gunshot that killed the assailant on the spot. A sense of desperation hovered over these unorganized attempts. In the same month, according to the Palestine Red Crescent Society, Israeli operations aimed at suppressing or dispersing demonstrations and protests where often stones, rocks and Molotov cocktails were thrown. An estimated 8,262 Palestinians were injured, 2,617 by gun wounds, 760 by live fire, 1,857 by rubber-coated steel bullets. See Ma'an News Agency, 'Red Crescent: Over 2,600 Shot with Live, Rubber Bullets in October', 1 November 2015. Available at: http://www.maannews.com/Content. aspx?id=768603.

64 In Palestinian society, until the 1920s, Bedouin men were distinguished from villagers and urban dwellers by their headgear, hattah or keffiyeh. Later, Yasser Arafat adopted a specific black-and-white *keffiyeh*. This newly acquired symbol of Palestinian liberation took on a new and significant meaning, becoming a symbol of Palestinian national identity. The black-and-white pattern became a popular motif in everyday Palestinian art and life where its meaning is understood as a sign of struggle for political identity among those who are familiar with the Palestinian situation. In Kiswani, Nerdeen. 'Why We Wear the Keffiyeh' (2015).

65 Following such individual acts of terror, the Israeli state also renewed procedures of house demolition that were first authorized as part of the Defence Emergency Regulations, instated by the British mandatory authorities in 1945. Under these regulations, military commanders possess a wide range of discretionary powers, including the authority to order house demolitions.

66 'Information contained in a high-resolution portrait of an individual', writes Azoulay, 'can be obscured and made unrecognizable when the person photographed is captured under what I suggest calling "the resolution of the suspect." Singled out, taken out of context, she or he no longer appears as an individual but rather as an outsider, a threat, presented as encapsulated in information that can be acquitted – if at all – only through systems of detection programmed by a specific military logic'. Azoulay, Ariella. *The Resolution of the Suspect*. Trans. from Hebrew by Tal Haran (Radius Books, 2016): 24–6.

67 Kane, Alex. 'Post, Share, Arrest', *The Intercept*, 7 July 2016. Available at: https://theintercept.com/2016/07/07/israel-targeting-palestinian-protesters-on-facebook/ (accessed 10 June 2018).

68 Ben Israel, Dori. 'Facebook is Sabotaging the Police's Work', *Hamizbala Blog*, 2 July 2016. Available at: http://mizbala.com/digital/social-media/112838 (accessed 5 June 2018).

69 Associated Press in Jerusalem. 'Facebook and Israel to Work to Monitor Posts That Incite Violence', *The Guardian*, 16 September 2016. Available at: https://www.theguardian.com/technology/2016/sep/12/facebook-israel-monitor-posts-incite-violence-social-media?CMP=twt_gu (accessed 10 May 2018).

Chapter 5

1 Esposito, Roberto. 'Community, Immunity, Biopolitics', *Journal of Theoretical Humanities*, Volume 18, 2013: 45.

2 Zitun, Yonatan. 'Soldier Who Shot Neutralised Terrorist Is Suspected of Murder', *Ynet*, 10 March 2016. Available at: https://www.ynetnews.com/articles/0,7340,L-4783059,00.html (accessed 25 March 2018).

3   Based on an interview Ruthie Ginsburg conducted with Abu Shamsia, Hebron, December 2016.

4   Keenan, Thomas. 'Mobilizing Shame', *The South Atlantic Quarterly*, Volume 103, Number 2/3, Spring/Summer 2004: 435–49.

5   Ibid., 438.

6   Bendet, Shabtai. 'Survey: 47 Per Cent of the Public Believe Azaria Was Tried Unjustly', *Walla*, 5 July 2016 [in Hebrew]. Available at: https://news.walla.co.il/item/2976259 (accessed 13 May 2018).

7   Israel Military Court. 'Appeal Court Ruling Protocol' [in Hebrew]. May 2017: 36.

8   Ibid., 40.

9   Weiner, Stuart. 'Soldier Elor Azaria Given 18 Months in Jail for Killing Wounded Stabber', *The Times of Israel*, 21 February 2017. Available at: https://www.timesofisrael.com/soldier-elor-azaria-given-18-months-prison-for-killing-wounded-assailant/ (accessed 25 June 2018).

10 Brown. 'The Defense Team Are Changing Strategy and Claims for Selective Enforcement'. Available at: https://www.haaretz.co.il/blogs/johnbrown/1.4002447.

11 Ibid.

12 According to Michal Tamir, the term 'selective enforcement' applies to a situation in which even though the law seems fair and impartial, it is applied, administered and enforced by the public authority in a discriminating way, in that the law is enforced only against certain individuals or groups, or in that there are different enforcement policies depending upon the identity or affiliation of the person or entity involved. Tamir, Michal. *Public Law as a Whole: The Case of Selective Enforcement and Racial Profiling* (New York University Press, 2015).

13 'Open Fire Regulations' are the official instructions of the IDF dictating when, and in what circumstances, a soldier should fire live ammunition. According to B'Tselem, until the outbreak of the al-Aqsa Intifada in September 2000, the Open-Fire Regulations in the Occupied Territories were based on Israel's penal code. Soldiers were only allowed to fire live ammunition when soldiers were in real and immediate life-threatening danger. When the 2000 intifada began, the IDF defined the events in the Occupied Territories as an armed conflict short of war," and expanded the range of situations in which soldiers are permitted to open fire. In B'Tselem, 'Trigger Happy: Unjustified Gunfire and the IDF's Open-Fire Regulations during the al-Aqsa Intifada', March 2002, B'Tselem. Available at: https://www.btselem.org/publications/summaries/200203_trigger_happy

14 Brown. 'The Defense Team are Changing Strategy and Claims for Selective Enforcement'. Available at: https://www.haaretz.co.il/blogs/johnbrown/1.4002447.

15 Cited in Anne McClintock. 'Paranoid Empire: Spectres from Guantanamo and Abu Ghraib Small Axe', Number 28 Volume 13, Number 1, March 2009: 50–74.

16 Butler, Judith. *Frames of War: When Is Life Grievable?* (Verso, 2009): 5, 13.

17   For Butler, the context of the production of a visual document of war is at risk
     of being severed by its circulation: The circulation of images, pertinent to their
     visibility, can potentially destroy the context of their production. 'The frame that
     seeks to contain, convey, and determine what is seen depends upon the conditions
     of circulability in order to succeed'. Ibid., 11.

18   Ibid.

19   Brown. 'The Defense Team Are Changing Strategy and Claims for Selective
     Enforcement'. Available at: https://www.haaretz.co.il/blogs/johnbrown/1.4002447.

20   Didi-Huberman, Georges. *Images In Spite of All: Four Photographs from Auschwitz*
     (Chicago University Press, 2008): 150.

21   Ibid., 121.

22   'The image is always an amalgam', writes Didi-Huberman, 'an impurity, visible
     things mixed with confused things, illusive things mixed with revealing things,
     visual forms mixed with a certain thought in action. It is therefore neither all nor
     nothing'. Ibid., 65.

23   Hoskins and O'laughlin. *War and the Media: After Diffused War* (Polity Press,
     2010): 21.

24   22 'The everyday, be this our connection with and our uses of media
     everyday', writes Grusin, 'are overlooked, given that they are routine and
     unexceptional and we do not ordinarily reflect upon such activities in themselves'.
     In Grusin, Richard. *Premediation: Affect and Mediality After 9/11* (Palgrave
     Macmillan, 2010): 27.

25   Shafir, Gershon. *A Half Century of Occupation: Israel, Palestine, and the World's
     Most Intractable Conflict* (University of California Press, 2016).

26   A dual legal system that separates Palestinians in the West Bank and the Jewish
     settlers: Palestinian cases are tried before different courts, Palestinian detainees fall
     under different rules of detention, search and interrogation, and Palestinians' freedoms
     of expression, protest and movement are constrained. By relegating Palestinians to a
     separate legal system, Israel has de facto created two laws for two peoples.

27   Yacobovich, Oren. 'Shooting Back: The Israeli Human Rights Group B'Tselem
     Gives Palestinians Video Cameras to Document Life under Occupation', *Democracy
     Now Website*, 2007. Available at: https://www.democracynow.org/2007/12/26/
     shooting_back_the_israeli_human_rights (accessed 30 June 2018).

28   Ibid.

29   Elsight: Expanding your Visual Reach. 'Documenting Soldier Project'. *Elsight
     website*. Available at: http://el-sight.com/project/documenting-warrior-project/
     (accessed 28 June 2018).

30   Elsight provided the IDF spokeperson's office with a state of the art live video
     streaming system as part of 'Documenting Warrior' project, designed to take close-
     up images during demonstrations, to ensure there is IDF material to respond to any
     criticism levied at the IDF while dispersing demonstrations.

31 Serwood, Harriet. 'Palestinian Children Woken in Night to be Photographed by Soldier', *The Guardian*. 28 September 2011. Available at: https://www.theguardian.com/world/view-from-jerusalem-with-harriet-sherwood/2011/sep/28/palestinian-territories-israel (accessed 28 June 2018).

32 Ibid.

33 As of June 2021, the IDF decided to discontinue the official 'mapping' tactics. Ben Zion, Illan. 'Israel to Halt Nighttime "Mapping" of Palestinians Homes', *AP*, 16 June 2021. Available at: https://apnews.com/article/israel-middle-east-bbcd7e2345ff7b0ea9db294111e20a29.

34 I employ the term obfuscation to unpack the ramifications of habitual media on the exercise of security. Drawing on Helen Nissenbaum, I contend that visual obfuscation aims to further increase the flow of data and to bring it to the point of excess, derailing attention from a particular photograph or video. For Nissenbaum, obfuscation is the deliberate addition of ambiguous information to interfere with data collection. 'At its most abstract', writes Nissenbaum, 'obfuscation is the production of noise to make data more unintelligible, and therefore less valuable'. Nissenbaum, *Obfuscation*, 53.

35 Altman, Yair. 'Documentation: What Did 40 Soldiers Do on the Rooftop in Hebron?' *Walla Website*. 29 May 2015 [in Hebrew]. Available at: https://news.walla.co.il/item/2858641 (accessed 20 January 2017).

36 Nissenbaum. *Obfuscation*, 53.

37 Espinosa. 'For an Imperfect Cinema', *Jump Cut*, Volume, Number 20, 1979: 24–6.

38 Steyerl, Hito. 'In Defence of the Poor Image'. *Journal #10*, November 2009, e-Flux.

39 Ibid.

40 Ibid.

Chapter 6

1 United Nations. 'Approaching the First Anniversary of the "Great March of Return" Protests in Gaza – OCHA Article', 27 March 2019. Available at: https://www.un.org/unispal/document/approaching-the-first-anniversary-of-the-great-march-of-return-protests-in-gaza-ocha-article/.

2 Goldenberg and Akram. 'Hamas claims Majority of the Palestinians killed near Border Fence', *Chicago Tribune*. 16 May 2018. Available at: https://www.chicagotribune.com/nation-world/ct-hamas-gaza-israel-20180516-story.html.

3 Garland, David. *Peculiar Institution: America's Death Penalty* (Harvard Press, 2010).

4 Kittler, Friedrich. *Optical Media* (Polity Press, 2009).

5 Lebow, Alisa. 'Shooting With Intent: Framing Conflict', in *Killer Images: Documentary Film, Memory, and the Performance of Violence*, Ed. Ten Brink and Oppenheimer (Columbia University Press, 2013): 42.

6   Butler, Judith. *The Force of Nonviolence: An Ethico-Political Bind* (Verso, 2020), 18.

7   Esposito, *Roberto. Community, Immunity, Biopolitics*. Trans. Rhiannon Noel Welch. (Fordham University Press, 2008), 14.

8   Roberto. *Community*, 40.

9   Robin, Corey. *Fear: The History of a Political Idea* (Oxford Press, 2006).

10 Robin, Corey. Fear: *The History of a Political Idea* (Oxford Press, 2006). 83. See Tocqueville and the Nature of Democracy, trans. John Waggoner (Rowman & Littlefield, 1996), 20.

11 Robin. *Fear*, 91.

12 Alexis de Tocqueville. *Democracy in America*, trans. George Lawrence, ed. J. P. Mayer (Harper and Row, 1969), 702.

13 de Tocqueville. *Democracy*, 705.

14 Robin. *Fear*, 98.

Conclusion

1   Chun, Wendy Hui Kyong. *Update to Remain the Same*, 32.

2   As I briefly mentioned in the third chapter, today social media platforms such as Facebook are forming a close collaboration with the Israeli state to monitor, locate and sometimes arrest Palestinian users who express political dissent online. In May 2018, for instance, the Palestinian poet Dareen Tatour was imprisoned for incitement after sharing a poem on her Facebook wall. And since 2016, others have been detained for similar reasons. Unpacking the ramifications of habitual media on the lives of Palestinians is therefore a pressing and timely issue. BBC. 'Dareen Tatour: Israeli Arab poet convicted of incitement', 3 May 2018. Available at: https://www.bbc.co.uk/news/world-middle-east-43990577.

Bibliography

Adamsky, Dima (2010) *The Culture of Military Innovation: The Impact of Cultural Factors on the Revolution in Military Affairs in Russia, the US, and Israel*, Stanford University Press.

Altman, Yair (2015) 'Documentation: What Did 40 Soldiers Do on the Rooftop in Hebron?' *Walla Website* [in Hebrew], 29 May. Available at: https://news.walla.co.il/item/2858641 [Last Accessed: 20 January 2017].

Andrejevic, Mark (2002) 'The Work of Watching One Another: Lateral Surveillance, Risk, and Governance', *Society & Surveillance*, Volume 2, Number 4. Pp. 479–97.

Arendt, Hannah (1954) 'The Crisis in Education: Eight Exercises in Political Thought', in *Between Past and Future: Eight Exercises in Political Thought*, Penguin Press, 2008.

Arendt, Hannah (1958) *The Human Condition*, Chicago University Press, 1998.

Arquilla, J. and Ronfeld, D. (1999) *Networks and Netwars: The Future of Terror, Crime, and Militancy*, Rand Publications.

Asa, C. and Yaari, Y. (2004) 'Dispersed War and Dynamic Molecules', *Maarachot Military Jounral*, Issue 395, August.

Azoulay, Ariella (2008) *The Civil Contract of Photography*, Zones Books.

Azoulay, Ariella (2016) *The Resolution of the Suspect*. Trans. Hebrew by Tal Haran. Radius Books.

Azoulay, Ariella and Ophir, Adi (2011) 'The Monster's Tail', *Roulette Magazine*. Issue 5, 2008. Available at: http://www.roulottemagazine.com/2011/04/the-monster%E2%80%99s-tail-ariella-azoulay-adi-ophir/.

B'Tselem (2002) 'Trigger Happy: Unjustified Gunfire and the IDF's Open-Fire Regulations during the al-Aqsa Intifada', *B'Tselem Website*, March. Available at: https://www.btselem.org/publications/summaries/200203_trigger_happy.

B'Tselem (2009) 'A Year to Cast Lead', *B'tselem Report*, Israel.

B'Tselem (2017) 'About B'Tselem video Project', *B'Tselem Website*, 19 November. Available at: https://www.btselem.org/video/about-btselem-video.

Bain, Lobovich (2013) 'Celcom's Military Training', *Ynet Online* [in Hebrew]. Available at: https://www.globes.co.il/news/article.aspx?did=1000884706 [Last Accessed: 15 June 2017].

Balibar, Etienne (2013) *Identity and Difference: John Locke and the Invention of Consciousness*. Trans. Warren Montag. Verso Press.

Barzilai, Gad (1999) 'War, Democracy and Internal Conflict: Israel in a Comparative Perspective', *Comparative Politics*, Volume 31, Number 3, Pp. 317–36.

Baudrillard, Jean (1995) *The Gulf War Did Not Take Place*. Trans. Paul Patton. Indiana Univesity Press.

Bauman, Zygmunt (2000) 'On Being Light and Liquid', in *Liquid Modernity*, Polity Press.

Bauman, Zygmunt and David Lyon (2013) *Liquid Surveillance: A Conversation*, Polity Press.

Beck, Ulrich (2006) 'Living in a World Risk Society', *Economy and Society*, Volume 35, Number 3, August. Pp. 329–45.

Belting, Hans (2016) *The Face and the Mask*. Trans. Thomas Hansen and Abby Hansen. Princeton University Press.

Ben Israel, Dori (2016) 'Facebook Is Sabotaging the Police's Work', *Hamizbala Blog*, 2 July. Available at: http://mizbala.com/digital/social-media/112838 [Last Accessed: 5 June 2018].

Ben Shaul, Nitzan (2006) *A Violent World: TV News Images of Middle Eastern Terror and War*, Rowman & Littlefield.

Bendet, Shabtai (2016) 'Survey: 47 Per cent of the Public Believe Azaria Was Tried Unjustly', *Walla* [in Hebrew], 5 July. Available at: https://news.walla.co.il/item/2976259.

Blas, Zach (2016) 'A Cage of Information', or, 'What Is a Biometric Diagram?' in *Documentary across Disciplines*. Ed. Erika Balsom and Hilla Peleg. MIT Press. Pp. 80–90.

Blum, Gabriella (2014) 'The Individualization of War: From War to Policing in the Regulation of Armed Conflicts', in *Law and War*. Ed. Austin Sarat, Lawrence Douglas and Martha Merrill Umphrey. Stanford Press. P. 53.

Bonen, Ze'ev (1991) 'The Missiles Are Coming', *Haaretz Newspaper*. Published 4 of February, 1991, p. 3b.

Bowditch, Henry Pickering (1894) 'Are Composite Photographs Typical Pictures?' *McClure's Magazine*.

Breaking the Silence (2014) *This Is How We Fought in Gaza: Soldiers Testimonies and Photographs from Operation Protective Edge*, Testimony 20. P. 34.

Breaking the Silence (2014) *This Is How We Fought in Gaza: Soldiers Testimonies and Photographs from Operation Protective Edge*, Testimony 33. P. 90.

Briner (2008) 'Mobile Phone Cameras? Not in Our Bases', *Walla Online*. Published 21 July. Available at: https://news.walla.co.il/item/1316618 [Last Accessed: 13 April 2018].

Briner, Yehushua (2010) 'Documentation: Soldier Humiliate Palestinian in Gaza', *Walla News* [in Hebrew], 24 October. Available at: https://news.walla.co.il/item/1747371 [Last Accessed: 13 June 2018].

Brown, Jon (2017a) 'The Defense Team Are Changing Strategy and Claims for Selective Enforcement', *Haaretz*, April 2017. Available at: https://www.haaretz.co.il/blogs/johnbrown/1.4002447.

Brown, Wendy (2010) *Walled Stated, Waning Sovereignty*, MIT Press.

Browne, Simone (2015) *Dark Matters: On the Surveillance of Blackness*, Duke University Press.

B'tselem (2017) 'About B'Tselem Video'. Available at: https://www.btselem.org/video/about-btselem-video [Last Accessed: 12 November 2017].

Buchbutt (2010) 'The IDF Declared War on Social Media', *NRG News* [in Hebrew], 23 December. Available at: http://www.nrg.co.il/online/1/ART2/192/452.html [Last Accessed: 20 September 2017].

Butler, Judith (2006) *Frames of War: Is Life Grievable?*, Verso Press.

Butler, Judith (2009) *Frames of War: When Is Life Grievable?*, Verso Press.

Caillois, Roger (1984) *Mimicry and Legendary Psychasthenia*. Trans. John Shepley. MIT Press.

Calliahu (2000) *How the Web Was Born: The Story of the World Wide Web*, Oxford Press.

Catignani, Sergio (2005) 'The Strategic Impasse in Low-Intensity Conflicts: The Gap Between Israeli Counter-Insurgency Strategy and Tactics During the Al-Aqsa Intifada', *Journal of Strategic Studies*, Volume 28.

Christison, Kathleen (1999) *Perceptions of Palestine: Their Influence on U.S. Middle East Policy*, UC Berkley Press.

Chun, Hui Kyong Wendy (2011) 'Crisis, Crisis, Crisis, or Sovereignty and Networks', *Theory, Culture and Society*, Volume 28. P. 91.

Chun, Wendy Hui Kyong (2016) *Updating to Remain the Same: Habitual New Media*, MIT Press.

Clausewitz, Karl Von (1832) 'On War', quoted in Mirzoeff's *The Right to Look* (2011), Duke Press. p. 37.

Cohen (1991) 'The Collapse of the Public Shelter', *Al Hamishmar Newspaper* [in Hebrew], 25 February.

Cohen (2013) 'Israeli Military Closes Probe into Death of Palestinian Protester Mustafa Tamimi', *Haaretz*, 5 December. Available at: https://www.haaretz.com/.premium-probe-into-palestinian-protester-s-death-closed-1.5297524 [Last Accessed: 12 March 2018].

Columbus (1990) *Home Alone* [film], United States: 20th Century Fox.

Cooksey, J (2017) *The Vest Pocket Kodak & the First World War: Camera & Conflict*, Ammonite Press.

Cordersman, Anthony (2008) *Arab-Israeli Military Forces in an Era of Asymmetric Wars*, Stanford Press.

Crary, Jonathan (2013) *24/7: Late Capitalism and the Ends of Sleep*, Verso Press.

De Landa, M (1991) *War in the Age of Intelligent Machines*, Zone Books.

Deleuze, G. and Guattari, F. (2010) *Nomadology: The War Machine* (Originally appeared in A Thousand Plateaus), Wormwood Distribution.

Demchak, C (2001) 'Technology's Knowledge Burden, the RMA and the IDF: Organizing the Hypertext Organization for Future "Wars of Disruption"?' *Journal of Strategic Studies*, Volume 24.

Der Derian, James (2001) *Virtuous War: Mapping the Military - Industrial-media-entertainment Network*, Westview Press.

Dewey, John (1922) 'From Human Nature and Conduct', in *The Essential Dewey, Volume 2: Ethics, Logic, Psychology*. Ed. Hickman, Larry and Alexander, Thomas. Indiana University Press, 1998. P. 28.

Didi-Huberman, Georges (2008) *Images in Spite of All: Four Photographs from Auschwitz*, Chicago University Press.

Doane, Marry Ann (2001) 'Information, Crisis, Catastrophe', in *The Historical Film: History and Memory in Media*. Ed. Marcia Landy. The Athlone Press. P. 276.

Doner, S (2013) 'Celcom Recruits Soldiers', *Ynet Online* [in Hebrew], 10 October 2005. Available at: https://www.ynet.co.il/articles/0,7340,L-3093481,00.html [Last Accessed: 12 March 2017].

Durham, John Peters (1999) *Speaking into the Air: A History of the Idea of Communication*, University of Chicago Press.

Edwards, Paul N (1996) *The Closed World: Computers and the Politics of Discourse in Cold War America*, MIT Press.

Eli, Y (2015) 'The Loner's Intifada', *Walla News* [in Hebrew]. 15 October. Available at: https://news.walla.co.il/item/2897602#!/wallahistory [Last Accessed: 20 September 2017].

Elsight: Expanding your Visual Reach (2018) 'Documenting Soldier Project', *Elsight Website*. Available at: http://el-sight.com/project/documenting-warrior-project/ [Last Accessed: 28 June 2018].

Esposito, Roberto (2008) *Community, Immunity, Biopolitics*. Trans. Rhiannon Noel Welch. Fordham University Press.

Esposito, Roberto (2011) *Immunitas: The Protection and Negation of Life*, Polity Press.

Fallon, K. (2016) 'Data Visualization and Documentary's (In)visible Frontiers', in *Documentary across Disciplines*. Ed. Erika Balsom and Hila Peleg. MIT Press.

Farkash, Zeev (2009) 'Preparedness of the Civil Front at Times of War', in *Research Report*. Ed. Meir Elran, 1 June, Institute for National Security Studies.

Flusser, Vilem (1985) *Into the Universe of the Technical Image*, 3rd ed., Minnesota Press.

Flusser, Vilém (1994) *The Freedom of the Migrant: Objections to Nationalism*. Trans. Kenneth Kronenberg. University of Illinois, 2003.

Foucault, Michel (1975) *Discipline and Punishment: The Birth of the Prison*. Trans. Alan Sheridan. Vintage Books.

Foucault, Michel (1982) 'The Subject and Power', *Critical Inquiry*, Volume 8, Number 4 (Summer). Pp. 777–95.

Galloway, Alexander R. (2004) *The Interface Effect. Are Some Things Unrepresentable?* MIT Press.

Galloway, Alexander R. and Eugene Thacker (2007) *The Exploit: A Theory of Networks*, *Electronic Mediations*, University of Minnesota Press.

Gates A., Kelly (2011) *Our Biometric Future: Facial Recognition Technology and the Culture of Surveillance*, New York University Press.

Gili, Cohen (2015) 'Feelings of Discrimination Driving Palestinian Youth to Terror', *Haaretz*, 11 November 2015. Available at: http://www.haaretz.com/israel-news/. premium-1.685485 [Last Accessed: 12 June 2018].

Gillham, NW (2001) *A Life of Sir Francis Galton: From African Exploration to the Birth of Eugenics: From African Exploration to the Birth of Eugenics*, Oxford University Press.

Gordon, Neve (2008) *Israel's Occupation*, University of California Press.

Grosz, Elizabeth (2013) 'Habit Today: Ravaisson, Bergson, Deleuze and Us', *Body & Society*, Volume 19, Number 2. P. 220.

Grusin, Richard (2010) *Premediation: Affect and Mediality After 9/11*, Palgrave Macmillan. P. 27.

The Guardian (2010) 'Soldier Who Shot Neutralized Terrorist Is Suspected of Murder', 19 November 2010. Available at: https://www.theguardian.com/world/2010/nov/19/ israeli-army-condemns-gaza-list: [Last Accessed: 20 September 2017].

The Guardian (2016) 'Facebook and Israel to Work to Monitor Posts That Incite Violence', September 16. Available at: https://www.theguardian.com/ technology/2016/sep/12/facebook-israel-monitor-posts-incite-violence-social-media?CMP=twt_gu [Last Accessed: 10 May 2018].

Gviratz, Yael (1991) 'The Military Spokesperson Calm Down the Atmposphere', *Yediot Achronot* [in Hberew], 25 January.

Haaretz (2017) 'I Would Gladly Kill Arabs - Even Slaughter Them', *Haaretz*, 19 August 2010. Available at: https://www.haaretz.com/1.5102386 [Last Accessed: 20 March 2017].

Hardt, Michael and Negri, Antonio (2005) *Multitude*, Penguin Press.

Harel, Amos (2015) 'East Jerusalem's Leading Role in Terror Attacks Catches Israel Off Guard', *Haaretz*, 17 October 2015. Available at: https://www.haaretz.com/.premium-e-jerusalem-terror-attacks-catch-israel-off-guard-1.5409887 [Last Accessed: 12 June 2018].

Harel, Amos (2017) 'The IDF Accelerated the Installment of Cameras in the West Bank and Monitors the Junctions', *Haaretz* [in Hebrew], 19 June. Available at: https://www. haaretz.co.il/news/politics/.premium-1.4179886.

Harel, Amos (2017) 'Israel Speeds Up Camera Placements in West Bank in Effort to Deter Terrorism', *Haaretz*, 22 June. Available at: https://www.haaretz.com/israel-news/.premium-idf-speeds-up-camera-placements-in-w-bank-in-effort-to-deter-terrorism-1.5485764 [Last Accessed: 12 March 2018].

Haselkorn, Avigdor (1999) *The Continuing Storm: Iraq, Poisonous Weapons and Deterrence*, Yale University Press.

Hazroni, Matan (2015) In at the Military base: Selfie Stand for Soldiers', *Mako Online* [in Hebrew], 2 December 2015. Available at: https://www.mako.co.il/news-military/ security-q4_2015/Article-99e4a4314f16151004.htm [Last Accessed: 10 April 2018].

Herrera, Linda (2016) *Revolution in the Age of Social Media*, Verso Press.

Hochberg, Gil (2016) *Visual Occupations: Violence and Visibility in a Conflict Zone*, Duke University Press.

Hodge, Nathan (2008) 'YouTube, Twitter: Weapons in Israel's Info War', *Wired Magazine*, December 30. Available at: https://www.wired.com/2008/12/israels-info-wa/.

Hoskins and O'laughlin (2010) *War and the Media: After Diffused War*, Polity Press.

IDF Archives (1948) 'The Danger of Areal Bombardment', 4 April 1948, IDFA 481/49/43.

IDF Archives (1948) 'From Mordechai Nimza-Bi to Yadin', 10 August 1948, IDFA 2384/50/40.

IDF Archives (1953) IDFA 481/53/10, extracted July 2017.

IDF Archives (2009) *The Fundamentals of Home Front Command*, Ministry of Defence Press.

Inbar, Efraim (2003) *The Gulf War Reconsidered*. Ed. Andrew J. Bacevich. Frank Cass Publishers.

Israel Military Court (2017) 'Appeal Court Ruling Protocol', May. P. 36

Kane, Alex (2016) 'Post, Share, Arrest', *The Intercept*, 7 July. Available at: https://theintercept.com/2016/07/07/israel-targeting-palestinian-protesters-on-facebook/ [Last Accessed: 10 June 2018].

Kaplan, Caren (2018) *Aerial Aftermaths: Wartime from Above,* Duke University Press.

Keenan, Thomas (1993) 'Windows: Of Vulnerability', in *The Phantom Public Sphere*. Ed. Bruce Robins. University of Minnesota Press. P. 133.

Kenan, Ido (2011) 'Eden Agerbil', *Room 404 Blog* [in Hebrew], July 2010. Available at: http://room404.net/?p=33295.

Kimmerling, Baruch (2001) *The Invention and Decline of Israeliness: State, Society, and the Military*, UC Berkley Press.

Kiswani, Nerdeen (2015) 'Why We Wear the Keffiyeh'.

Krämer, Gedrun (2008) *A History of Palestine: From the Ottoman Conquest to the Founding of the State of Israel*, Princeton University Press.

Kramp, Arie (2018) *The Israeli Path to Neoliberalism: The State, Continuity and Change*, Oxford Press.

Kuntsman, Adi and Stein, Rebecca (2016) *Digital Militarism: Israel's Occupation in the Social Media Age*, Stanford Studies in Middle Eastern and Stanford University Press. P. 72.

Landsberg (2003) 'The Military Frontline in Today the Television, and the IDF is Failing the Battle. Imagine 500 Cameramen Documenting the War', *Maarachot -Mabat Ishi* [in Hebrew].

Lemke, Thomas (2001) 'The Birth of Bio-politics": Michel Foucault's Lecture at the Collège de France on Neo-liberal Governmentality', *Economy and Society*, Volume 30, Number 2, May. Pp. 190–207

Levi (1991) 'Mask for Each Citizen', *Davar*, 5 February.

Levinas, Emmanuel (1985) *Ethics and Infinity*. Trans. Richard Cohen. Duquesne University Press.

Lissak, Moshe (1993) 'Civil Components in the National Security Doctrine', in *The National Security and Democracy in Israel*. Ed. Avner Yaniv. Los Angeles Press. Pp. 66–8.

Loevy, Karin (2016) *Emergencies in Public Law: The Legal Politics of Containment*, Cambridge University Press.

Lovink, G. (2016) *Social Media Abyss: Critical Internet Cultures and the Force of Negation*, Amsterdam Press.

Lowe, Paul (2016) 'The Forensic Turn: Bearing Witness and the 'Thingness' of the Photorgaph', in *Violence of the Image: Photography and International Conflict*. Ed. Liam Kennedy and Caitlin Patrick. I.B.Tauris. P. 213.

Malabou, Catherine (2008) 'Addiction and Grace: Preface to Félix Ravaisson's on Habit', in *Of Habit*, Ed. Felix Ravaisson. Continuum Press. P. vii.

Masco, Joseph (2014) *The Theater of Operations: National Security Affect from the Cold War to the War on Terror*, Duke University Press. Pp. 47–56.

Massumi, Brian (2016) *Ontopower: War, Powers, and the State of Perception*, Duke University Press. Pp. 69.

McEnaney, Elaine (2000) *Civil Defense Begins at Home Militarization Meets Everyday Life in the Fifties*, Princeton University Press. Pp. 121–31.

Mehozay, Yoav (2016) *Between the Rule of Law and States of Emergency: The Fluid Jurisprudence*, SUNY Press.

Michel, Foucault (2010) *The Birth of the Biopolitcs Lectures at the Collage de France 1978–79*. Trans. Graham Bur-chell. Palgrave Macmillan.

Mirzoeff, Nicholas (2005) *Watching Babylon: The War in Iraq and Global Visual Culture*, Psychology Press.

Mirzoeff, Nicholas (2011) *The Right to Look: A Counterhistory of Visuality*, Duke University Press.

Negri, Antonio and Hardt, Michael (2012) *Declaration*, Argo Navis Author Services. P. 18.

Neyrat, Frédéric (2010) 'The Birth of Imnunopolitics', Trans. Arne de Boever, in *Parrheisa*, Issue 10. Pp. 31–8.

Nissenbaum, Helen (2015) *Obfuscation: A User's Guide for Privacy and Protest*, MIT Press.

Oaks, Guy (1994) *The Imaginary War: Civil Defense and American Cold War Culture*, Oxford University Press.

Orr, Jackie (2006) *Panic Diaries: A Genealogy of Panic Disorder*, Duke University Press.

Pasquale, Frank (2015) *The Black Box Society: The Secret Algorithms That Control Money and Information*, Harvard University Press.

Peters, John Durham (2016) *The Marvellous Clouds: Toward a Philosophy of Elemental Media*, University of Chicago Press.

Quatelet, Adolphe (2013) *Treatise of Man and the Development of His Faculties*, Cambridge Press.

Rahman, Omar (2011) 'Nabi Saleh Protester Hit by Tear Gas Canister Dies from Wounds', *+972 Magazine*, 9 December 2011. Available at: https://972mag.com/nabi-saleh-palestinian-shot-in-head-with-tear-gas-canister/29317/.

Rancière, Jacques (2006) *Film Fables*, Berg Press.

Rancière, Jacques (2006) *The Politics of Aesthetics: The Distribution of the Sensible*. Trans. Gabriel Rockhill. Continuum Press.

Ranciere, Jacques (2010) *Dissensus: On Politics and Aesthetics*. Trans. and ed. Steve Corcoran. Continuum Press.

Rasmussen, Terje (2014) *Personal Media and Everyday Life: A Networked Lifeworld*, Palgrave Mcmillan.

Ravaisson, Felix (1838) *Of Habit*, Continuum Press.

Reut, (2009) *Civil Resilience Network - Conceptual Framework for: Israel's Local & National Resilience*, Version B.

Rid, Thomas and Hecker, Mark (2009) *War 2.0: Irregular Warfare in the Information Age*, Praeger Security International.

Roadstrum Moffett, Martha (1989) *Perpetual Emergency: A Legal Analysis of Israel's Use of the British Defence (Emergency) Regulations, 1946, in the Occupied Territories*, Al-Haq.

Rose Shell, Hanna (2012) *Hide and Seek: Camouflage, Photography, and the Media of Reconnaissance*, MIT Press.

Rotner, Rachel (2014) 'The David Hanachlawi Facebook Campaign', *Walla Tech* [in Hebrew], 1 May. Available at: https://tech.walla.co.il/item/2742383 [Last Accessed: 20 September 2017].

Sekula, Allan (1985) 'The Body and the Archive', *October*, Volume 39, Winter 1985. Pp. 3–64.

Serwood, Harriet (2011) 'Palestinian Children Woken in Night to be Photographed by Soldier', *The Guardian*. 28 September. Available at: https://www.theguardian.com/world/view-from-jerusalem-with-harriet-sherwood/2011/sep/28/palestinian-territories-israel [Last Accessed: 28 June 2018].

Shafir, Gershon (2016) *A Half Century of Occupation: Israel, Palestine, and the World's Most Intractable Conflict*, University of California Press.

Shaul (1991) 'If You Must, Record Everything', *Davar Newspaper* [in Hebrew], 21 January. p. 3c.

Shavit, Michal (2017) *Media Strategy and Military Operations in the 21st Century: Mediatizing the Israel Defence Forces*, Taylor and Francis: Contemporary Security Studies.

Sher (2013) *The Land Division Military Journal*. Issue 34. Published 14 March, IDF Publishing.

Shoval, Lilach (2011) 'In Case of Ground Operation, the IDF Will Allocate Cameras to Soldiers', *Israel Hayom* [in Hebrew], 6 April. Available at: http://www.israelhayom.co.il/site/newsletter_article.php?id=10819&newsletter=10.04.2011.

Sivan (2013) 'Documentation at War', *Maarachot Military Journal* [in Hebrew], Number 18, 25 December.

Sluzky, Yehuda (1986) *A Short History of the Hagana* [in Hebrew], The Israeli Defense Ministry Publishing.

Smith, Shawn Michelle (2013) *At the Edge of Sight*, Duke University Press.

Struk, Jenina (2011) *Private Pictures: Soldiers' Inside View of War*, I.B. Tauris.

Switzer (1991) 'Private Homes Would Be the First Destination of Chemical Warheads: Security Experts Claim', *Haaretz* [in Hebrew], 10 Febuary, P. 1b.

Tagg, John (1993) *The Burden of Representation: Essays on Photographies and Histories*, University of Minnesota Press.

Tamir, Michal (2015) *Public Law as a Whole: The Case of Selective Enforcement and Racial Profiling*, New York University Press.

Tawil-Souri, Helga (2015) *In Signal Traffic: Critical Studies of Media Infrastructures (The Geopolitics of Information)*. Ed. Lisa Parks and Nicole Starosielski. University of Illinois Press.

Teyssot, Georges (2013) *A Topology of Everyday Constellations*, MIT Press.

Thomas, Rid and Hecker, Marc (2009) *War 2.0: Irregular Warfare in the Information Age*, Praeger Security International.

Virilio, Paul (1984) *War and Cinema: The Logics of Perception*. Trans. Patrick Camiller. Verso Press, 2000.

Virilio, Paul (1991) *Desert Screen: War at the Speed of Light*, The Anthole Press.

Weber, Samuel (2005) *Targets of Opportunity: On the Militarization of Thinking*, Fordham Press. Pp. 90–190.

Weiner, Stuart (2017) 'Soldier Elor Azaria Given 18 Months in Jail for Killing Wounded Stabber', *The Times of Israel*. 21 February. Available at: https://www.timesofisrael. com/soldier-elor-azaria-given-18-months-prison-for-killing-wounded-assailant/ [Last Accessed: 25 June 2018].

Weiss (1991) 'Your House Will be Destroyed is a Harsh Insult', *Davar Newspaper* [in Hebrew], 2 January, p. 17.

Weizman, Eyal (2007) *Hollow Land: Israel's Architecture of Occupation*, Verso Press. P. 117.

Wendy, Brown (2016) *Undoing the Demos: Neoliberalism's Stealth Revolution*, MIT Press.

Werman, Robert (2004) *Notes from a Sealed Room: An Israel View of the Gulf War*, Southern Illinois University Press.

Yaacov Yadgar (2004) *Our Story: National Narratives in the Israeli Press*, Haifa University Press.

Yacobovich, Oren (2007) 'Shooting Back: The Israeli Human Rights Group B'Tselem Gives Palestinians Video Cameras to Document Life Under Occupation', *Democracy Now Website*. Available at: https://www.democracynow.org/2007/12/26/shooting_back_the_israeli_human_rights [Last Accessed: 30 June 2018].

Yaniv, Avner (1993) 'A Question of Survival: The Military and Politics under Siege', in *National Security and Democracy in Israel*. Ed. Avner Yaniv. Lynne Rienner Publishing.

Zimmerman, Patricia (1995) *Reel Families: A Social History of Amateur Film*, Indiana University Press.

Zitun, Yonatan (2016) 'Soldier Who Shot Neutralized Terrorist Is Suspected of Murder', *Ynet*, March 10. Available at: https://www.ynetnews.com/articles/0,7340,L-4783059,00.html [Last Accessed: 25 March 2018].

Ziv, Amitai (2014) 'Israel's Defense Ministry Signs Deal for Military-grade Smartphones', *Haaretz*, 3 January. Available at: https://www.haaretz.com/.premium-idf-smartphones-on-the-way-1.5307579 [Last Accessed: February 2016].

Zylinska, Joanna and Sara, Kember (2012) *Life after New Media: Mediation as a Vital Process*, MIT Press.

Index